RESPONSIBLE
GOVERNMENT
IN ONTARIO

CANADIAN GOVERNMENT SERIES

General Editors

R. MacG. Dawson, 1946–58

J. A. Corry, 1958–61

C. B. Macpherson, 1961–

1. *Democratic Government and Politics.* By J. A. Corry and
   J. E. Hodgetts

2. *The Government of Canada.* By R. MacGregor Dawson;
   revised by Norman Ward

3. *Constitutional Amendment in Canada.* By Paul Gérin-Lajoie

4. *The Canadian House of Commons: Representation.*
   By Norman Ward

5. *The Government of Prince Edward Island.* By Frank MacKinnon

6. *Canadian Municipal Government.* By Kenneth Grant Crawford

7. *Pioneer Public Service: An Administrative History of the United
   Canadas, 1841–1867.* By J. E. Hodgetts

8. *The Government of Nova Scotia.* By J. Murray Beck

9. *The Office of Lieutenant-Governor.* By John T. Saywell

10. *Politics in New Brunswick.* By Hugh G. Thorburn

11. *The Public Purse.* By Norman Ward

12. *Procedure in the Canadian House of Commons.* By W. F. Dawson

13. *The Canadian General Election of 1957.* By John Meisel

14. *The Government of Manitoba.* By M. S. Donnelly

15. *The Modern Senate of Canada.* By F. A. Kunz

16. *Responsible Government in Ontario.* By F. F. Schindeler

Responsible Government in Ontario

F. F. Schindeler

UNIVERSITY OF
TORONTO PRESS

© University of Toronto Press 1969

Printed in Canada

SBN 8020 5204 5

To Mid

PREFACE

BY CONSTITUTIONAL PROVISION and judicial decision, many fields of government activity which have experienced the most rapid growth in Canada since the second world war fall under the jurisdiction of the provincial governments. The result has been a phenomenal growth in the scope of provincial government functions and a decided shift in power in the finely balanced Canadian federal system. This study arose out of the realization that although the latter subject has been the occasion for a number of studies – not the least of which has been the Royal Commission on Bilingualism and Biculturalism – very little attention has been paid to the problem of the effect the growth of government activity has had on the political process at the provincial level.

Perhaps the crucial question to be asked when investigating changes in parliamentary institutions at any level of government is: To what extent have these changes affected legislative-executive relations? For, if democratic procedures are to be maintained and personal liberties safeguarded, the role of the legislature as a check on the executive must be preserved. This is not to say that informal checks are insignificant or even of secondary importance to institutional controls; it is only to affirm that informal procedures, which do not rest upon a popular base that plays a recognized part of the constitutional structure of government, are a fragile defence against the abuse of executive powers. As Justice Frankfurter noted: "The history of liberty has largely been the history of observance of procedural safeguards." In keeping with this line of reasoning, this study focuses on governmental institutions in Ontario and, more particularly, on legislative-executive relations in the province. The *terminus ad quem* set for the study is 1965 and, although the important changes that have been made since that time are noted in passing, the bulk of the analysis relates to the situation that existed prior to 1966. It is still too early to say whether or not these changes will fundamentally affect the style of government in Ontario.

Ontario provides excellent material for a case study on this subject not only because it was one of the original provinces, but because it has from the beginning remained the largest and most prosperous of the provinces. To a large extent Ontario establishes the trends which eventually occur in the other regions of the country.

The procedure followed in the study was, first, to investigate the ways in which the executive branch of the government of Ontario was adapted to cope with its increased responsibilities and, second, to explore the ways in which the legislative branch was modified to enable it to understand, criticize, and so control the executive. At the same time, in order to create a standard for evaluating Ontario's institutions, they were compared with the larger and more familiar models of parliamentary government at Westminster and Ottawa.

As Norman Ward has made clear in *The Public Purse*, the struggle for responsible government is a continuing one. The general conclusion of this study is that, as the functions of government have increased in scope and complexity, the realities of the political process have made the ideal of responsible government increasingly remote. The legislative branch, which is the *sine qua non* of responsible government, has become almost completely dominated by the executive, which has been more easily modified to meet the demands of the modern welfare state.

The paucity of available written materials on almost all aspects of Ontario government has meant that I have been dependent for information upon a multitude of political actors, from ex-premiers and deputy ministers to clerks and vault keepers. However, four public servants were particularly generous with their time and talents: Roderick Lewis, QC, clerk of the Legislative Assembly and chief election officer; W. M. McIntyre, secretary of the cabinet and deputy-minister of the Department of the Prime Minister; L. R. MacTavish, senior legislative counsel; and C. E. Brannan, secretary of the Treasury Board. On occasion these men have taken strong issue with my own views on certain subjects, but they have, without exception, been most patient and tolerant. Special thanks are also due to Professors Paul Fox, Wilbur Grasham, and Douglas Verney, who read the manuscript in its entirety and made numerous suggestions for its improvement. And, finally, to Linda Rose, who laboured over a number of details, including the index, and to my wife, who endured the whole ordeal and proofread the manuscript, I express my deepfelt gratitude. If, in spite of the help of all of these, and of others too numerous to name, there remain any errors or inexcusable omissions, the responsibility is mine alone.

This work was supported by research grants from the Ontario Government and York University. It has been published with the help of a grant from the Social Science Research Council of Canada using funds provided by the Canada Council, and with the assistance of the Publications Fund of the University of Toronto Press. Professor Albert Abel, editor of *Canadian Public Administration*, has kindly granted permission to include material previously published in that journal.

F. F. S.

CONTENTS

FIGURES

TABLES

RESPONSIBLE GOVERNMENT IN ONTARIO

INTRODUCTION

1

IN THE MID-NINETEENTH CENTURY, when the Province of Ontario was being formed out of the western half of the old colony of Canada, the prevailing political philosophy in the English-speaking world was that the activities of government should be limited generally to the preservation of peace or the waging of war in external affairs, the maintenance of justice and order in domestic affairs, and the provision of those public works that could be obtained in no other way. General laws were to be devised to prohibit conduct disruptive of order, and the courts and the police force were to be relied upon to see that offenders were dealt with according to their just deserts. Within these limits individuals were to be free to compete in the never-ending struggle of life out of which would eventually evolve the good society. The advocates of this concept of the negative state were never able to restrict the functions of government to the narrow sphere prescribed in their ideal model but, as Professors Corry and Hodgetts have pointed out, "they had a profound influence on the scope of government action throughout the greater part of the nineteenth century. The negative state was not merely an academic theory; it was largely realized in the scope and character of nineteenth-century governments."[1] In the new provinces of Canada there were more concrete limitations on the extent of their operations than political philosophy: the central government took from them all of their "great functions" and approximately 83 per cent of their former revenues.[2]

[1]J. A. Corry and J. E. Hodgetts, *Democratic Government and Politics* (3rd ed. rev.; Toronto: University of Toronto Press, 1959), p. 116.
[2]R. M. Dawson, *The Government of Canada* (4th ed. rev. by Norman Ward; Toronto: University of Toronto Press, 1963), p. 105. The "great functions" of

Eventually the laissez-faire philosophy succumbed: first to the demands of the business community, and later in response to the social conscience of an awakened populace. As production and transportation techniques improved, international competition for markets was heightened, and manufacturers pressed their governments to regulate trade by means of tariffs and licenses. Unregulated economic activity had repercussions domestically as well, and by the turn of the century the newly enfranchised classes were making their wills felt and governments were called upon to regulate relations between employers and employees. With increasing specialization and division of labour, industrial society became a series of complex, interdependent relationships ordered, and to some extent adjusted, by the common arbiter, the state. The government was also enlisted to provide the services which became expected by all classes, and eventually public education and health and welfare programmes began consuming large portions of the state's revenues. Once begun, the readiness to turn to the state had a multiplier effect. Having tasted the fruit of co-operation, the people became less enamoured with the individualists' slogan: "That government governs best which governs least." Instead of looking upon the state as a great beast with an all-consuming appetite, they began to see it as a ready instrument for obtaining collectively the security and prosperity that had formerly been jeopardized by the exigencies of the free market.

Although the Fathers of Confederation had deprived the provinces of what were considered to be the important areas of government activity, sections 92, 93, and 95 of the British North America Act gave the provinces responsibility for a number of subjects which, since the advent of the positive state, have become some of the most extensive and expensive functions of government. Mention need only be made of subjects such as education, agriculture, and "hospitals, asylums, charities and eleemosynary institutions" to indicate the profound effects that the new view of the functions of the state has had on the operations of government at the provincial level, particularly since the end of the second world war. During the last year of the war, the current income of the federal government was still three times the combined incomes of the provinces and municipalities. But by 1963 the incomes of the "junior" governments totalled 15 per cent more than the federal income.[3] And not only do the provinces and their

---

government were regarded by the Fathers to be: national security, national development, and the fostering of trade and commerce by appropriate regulation. *Report of the Royal Commission on Dominion-Provincial Relations* (Ottawa: King's Printer, 1940), vol. 1, p. 43.

[3]Federal transfers to provinces and municipalities are added to the income of the

creatures, the municipalities, spend more, but they spend it on services which often affect the ordinary citizen more directly and more frequently than do the services provided by the central government.

However, in spite of these facts, in many respects the provincial governments remain untouched by the administrative reforms that have accompanied the growth of federal government functions. This is largely attributable to the fact that, although the provincial governments collectively constitute a major factor in the Canadian economy, individually they are relatively minor when compared to the significance of the central government. With a few exceptions, until quite recently they have not had the necessary resources to recruit the staff and sponsor the research that would enable them to streamline their procedures. Political economists have also tended to turn their attention either to the central government or to the problems of the relations between the central and provincial governments in the federal structure. Even the general public has tended to concentrate on issues associated with the central government or on the problems of federalism.

Given circumstances such as these it is understandable that the classic problem of how to control the executive branch of government has become particularly acute at the provincial level. From their very inception, when it was seriously contended that their cabinets should not be responsible to elected assemblies,[4] the provincial governments have been dominated by their respective executive branches, and this situation has been aggravated over the years. Generally neglected by those who have been interested in the reform of our parliamentary system, the institutions of the provincial governments have evolved only slightly since their creation; hence they sometimes appear anachronistic in modern society: Prince Edward Island maintained a property franchise and a multiple vote for owners of property in more than one district until 1963;[5] Quebec maintains a redundant, appointed upper house; Alberta has never developed that sophisticated political institution, Her Majesty's Loyal Opposition;[6] and none of the provinces has ever significantly altered its basic machinery of government.

---

junior governments and deducted from federal total income. These calculations were given by Jacques Parizeau in an address, "Economic Policy in a Federation," given at the annual meeting of the Canadian Political Science Association, Charlottetown, June 11, 1964.

[4]*Infra*, pp. 87–88.

[5]Frank MacKinnon, *The Government of Prince Edward Island* (Toronto: University of Toronto Press, 1951), pp. 104, 112, and 216; *idem*, "Prince Edward Island," in J. T. Saywell, ed., *Canadian Annual Review for 1963* (Toronto: University of Toronto Press), 1964, p. 143.

[6]See C. B. Macpherson, *Democracy in Alberta: The Theory and Practice of a Quasi-Party System* (Toronto: University of Toronto Press, 1953), esp. p. 4.

Ad hoc measures have been devised in order to cope with the burdens of administering their ever-increasing responsibilities, but these devices have invariably remained under the jurisdiction of the executive or, worse, have been delegated to bodies which are completely irresponsible – in the legal, institutional sense. The legislative apparatus has not been altered, and the role of the legislative branch has become ever more frustrating. The Honourable Leslie Frost, when he was Premier of Ontario, claimed that "one of the weaknesses of Parliamentary government has been the tendency to concentrate powers in the Executive . . . without regard to the membership of the House."[7]

In the light of all of the criticism currently being levied against the operations and performance of the "Mother of Parliaments" in Westminster, it is sobering to reflect upon the fact that the Canadian provinces have not even adopted the most basic of the many reforms introduced in the United Kingdom. If, even after the many innovations made in Britain, Ramsay Muir could say in 1931 that "there is no country in North-Western Europe in which the control exercised by Parliament over the Government – over legislation, taxation, and administration – is more shadowy and unreal than it is in the United Kingdom,"[8] then what should one say about the parliament of Ontario which still follows the procedures developed in Britain in the mid-nineteenth century?

The purpose of this study will be to describe briefly the development of cabinet government in Ontario and to evaluate the various institutions and procedures which have been used for controlling the executive branch of government. Any analysis of legislative-executive relations must be concerned primarily with the role played by the legislative branch but, since the Legislature has final responsibility for defining the roles played by many of the other institutions which serve as checks on the executive, this study will be concerned also with such subjects as the judicial review of decisions made by administrative tribunals and the internal controls set up within the executive branch itself. However, those informal checks on the executive which are exercised by groups or individuals from bases outside of the institutional framework of government do not fall within the scope of this work.

Since there has been very little published on the subject of the government of Ontario, it will be necessary to describe the main institutions in

[7]Ontario, Legislative Assembly, *Debates*, Feb. 1, 1960, p. 79.

[8]Great Britain, *Parliamentary Papers*, vol. VIII (*Reports*; Committees, vol. IV) no. 161, 1931, "Special Report from the Select Committee on Procedure on Public Business," pp. 255–6. Quoted in Robert N. Kelson, *The Private Member of Parliament and the Formation of Public Policy: A New Zealand Case Study* (Toronto: University of Toronto Press, 1964), p. 3.

some detail before going on to discuss the relationship between the legislative and executive branches. The general outline of the study is as follows. Chapter 2, "The Growth of Government Functions," will describe the changes that have taken place in the socio-economic context within which the institutions of Ontario government must operate. The next chapter will indicate the adaptations that have been made in the executive branch to enable it to meet the needs of this changing society, and chapter 4 will do the same for the legislative branch. Chapters 5, 6, and 7, which form the bulk of the study, will be devoted to the various means available to the legislative branch to exercise some control over the executive. Two of these chapters will examine the opportunities to control the executive that are afforded the legislative branch in the ordinary formal legislative process: the general debates, private member's time, and by the use of certain special procedures. The methods that have been developed to enable the legislature to control the use of delegated powers and to supervise government expenditures will be dealt with in chapter 7. Finally, the last chapter will bring together the conclusions, both diagnostic and prescriptive, that have emerged in the body of the study and will attempt to relate the one to the other in a meaningful manner.

While this work is not meant to be historical in nature, the paucity of available literature on political institutions in Ontario has necessitated the inclusion of some historical data. It would be difficult, for example, to appreciate the sheer magnitude of current government activities and the concomitant immensity of existing executive powers without some knowledge of the scale of government operations in the early history of the province and some understanding of the changes that have taken place over the years. Similarly, it would be foolhardy to attempt to describe the present status of the Legislative Assembly without giving some indication of its origins and history. Nevertheless, the primary object of this study is to give a still picture of a subject which is admittedly in a constant state of flux. Most of the detailed analysis will therefore be confined to the modern, that is, postwar, period. The chief reasons for choosing the second world war as the *terminus a quo* for a detailed study are that the years following it are those of greatest expansion of government in Ontario and are co-extensive with the current period of dominance by the Progressive Conservative party. At the same time there has been so little change in some areas of government in the last forty years that the description of the currently existing situation will prove sufficient.

To avoid any possible confusion of terms, working definitions of two key words – executive and legislative – should be borne in mind. The term "executive" will be used to refer primarily to what Bagehot described as the "efficient" executive: the cabinet.[9] However, since the administration, or the public service, operates under the control and direction of the cabinet, no attempt has been made to separate it from the executive as a separate branch of government organization, and the term "executive" should be understood to include the public service. This admittedly arbitrary grouping of functions still leaves those relatively recent bodies – the semi-independent boards and commissions – out in their own political limbo. It would be heretical to describe them as legislative bodies, although some of them perform legislative functions, and, although some of them operate in a quasi-judicial fashion, it would be absurd to lump them together with the third classical division of government, the judiciary. However, since the types of functions carried out by these agencies could be, and on occasion have been, performed by the usual departments of government, and since they are usually under control of the cabinet to some degree, either directly or indirectly, they have also been considered a part of the executive branch for the purposes of this study.

On the face of it, "legislative," refers to all of the members of the Legislative Assembly of Ontario, except those in the cabinet, and in general this is correct. But when one speaks of "legislative-executive relations" or the "control of the executive," the realities of the party system which underlie the cabinet form of government are such that "legislative" for most practical purposes embraces only Her Majesty's Loyal Opposition, because as far as the formal institutions of government are concerned, the Government backbencher is not much more than a cipher: "The Government's majority exists to support the Government."[10] This is not to imply that an individual MPP[11] in the governing party has no say over the policy adopted by the Government and no opportunities to influence the day-to-day administration of the affairs of the province. Indeed, if his party has the trappings of democracy, or if the MPP is influential in his party, he may play a very significant part in shaping the pattern of the political life of the province. What is suggested is that once the cabinet has embarked on a course of action, it is highly unlikely that the ordinary Government MPP will voice publicly any criticisms, let alone use the available institutions of government, in order to force the cabinet to change its collective mind. Thus, while the term "legislative," as used here, embraces

[9]Walter Bagehot, *The English Constitution*, with an introduction by the First Earl of Balfour (London: Oxford University Press, 1958), p. 9.

[10]Sir William Ivor Jennings, *Cabinet Government* (3rd ed.; Cambridge: Cambridge University Press, 1959), p. 472.

[11]In Ontario, members of the Legislative Assembly are referred to as Members of the Provincial Parliament or by the initials MPP.

all private members of the legislature, in most instances it has relevance only for the Opposition members.[12]

Underlying and guiding this investigation of responsible government in Ontario is an assumption that man is imperfect and that this imperfection is not limited to any particular political party. It then follows that the problem of executive abuse cannot be solved simply by electing a different group of executives and that, if there is to be a long-run solution, control over the executive must come through containment and not conversion. In short, the only long-run defence against the irresponsible use of Government authority, to the disparagement of democracy and the detriment of public well-being, is not simply to "vote the rascals out," but to surround the cabinet with institutional checks in order to regulate the exercise of its authority and to make institutional provision for appeals from administrative decisions.

It should also be made absolutely clear from the outset that it is not being proposed that we should go back to a form of "government by the people," if indeed there ever was a time when a state was so governed. Nor is it even suggested that we can resurrect representative or "parliamentary" government, if by that is meant a system of government wherein an assembly of legislators decides policy matters and creates laws. If anything is advocated here, it is a system of responsible "cabinet" government with distinctive political parties putting forward contenders for office who, when successful, rule according to their own sense of good government for a limited period according to strictly circumscribed procedures and with adequate provision for appeal.[13]

[12]On the question of the role of the government backbencher as compared to that of the private member on the opposition side see Kelson, *The Private Member*, and Peter Richards, *Honourable Members: A Study of the British Backbencher* (London: Faber and Faber, 1959).

[13]That this is as close as we can come to classical democracy is made evident in writings such as H. H. Gerth and C. W. Mills, *From Max Weber: Essays in Sociology* (New York: Oxford University Press, 1946), esp. p. 226; Joseph A. Schumpeter, *Capitalism, Socialism and Democracy* (3rd ed.; New York: Harper and Row, 1962), esp. chap. XXI and p. 269; S. M. Lipset, *Political Man* (New York: Doubleday, 1960), esp. pp. 27–8; S. M. Lipsett, M. H. Trow, and I. S. Coleman, *Union Democracy* (Glencoe: Free Press, 1956), pp. 405–12. My own feeling is that the term "democratic" should continue to be applied to those systems of government in which executives are freely elected and in which they continue to govern in accordance with appropriate understandings and procedures providing for popular participation and consent. But, when referring to that classical democracy which Lincoln defined as government of, for, and by the people, a distinctive term ought to be used, e.g., "ochlocracy," or perhaps "plethocracy." Consistently making some distinction such as this would help to dispel the popular myth that it is the people who govern modern "democracies."

Today the province has a system of cabinet government that operates on the basis of a supposed responsibility to the legislature. But this doctrine of responsible government lost much of its meaning with the development of the party system in Ontario following the breakdown of the original coalition government of the province. On the one hand, the fact that the cabinet commands the loyal support of a majority in the House takes the teeth out of any possible restraint which the legislature might otherwise exercise over the executive; while, on the other hand, the cabinet asserts the doctrine of ministerial responsibility to counter demands for independent inquiries into alleged abuses of administrative powers and to impede suggested procedural reforms which might give private members greater influence in the legislative process. If the principle of ministerial responsibility is to have any relevance in Ontario, the institutions and procedures of government must ensure that there is ample opportunity for the legislature to review administrative decisions and to criticize the executive, regardless of the size of the Government's majority in the House. One of the purposes of this study will be to evaluate the degree to which procedures and institutions approximated this goal up to 1965.

In order to set the Ontario model in its broader context and raise this examination above the level of the purely descriptive and parochial, the comparative method is adopted and reference is made to other systems of government, particularly those in operation at Ottawa and Westminster. While one might despair at attempting a comparative approach to such a subject for fear of creating a many-headed and unmanageable monster, there is really no alternative, for what Durkheim said about sociology applies to political institutions as well: "Comparative sociology is not a particular branch of sociology; it is sociology itself, in so far as it ceases to be purely descriptive, and aspires to account for facts."[14]

Furthermore, the author does not subscribe to the view that political institutions and political theory are two quite separate fields of study. Hence, along with the purely descriptive material, dealing with the hitherto undescribed institutions of Ontario government, and the comparative material, meant to provide an explanatory frame of reference from which Ontario's institutions may be viewed, there is also implicit in this work a theoretical approach aimed at adapting orthodox democratic theory to the realities of democratic practice at the provincial level.

[14]Emile Durkheim, *The Rules of Sociological Method*, translated by Sarah A. Soloway and John H. Mueller and edited by George E. G. Catlin (8th ed.; Glencoe: Free Press, 1938), p. 139.

THE GROWTH OF
GOVERNMENT
FUNCTIONS

2

WHEN THE CANADIAN FEDERATION was formed in 1867, even the most ardent advocates of provincial powers and the most visionary of Canadian statesmen could not have surmised the phenomenal expansion in the scope of government activities that was to take place in the province of Ontario during the first century of its existence. In 1867 most of the traditional functions of the state were taken over by the central government, the great bulk of the former colony's revenue was transferred to the federal government, and most of the leading politicians of Upper Canada chose to serve in the new Parliament at Ottawa. Although the contenders for a legislative union had not had things completely their way, they were content that the provincial administrations were to be so strictly curtailed in their responsibilities and means as to be little more than glorified county councils.

A number of factors have worked together to demolish this conception of the place of Ontario in the Canadian federation. In the first place, administrative and financial responsibilities in certain legislative fields have simply grown in proportion to the increase in population. While this is not a sufficient explanation, it has been a significant factor in the expansion of functions in fields such as education and public works. Between 1871 and 1961 the population of Ontario quadrupled, with by far the greatest increase taking place after the second world war. In fact, as a result of the flow of immigrants and a higher birth rate – from 17 to 27 per thousand[1] – more people were added to Ontario's population in the

---

[1]G. E. Gathercole, "Fiscal Policy in Ontario." An address delivered at the 1961 Senior Officers' Conference, p. 3. (The Senior Officers' Conference is sponsored by the Training and Development Division of the Ontario Department of Civil Service for the benefit of the senior administrators in the provincial civil service).

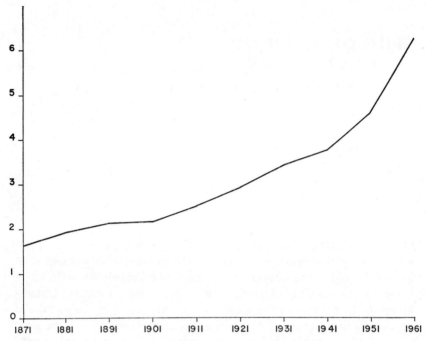

FIG. 1.   The population of Ontario, 1871–1961, in millions.

twenty-year period from 1941 to 1961 than in the whole previous history of the province.[2] Or, the increase in population between 1941 and 1961 was greater than the total population had been at the turn of the century (Figure 1)[3]. Even more significant is the fact that, while the aggregate population increased by 50 per cent in the decade and a half following the war, the number of children increased by more than 100 per cent. As a result, school enrolment rose from 660,000 in 1946 to 1,400,000 in 1961 and university enrolment from approximately 13,000 to more than 31,000.

A second factor in the increase in provincial responsibilities has been the tendency of judicial decisions, particularly since 1882, to favour the provincial rather than the federal jurisdiction.[4] Whether through inten-

[2]In the decade 1951–61, the rate of increase in the population of Ontario was 3 per cent, compared to 1.8 per cent for North America, 2 per cent for Asia, and 2.1 per cent for Africa. From a report of a study made by the Department of Public Welfare in the Toronto *Globe and Mail*, Aug. 22, 1964, p. 5.

[3]Canada, Dominion Bureau of Statistics, *Canada Year Book*, 1956, p. 149; *Canada Year Book*, 1965, p. 160.

[4]Still perhaps the best analysis of this trend is to be found in Canada, Senate *Report to the Honourable Speaker of the Senate on the British North America Act* (O'Connor Report) (Ottawa: King's Printer, 1939).

tional malice towards the central government or simply because of an over-emphasis on the letter as opposed to the spirit of the constitution, the Judicial Committee of the Privy Council practically reversed the intentions of Canada's founding Fathers. The clause in section 91 of the British North America Act that was meant to give the central government not only the residual powers (conferred also by clause 91:29) but also a general power to legislate for the "Peace, Order and good Government of Canada" was relegated to the position of an emergency clause, while clauses 13 and 16 of section 92, which gave the provinces control over "Property and Civil Rights" and "all Matters of a merely local or private nature in the Province," became the *de facto* residual clauses of the constitution. The learned judges found it increasingly difficult to find any subject matter that did not touch upon property or civil rights or was not essentially a local problem. This process, which began during Oliver Mowat's premiership, has continued and has resulted in the provinces acquiring most of the new territory that has come under the aegis of government control. Thus the provinces have been assigned responsibility for the regulation of intraprovincial production, trade, and marketing; wages; hours of labour; unemployment insurance (transferred to the federal government by constitutional amendment in 1940); workmen's compensation; industrial disputes; trade union legislation; health regulations; and insurance legislation.[5]

Many fields of provincial jurisdiction have been enhanced as the Canadian society has matured. As the society has become more sophisticated and self-conscious the provincial government has had to extend services such as those provided by the Ontario Council for the Arts, the Ontario Human Rights Commission, the Water Resources Commission, the Ontario Research Foundation, and the Department of Tourism and Information. The factor that has most profoundly influenced this change in the scope of government operations has been the gradual change in the social attitudes of the people. Increased specialization in agriculture and industry, improved means of transportation and communication, and the massive rural to urban population shift have made men less self-sufficient than they were in 1867. Economic and social interdependence have been an impetus to government intervention, and gradually the people have come to expect the government to take a creative part in establishing a viable economy and the "good society." They have demanded that their government take steps to mitigate the more pernicious by-products of the free market; they have insisted that education should be made universally available, free of charge; and they have urged that public funds be used to

[5]R. M. Dawson, *The Government of Canada* (4th ed. rev. by Norman Ward; Toronto: University of Toronto Press, 1963), p. 101.

sustain them and assist them when they fall prey to the inescapable hardships of life. Some of these new-found functions of government were unquestionably provincial responsibilities; others required action at all three levels of government. But, in general, the burden of the new activities has been, and in all probability will continue to be, shifted to the governments of the provinces. For example, to provide employment for an average of 60,000 new entrants to the Ontario labour force each year,[6] action must be taken to ensure a steady and substantial rate of economic growth. In the past, economic growth has generally been ascribed to the utilization of natural resources and the formation of physical capital by expenditures on new structures, machinery, equipment, and inventories. Increasingly emphasis has been shifted to the dynamic influences of investment in human capital, so that now it is recognized that a large part of the growth of our gross national product is attributable to increases in intangible assets, such as improvements in the efficiency of labour because of the investment in health, education, and training, and because of the resultant scientific and technological advance. As Premier Robarts explained, this means "much greater emphasis on the activities of provincial and municipal governments, which are primarily responsible for investments in people."[7]

Whatever the causative factors, the resulting growth in the responsibilities of the government of Ontario has been enough to stagger the imagination of the voters and confound the wisdom of the bureaucrats. This growth can be seen in sharper focus when one isolates certain of its manifestations: the increase in government expenditures, the enlargement of the public service, and the proliferation of ministries and departments.

Expenditures

Looked at in terms of unadjusted dollars, the Ontario government's net current and capital expenditures have increased at such an accelerated rate since 1945 as to make ludicrous any comparisons with expenditures in the nineteenth century. For example, if no allowance is made for changes in the value of the dollar, it may be said that government expenditures in each *day* of 1963 were over twice as much as the total government expenditures in the whole first *year* of the province's existence. The raw figures for selected years are given in Table 1.

---

[6]This figure was given by Prime Minister Robarts in his opening statement at the Federal-Provincial Conference in Ottawa, November 26, 1963. *Federal-Provincial Conference, 1963* (Ottawa: Queen's Printer, 1964), p. 23.
   [7]*Ibid.*

TABLE 1

EXPENDITURES OF THE GOVERNMENT OF ONTARIO, 1868–1965

(selected years)

1868	$ 1,484,506	1920	$ 82,844,790
1870	1,883,640	1925	129,225,425
1875	3,617,522	1930	212,786,765
1880	2,531,166	1936	95,856,130
1885	3,040,139	1940	141,643,788
1890	3,907,428	1945	144,662,429
1895	3,758,595	1950	336,447,678
1900	4,300,759	1955	522,203,215
1905	5,396,016	1960	970,318,311
1910	12,591,529	1965	2,494,699,237
1915	19,439,988		

SOURCES: The figures for the years 1868 to 1891 are taken from Ontario, Royal Commission on the Financial Position of Ontario, *Report*, 1901, Sessional Paper 50, Statement 3. The amounts for the other years are from the *Public Accounts of the Province of Ontario* for the years concerned.

In illustrating this increase it has been necessary to use a semi-logarithmic graph in order to embrace the range of expenditures since 1868 and still give some accurate picture of the changes that have taken place (Figure 2)[8]. In the first full year of operation, the provincial government spent a total of $1,484,506, less than $1 per capita. In 1961 total expenditures were 664 times higher, at $985,694,178, or $158 per capita. Even if we translate the 1868 figure into 1961 dollars, the per capita expenditure of that year is still only approximately $3.70.[9] Ontario never spent more than $4.5 million in any year in the nineteenth century, and with one or two exceptions the province's expenditures did not exceed $150 million per annum until after the second world war. During most of this period the federal government's share of total government expenditures tended to decline in proportion to the expenditures of the junior governments. The chaos of the thirties and the requirements of war in the first half of the forties reversed the trend so that by the end of the war the federal government was spending three times as much as the provincial and municipal governments combined.

However, in 1946 the federalization of revenues and expenditures began again, until by the sixties provincial and local governments together were spending more than the central government. This development, as well as the general increase in government expenditures, is depicted in Figures 3 and 4. Figure 3 shows the trends in expenditures for each of the

[8]The amounts for the years 1868–91 are from Ontario, Royal Commission on the Financial Position of the Province of Ontario, *Report*, 1901, sessional paper no. 50, statement no. 3. Amounts for the other years are from the respective *Public Accounts of the Province of Ontario*.

[9]W. E. Grasham, "Provincial Government," an unpublished manuscript, p. 17.

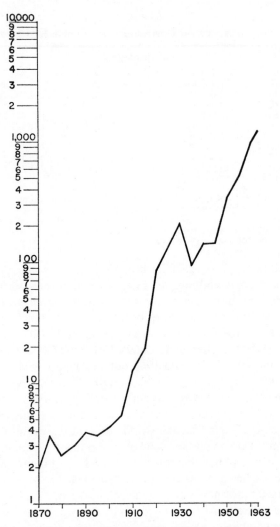

Fɪɢ. 2. Ontario provincial expenditures, 1868–1963, in millions of dollars.

three levels of government and the total expenditures for all levels of government combined for the years 1945–63. Again, using a semi-logarithmic type of graph gives a more accurate expression of the rates of increase in expenditures at the three levels.[10] In Figure 4 only two sets of

[10]Amounts for the years 1945–56 are from *National Accounts: Income and Expenditure, 1926 to 1956* (catalog no. 13–502); those for the years 1957–62 are from *National Accounts: Income and Expenditure, 1962* (catalog no. 13–201); those for 1963 are from *National Accounts: Income and Expenditure, 1963* (catalog no. 13–201), Dominion Bureau of Statistics, Research and Development Division.

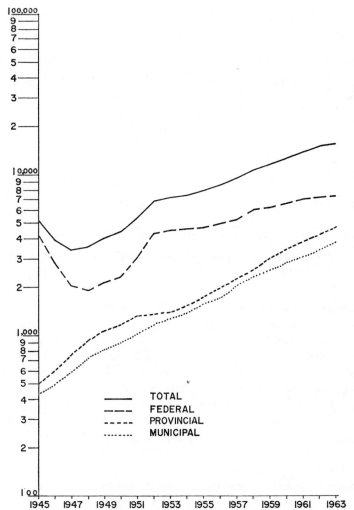

FIG. 3. Government expenditure by level of government, 1945–63, in millions of dollars.

data are depicted: the expenditure of the federal government, and the combined amounts spent by the two junior levels of government.[11] The latter graph gives a clearer portrayal of the adjustments that are being made in Canadian federal financial relations.

[11]Amounts for the years 1945–56 are from *National Accounts: Income and Expenditure, 1926 to 1956*, (catalog no. 13–502); those for the years 1957–1962 are from *National Accounts: Income and Expenditures, 1962* (catalog no. 13–201); those for 1963 are from *National Accounts: Income and Expenditure, 1963* (catalog no. 13–201), Dominion Bureau of Statistics, Research and Development Division.

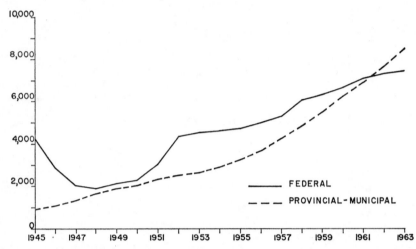

FIG. 4. Government expenditure, federal and provincial–municipal, 1945–63, in millions of dollars.

Between 1955 and 1962 federal government expenditures increased by 55 per cent. The annual increase varied between 3.7 per cent and 6.9 per cent, if one omits the unusual increase of 14.1 per cent in the election year of 1958. During the same period the expenditures of the provincial governments increased by 146.3 per cent, the annual increase varying between 11.2 per cent and 16.7 per cent. The expenditures of the local governments went up by 120.2 per cent, their annual rates of increase fluctuating between 8.7 per cent and 14.5 per cent.[12] In Ontario, during this same period, net ordinary and net capital expenditures by the provincial government increased from $522,203,215 in 1955 to $1,071,011,826 in 1962, a total of 105.1 per cent or an average of 11.8 per cent per year. From 1945–46 to 1963–64 Ontario government expenditures increased more than nine-fold, from $132 million to $1,267 million.

While it is informative to see this increase in provincial expenditures in current dollars, this does not really give an accurate picture, since a part of the over-all increase is attributable to the depreciation in the purchasing power of the dollar. It is more useful to see this growth in relation to increases at the other two levels of government as outlined in Figure 3. But for the purposes of this chapter, it is perhaps most profitable to view

[12]Quebec, Department of Industry and Commerce, *Statistical Study of the Expenditures of the Quebec Government: Comparisons with Other Provinces* (1963), p. 5.

the growth of government expenditures as a percentage of personal income in the province and as a percentage of the gross provincial product (Table 2).

In terms of the gross provincial product, in 1963–64, the last year for which reasonably precise figures are available, total disbursements by the Ontario government were approximately 6.9 per cent of the estimated GPP, compared with 2.7 per cent in 1945–46;[13] in the 1930s the province's expenditures approximated 5 per cent. During the war years, and also for many years after the war, the proportion was lower, but since 1957 the province's expenditures as a proportion of GPP have exceeded the prewar levels and continue to rise.

Looking at the expenditures of the province as a percentage of personal income does not disclose much more about trends *within* the province than is revealed by looking at expenditures as a percentage of the GPP, because the two ratios parallel each other quite closely. However, since personal income figures are available for the other provinces, using this method does make possible comparisons *between* the provinces.[14] Such comparisons can be very useful, if for no other reason than to check the tendency to magnify the significance of increased expenditures in Ontario, which can so easily lead to unfounded conclusions. For instance, it does indeed give cause for thought to note that expenditures in Ontario in 1962

[13]It will be noted that the "total expenditures" listed in Table 2 differ substantially from the expenditures given for the same years in Table 1. The chief reason for this is that Table 1 gives *gross* figures and Table 2 gives *net* figures. To arrive at net expenditures one usually subtracts from gross expenditures such items as the following: (*a*) all revenues of institutions coming under the provincial government, (*b*) revenues in the form of interests, premiums and discounts, (*c*) grants-in-aid and shared-cost contributions (see, for instance, *Statistical Study of the Expenditures of the Quebec Government*, p. 4). Thus the classification "net" expenditures differs from the classification "gross" expenditures in that it reflects the fiscal burden rather than the administrative one. However, even when one uses the same classification throughout, minor discrepancies in figures will still occur. For instance, the DBS publication, *National Accounts*, differs from the *Public Accounts of Canada* in reporting total expenditures for the federal government. The differences are explained by the numerous items mentioned in the *National Accounts* that are not found in the *Public Accounts*. These items include expenditures of an extrabudgetary nature made from certain funds, e.g., old age pension payments, expenditures of crown corporations, the adjustments for the change from the fiscal to the calendar year, etc. Similar difficulties are encountered with provincial statistics. Indeed, it is difficult to find two sources that give exactly the same figures for any one item, unless one source is copied from the other. Happily, such discrepancies are seldom large enough to hamper most common calculations or, if they are, the sources of the variances are usually quite easily isolated so that the necessary adjustments may be made.

[14]The figures for the years 1926–55 are given in *Canadian Fiscal Facts: Principal Statistics of Canadian Public Finance* (Toronto: Canadian Tax Foundation, 1957). Figures for 1954–62 are to be found in *Statistical Study of the Expenditures of the Quebec Government*, p. 14.

TABLE 2

PROVINCE OF ONTARIO
NET ORDINARY EXPENDITURE AND NET CAPITAL DISBURSEMENTS AS A PERCENTAGE
OF PERSONAL INCOME AND GROSS PROVINCIAL PRODUCT[a]

	Net ordinary expenditure	Net capital disbursements[b]	Total expenditures	Total expenditures as a percentage of	
				Personal income	GPP[c]
	(millions of dollars)			(percentages)	
1945–46	126.8	5.5	132.3	3.6	2.7
1946–47	140.9	23.0	163.9	4.4	3.4
1947–48	166.1	35.0	201.1	5.0	3.7
1948–49	206.3	41.7	248.0	5.4	4.0
1949–50	219.9	54.5	274.4	5.6	4.1
1950–51	249.8	55.6	305.4	5.8	4.1
1951–52	301.3	71.0	372.3	6.1	4.3
1952–53	348.4	86.2	434.6	6.4	4.4
1953–54	372.0	58.9	430.9	6.0	4.2
1954–55	399.2	53.6	452.8	6.1	4.4
1955–56	425.5	82.2	507.7	6.4	4.6
1956–57	478.0	113.7	591.7	6.9	4.7
1957–58	591.0	80.3	671.3	7.1	5.1
1958–59	642.1	94.5	737.6	7.4	5.5
1959–60	701.6	115.7	817.3	7.7	5.7
1960–61	739.0	132.6	871.6	7.9	5.9
1961–62	824.9	152.6	977.5	8.5	6.4
1962–63	933.0	113.5	1,106.5	9.0	6.7
1963–64	1,078.2	102.5	1,180.7	9.0	6.6
1964–65	1,236.8	68.7	1,305.5	9.3	6.7

[a]This information was supplied by the Research and Statistics Branch of the Ontario Treasury Department.
[b]Net capital disbursements on physical assets after deducting expenditures for highway construction account, and capital disbursements financed out of ordinary revenue.
[c]Following the technique devised by the Ontario Treasury Department, the gross provincial product is here assumed to be 41 per cent of the gross national product. No accurate independent calculation of Ontario's GPP is attempted either by the Dominion Bureau of Statistics or by any provincial organization.

had risen to 9.6 per cent of the personal income of the province from 3.6 per cent in 1945–46. But before any hasty conclusions about the increasing role of government in Ontario's economy are drawn from these statistics it would be well to reflect on the fact that government expenditures in Quebec had reached 9.5 per cent of the province's personal income in 1959 and were 13.1 per cent in 1962, nearly four percentage points higher than the corresponding figure for Ontario. The other provinces were already spending an average of 9.7 per cent of their personal incomes on government services in 1954 and by 1962 this had been raised to 12.1 per cent. Nor is this a recent trend: from 1926, government disbursements in Ontario have been below the Canadian average both in per capita terms and in relation to aggregate personal income.[15] The expenditures of the Ontario government are compared to the expenditures of the other provinces in Table 3.

There are four main factors which account for the relatively low government expenditure in Ontario. The one which is most frequently cited is that Ontario has been governed by essentially conservative parties ever since the defeat of the United Farmers Government in 1923. That there is an element of truth in this would not be denied even by the current Conservative Government which has held office during the whole of the postwar era with which this study is primarily concerned. So far as comparisons with Quebec are concerned, one of the major reasons for the greater rate of expenditure there has been the desire on the part of that province to assume financial responsibility for certain functions which the other provinces have gladly shared with the central government or left to private initiative.[16] With the change of Government in Quebec in 1960, however, a new factor was added, and the augmentation of government activity in virtually every aspect of life in the province has meant a substantial increase in expenditures. From 1960 to 1962 the average rate of increase in Quebec government expenditures was 18.5 per cent, compared to 10.6 per cent for the Ontario government, and 7.9 per cent for the governments of the other provinces. Ontario's expenditures as a percentage of personal income are lower than those in other provinces because of the size and prosperity of her population: the cost of administering certain standard services does not increase in direct proportion to the number or affluence of those served; hence, the percentage of personal income needed to maintain these services should decline as the population and wealth of the province increase. Also, because of the highly developed municipal-government system in Ontario, a number of the demands that are made on the provincial governments in other provinces are met at the municipal level in Ontario.

Although the increase in expenditures by the Ontario government has not kept pace with the increases in the other provinces, it has been substantial, mirroring the government's response to the change in attitudes towards its responsibilities in the province. To cope with the demands of this changing society the government has not simply had to expand its

[15]Cecil E. Wood, "A Study of Provincial Government Finance in Ontario from 1926 to 1960" (unpublished MA thesis, Queen's University, 1962), p. 6. Two other MA theses at Queen's University, by H. H. F. Benhammer and R. H. Johnson, deal with Ontario government revenues and expenditures, respectively.

[16]For example, Quebec has seen fit to invest proportionately more in the development of natural resources and social welfare. *Statistical Study of the Expenditures of the Quebec Government*, p. 8.

TABLE 3

Net General Expenditure as a Percentage of Personal Income and Per Capita: Quebec, Ontario, Other Provinces, 1954–62

	Personal income ($ millions)			Expenditure as a percentage of personal income (percentages)			Population (thousands)			Expenditure per capita ($)		
	Ontario	Quebec	Others	Ontario	Quebec	Others	Ontario	Quebec	Others	Ontario	Quebec	Others
1954	7,397	4,647	6,325	5.7	7.5	9.7	5,046	4,388	5,734	83.43	79.76	106.93
1955	7,918	4,847	6,918	6.2	8.2	9.9	5,266	4,517	5,886	92.85	88.49	116.29
1956	8,617	5,318	7,880	6.4	8.2	10.0	5,405	4,628	6,017	102.16	93.66	130.49
1957	9,399	5,742	7,977	7.0	8.6	11.1	5,622	4,758	6,178	116.77	103.69	143.00
1958	9,978	6,071	8,553	7.4	8.8	11.1	5,803	4,884	6,328	128.75	109.14	150.15
1959	10,566	6,353	9,025	8.5	9.5	11.6	5,952	4,999	6,457	150.91	120.21	161.70
1960	11,002	6,725	9,577	8.5	11.1	12.3	6,111	5,142	5,581	153.38	145.72	179.54
1961	11,540	7,159	9,700	9.0	11.8	12.4	6,236	5,259	6,706	166.29	160.68	179.86
1962	12,292	7,603	10,779	9.6	13.1	12.1	6,342	5,366	6,823	185.19	186.00	191.67

SOURCE: Quebec, Department of Industry and Commerce, Statistical Study of the Expenditures of the Quebec Government; Comparisons with Other Provinces (1963), p. 14.

financial commitments; it has also been necessary to enlarge and adapt its institutional structure. But the significant point here is that enlarging and improving the legislative branch of government is of very little immediate or obvious benefit so far as the provision of services is concerned, because to create and administer new social policies is not a function of the legislative institutions of government. Hence, as will be shown in the following chapters, there has been very little enlargement of the legislative branch of government in Ontario, and its organization has remained virtually unchanged until quite recently. It is in the executive branch – the cabinet and the public service – that the growth in government has taken place, that the new functions of government have been centred, and that modifications have been made in the original institutions.

Public Service

One of the most sensitive indicators of increased government activity is the size of the public service. Assuming that Parkinson's "law"[17] was at least no less valid in 1867 than in 1964, any enlargement of the administrative branch should serve as a rough measure of the extension of government functions. In the early years of the province's history, the public service consisted of a few hundred men and women, usually hand-picked by a Government grateful for electoral support. The employees were known individually by their respective ministers, and even the premier was approachable by those seeking positions or preferment.[18] By 1904 there were only 704 provincial employees in Ontario, or 7 civil servants for each member of the Legislative Assembly. The second decade of the twentieth century saw a rapid expansion in the size of the public service, reaching a total of 4,066 in 1919; the total increase in staff in the twenties was 37 per cent in spite of the decline during the recession years of 1921–22. During the thirties there was a net increase of only 5 per cent, but the

[17] The reference here is to his contention that work expands to fill the time available for its completion and not to his statement that, in any public administrative department not actually at war, staff increase will be from 5.17 to 6.56 per cent annually irrespective of any variation in the amount of work (if any) to be done. In reference to the latter "law," it is interesting to note that the number employed by the Ontario government has declined twice in this century during times of peace—from 1921–22 and from 1932–37. In the latter period the reduction was from 7,760 to 6,963.

[18] The classic illustration of this is the story of Sir J. P. Whitney, premier of Ontario at the turn of the century. Sir James made a habit of riding a bicycle to his office and one morning he was overtaken by a man who informed him that a sheriff of Manitoulin Island had died and asked if he could take his place. The unperturbed Premier replied that it was all right with him, if the undertaker did not mind.

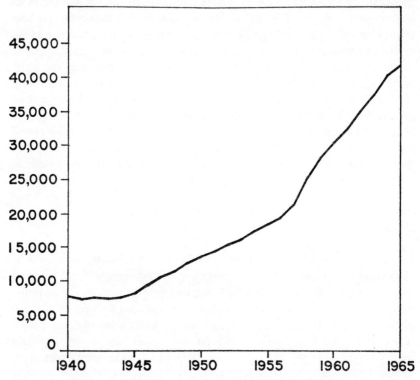

FIG. 5. Public employees of the Ontario government, 1940–65.

turnover was considerable: Premier Hepburn fired the "Tories" as a supposed economy measure following his election of 1934, but he rebuilt the civil service to more than its 1930 complement by the end of the decade, presumably with employees more sympathetic to his style of government. The trend since then is depicted in Figure 5. In spite of the decrease in the size of the service during the war years, the net increase in the forties was 66 per cent. The impact of "big government" on the civil service was especially felt during the years from 1944 to 1964, when the staff increased from 7,712 to 41,074 or 433 per cent; the increase in the twenty years before had only been from 5,528 to 7,712, or 39.5 per cent.[19]

[19]This information was provided by Mrs. A. H. Malkin, statistician in the Administrative Service Branch of the Ontario Department of Civil Service. Each figure is as of March 31 of the year indicated, except the years 1960–65, inclusive, which are as of April 30. In 1951 the employees of the Liquor Control Board of Ontario were brought under the jurisdiction of the Civil Service Commission, but they are omitted from these figures to make comparisons with previous years more meaningful.

Some indication of the problems this growth in the administration poses for the legislature – which considers one of its functions to be the continuous supervision of administrative actions – is found in the simple fact that in 1924 there was one MPP for every 49 civil servants, in 1944 there was one for every 85, but in 1963, when the House was the same size as it was in 1902, the ratio was one MPP to 402 civil servants. It would be erroneous and foolish to conclude on the basis of this evidence that the members' task of keeping an eye on the operations of the civil service was ten times more difficult in 1963 than in 1944, but certainly the facts do illustrate the increasing complexity of functions traditionally ascribed to members of legislative assemblies.[20] When the staffs of the various boards and commissions are added to the total the magnitude of the problem becomes even more awesome.

Ministries

A further indication of the expansion of government activity in Ontario and one which, like the last mentioned, has direct significance for a study of legislative-executive relations, is the growth in the size of the cabinet itself. Neither the Quebec Resolutions of 1864, nor the London Resolutions of 1866 made any provision for an executive council of Ontario, stipulating only that "The Local Government and Legislature of each Province shall be constructed in such manner as the Legislature of each such Province shall provide."[21] During the debate on the local constitutions, Mr. M. C. Cameron objected to this lack of precision, but Sir John A. Macdonald "explained that the general terms of the well understood principles of the British Constitution were sufficiently explicit to define the necessity for a constitutional Ministry. But the number of Departments has been left to be determined by the local Parliament."[22] Nevertheless,

[20]The difficulty the MPP experiences attempting to "keep an eye on the civil service" is also increased by the decentralization of service. Although a large part of the bureaucracy is situated at Queen's Park in Toronto, some of it is scattered in offices throughout the city, and much of it is outside of Toronto altogether. Besides the half dozen buildings at Queen's Park there are another 5,360 government-owned buildings, ranging in size from roadside salt sheds to such major institutional buildings as the hospital located in Orillia. Office space is also leased by the province in approximately 350 different locations.

[21]Quebec Resolution 41, and London Resolution 40.

[22]Canada, Parliament, House of Commons, *Debates, 1866–1870* (microfilm of newspaper accounts reported by the *Ottawa Times*, Toronto *Globe*, and Toronto *Mail* in the Library of Parliament, filmed by the Canadian Library Association, July 27, 1866, p. 61.

the British North America Act did make provision for executive councils in Ontario and Quebec and, furthermore, limited the number of officers in the former to five in the first instance: the attorney general, the secretary and registrar of the province, the treasurer of the province, the commissioner of crown lands, and the commissioner of agriculture and public works.[23] By section 134 of the British North America Act the lieutenant governor was also authorized to "appoint other and additional Officers to hold office during Pleasure," but this opportunity to appoint "Ministers without portfolio" was not used very extensively in the early history of the province.[24]

The first expansion of the cabinet took place in 1871 when Edward Blake became president of the Council, without salary, and assigned the five portfolios provided for in the constitution to the other members of the executive council. This was exactly what Sir John A. Macdonald had urged John Sandfield Macdonald to do in order to stave off defeat, and so it was to be expected that Sandfield was chagrined at the innovation and its success.[25] His resolution condemning the increase was defeated in the Assembly by a vote of 50 to 12. In 1872 statutory provision was made for an executive council of six members.[26] Nevertheless, when Sir Oliver Mowat took office later in the same year, he reduced the cabinet to its former size and took the post of attorney general which, with the exception

23British North America Act. s. 63. Quebec was provided with two additional officers, the speaker of the legislative council and the solicitor general. It was not necessary to provide for the executive councils of Nova Scotia and New Brunswick, whose constitutions were to continue as they existed.

24Only three ministers without portfolio were appointed before 1900: Erskine H. Bronson (1890), Elihu J. Davis (1896), and James T. Garrow (1898).

25A few days after Sandfield Macdonald's defeat, Sir John A. Macdonald wrote to a member of the defeated cabinet: "There is no use in crying over spilt milk, but it is vexatious to see how Sandfield threw away his chances. He has handed over the surplus [there had been a series of budgetary surpluses] which he had not the pluck to use, to his Opponents, and although I pressed him . . . to make a President of the Council and a Minister of Education, which he had promised to do, yet he took no steps towards doing so. With these two offices and that of the Solicitor General and the Speakership he had the game in his hands. You see that, as I prophesied would be the case, the first act of the new government was to increase the Cabinet." Quoted from Charles Clark, *Sixty Years in Upper Canada, with Autobiographical Recollections* (Toronto: William Briggs, 1908), p. 157.

26*Statutes of Ontario (SO)* 1871–72, c. 3, An Act further to secure the Independence of the Legislative Assembly. Mr. M. C. Cameron moved, in amendment to the provision for six ministers, "that in case any member of the Legislative Assembly hereafter becomes a member of the Executive Council, his election shall be void and his seat vacant." If this peculiar resolution meant anything, it was the abolition of responsible government; an end that appealed to a significant number of the province's constitution-makers (*infra*, chap. 4). Only four other members voted with Cameron in support of the amendment.

of Blake's Ministry, traditionally went to the prime minister of the province.[27]

In 1874 a slight change in the provisions for the executive council made it no longer necessary that the commissioner of agriculture and the commissioner of public works should be the same person.[28] This, however, did not necessarily mean an increase in the size of the cabinet, since either one of these functions could be given to someone already responsible for one of the other departments. Similarly, the creation of the position of minister of education in 1876 did not necessarily need to result in an enlargement of the cabinet but did in fact have that effect.[29] Following this change, the number of positions listed in the Executive Council Act remained at seven until 1905 when the position of "President of the Council" was finally given statutory recognition.[30] Since that time the number of positions has continued to increase. The names of some of these new positions are themselves indicative of the changes in the scope of government activities since 1905: the ministers of the Departments of Citizenship, Highways, Labour, Health, Public Welfare, Municipal Affairs, Economics and Development, Tourism and Information, Reform Institutions, Transport, Energy and Resources Management, and University Affairs.[31] The largest cabinet in the history of the province was appointed on November 21, 1960, when twenty-two ministers took the oath of office.

Enough has now been said about the growth of government functions in Ontario to set the scene for a discussion of how and to what extent the formal institutions of government have been modified in response to this new situation. The next chapter will describe the changes that have been made in the executive branch.

[27]The practice of the prime minister also becoming attorney general ended in Ontario in 1899 when Premier Ross chose the position of provincial treasurer instead.
[28]SO, 1874, c. 2, An Act respecting the Executive Council.
[29]SO, 1875–76, c. 16, An Act respecting the Eduction Department.
[30]SO, 1905, c. 5, An Act to amend the Act respecting the Executive Council.
[31]SO, 1964, c. 28, An Act to Amend the Executive Council Act.

THE EXECUTIVE
BRANCH

3

THE LOCUS OF POWER and responsibility in the governmental structure of Ontario is the cabinet. Sir Ivor Jennings resorted to analogy to define the British cabinet as "the board of directors for Great Britain and all those parts of the Commonwealth which do not possess self-government."[1] Similarly, the Hon. Leslie M. Frost, a former premier of Ontario, has referred to the principles of cabinet government obtaining in the province as being very similar to those of corporate administration.[2] However, while the Ontario cabinet may be very similar to others throughout the Commonwealth in its functions, its legal position is quite different from the Westminster prototype and, to a lesser extent, from the Ottawa model.

In the first place, like its New Zealand counterpart, the Ontario cabinet differs from the British, Australian, and Canadian cabinets in the fact that its membership is identical to that of the executive council, the Ontario equivalent of the privy councils at Westminster and Ottawa.[3] The corollary

[1]Sir William Ivor Jennings, *Cabinet Government* (3rd ed.; Cambridge: Cambridge University Press, 1959), p. 228.
[2]From an interview with the Hon. Leslie M. Frost, January 27, 1965.
[3]Much of the detailed information in this chapter has been obtained by means of interviews and correspondence with persons who have been closely associated with the Ontario cabinet in some official capacity. I am particularly indebted to the following: Mr. Ernest C. Drury, premier of Ontario, 1919–23; the Hon. Leslie M. Frost, premier of Ontario, 1949–61; Mr. W. M. McIntyre, secretary of the cabinet and deputy minister of the Prime Minister's Department; the Hon. Roland D. Michener, a former provincial secretary of Ontario; Mr. L. R. McDonald, general council for the Hydro-Electric Power Commission of Ontario and a former secretary of the cabinet; Mr. L. R. MacTavish, QC, senior legislative council; Mr. H. H. Walker, associate deputy minister of the Treasury Department and a former secretary of the Treasury Board; Mr. C. E. Brannan, secretary of the Treasury Board; Mr. A. N. Stone, registrar of regulations; Mr. J. J. Young, clerk of the executive

of this is the fact that when a person leaves the cabinet he also leaves the executive council and hence loses his right to the title "Honourable." In Britain and at the federal level in Canada, once a person takes the privy councillor's oath he remains a privy councillor for life, retaining also the titles "Right Honourable," in Britain, and "Honourable" in Canada.

Although there is no difference between the personnel of the cabinet and the executive council in Ontario, it is nevertheless possible to distinguish between the functions of the two bodies, as indeed is done in the *Manual of Administration* prepared by the Organization and Methods Services Branch of the Treasury Board. The executive council is the only one of the two that has any statutory existence and is responsible for giving formal advice to the lieutenant governor, taking action in conjunction with him by means of orders in council, and administering the work of the departments. The cabinet, on the other hand, exists only by convention and represents the political reality underlying the constitutional form. Its functions are political in nature and include such things as the determination of Government policy and the devising of strategy to ensure the implementation of that policy.

Making this distinction between the functions of the executive council and those of the cabinet no doubt helps to clarify the relationship between the formal institutions of government and the political process that gives them meaning in a democracy, but it must be borne in mind that in Ontario the distinction is quite artificial. The members of the executive council certainly do not make any such distinction and even if the attempt were made it would be difficult to find criteria by which the dividing line between the two sets of functions could be determined. For instance, all members of the executive council take the same three oaths: the Oath of Allegiance, the Oath of Member of the Executive Council, and the Oath of Office (except ministers without portfolio who naturally would not take the latter oath).[4] Consequently in this study the terms executive council and cabinet are used interchangeably, although the choice of term in any given context may reflect a judgment as to whether the activity discussed tends to be formal or political in nature.

A second distinctive feature of the Ontario cabinet, when contrasted with the British or Australian cabinets – but not the Canadian federal cabinet or the New Zealand cabinet – is that it is synonymous with the "ministry." Everyone who is in the ministry is automatically in the cabinet, even if he has no portfolio to administer. In fact, the term "minis-

---

council, and the staff of the Organization and Methods Services Branch of the Treasury Board.

4See Appendix A for the wording of these oaths.

try" is not commonly used in the province. Instead, preference is given to either the American word, "administration" or the general term, "government," as in "the Frost administration" or "the Robarts government."[5]

The Ontario executive council is provided for in the Executive Council Act,[6] but a number of other acts also affects its composition and functions. For instance, until 1926 the terms of the Legislative Assembly Act made it necessary for anyone accepting a portfolio in the executive council to relinquish his seat in the Assembly and stand for re-election.[7] The Financial Administration Act provides for a permanent committee of the executive council, the Treasury Board, and sets out its functions and responsibilities.[8] Besides these general acts there are the individual acts establishing the various government departments, the ministerial heads of which compose the executive council. And, finally, there are the myriad acts which grant specific powers to the "Lieutenant Governor in Council," all of which would have to be considered if one were to attempt a complete description of the powers and responsibilities of the executive council. However, the main functions of the Ontario cabinet are still essentially those that were set out for the British cabinet by the Machinery of Government Committee in 1918:

(a) the final determination of the policy to be submitted to Parliament;
(b) the supreme control of the national executive in accordance with the policy prescribed by Parliament; and
(c) the continuous co-ordination and delimitation of the authorities of the several Departments of State.[9]

It will be noted that this statement makes no distinction between what may be called the "political," the "legislative," or the "administrative" functions of the cabinet, and this certainly reflects the situation in Ontario. From the time that a given policy proposal is agreed to by the cabinet, through all of the stages in the legislative process which finally issue in statutory provisions for the achievement of that policy, to the time that those laws are actually administered, the cabinet is the dominant institu-

5Although by no means uniform, official publications tend to favour the term "ministry."

6Revised Statutes of Ontario (RSO), 1960, c. 127.

7RSO, 1914, c. 11, s. 15. In 1926 an amendment to the Legislative Assembly Act provided that a member of the Assembly could be appointed to the executive council within three months of a general election without having to vacate his seat (SO, 1926, c. 5, s 4). Later, in 1941, the three-month period was eliminated so that an MPP could be appointed to the executive council at any time without needing to go through the formality of a by-election (SO, 1941, c. 26, s. 1).

8RSO, 1960, c. 142, s. 2.

9Report of the Machinery of Government Committee, Cd. 9230/1918, p. 5, as quoted in Jennings, Cabinet Government, p. 232.

tion. As the leaders of the party in power the members of the cabinet are primarily responsible for the formulation of party policy, and as the ministers of the crown they are ultimately held responsible for all the activities of government, whether these are performed by civil servants, by individual ministers, or by the cabinet itself.

Size of the Cabinet

Because the cabinet serves as the hub of the wheel of government and because the functions of government have expanded, the cabinet has increased in size. This phenomenon of modern government poses a great many problems, not only for those who are concerned with controlling the powers of the executive, but also for those whose primary concern is simply efficiency of administration. Anyone who has ever attempted to get some twenty individuals to discuss an issue and agree on a course of action has difficulty imagining how modern cabinets, composed as they are of loquacious politicians, manage to reach any decisions at all. But to see the significance of this growth for a study of legislative-executive relations, it is useful to view the size of the cabinet in relation to the size of the Legislative Assembly and, perhaps more significantly, in relation to the size of the majority party caucus. Other things being equal, the greater the proportion of the House or the party taken up by the cabinet, the easier it will be for it to dominate proceedings. While increases in the size of the Ontario cabinet are in keeping with general trends, the problem of size is not as acute as in some other jurisdictions where the size of the legislatures has remained relatively static. In Newfoundland, for instance, from 1949 to 1954 the members of the cabinet accounted for approximately 46 per cent of the seats in the Assembly – which did not leave very many backbenchers in the Government.[10] In Prince Edward Island since the end of the war the cabinet has usually encompassed close to one-third of the House.[11]

In Ontario the membership of the Legislative Assembly increased from 82 in 1867 to 108 in 1963, or 32 per cent. In the same period the cabinet increased from 5 ministers to a maximum of 22, or 440 per cent: whereas the cabinet only accounted for 6 per cent of the total membership of the House in 1867, it included over 22 per cent of the House in 1960 when the Assembly totalled 98 members. When Mr. Robarts became premier in 1961 he took advantage of the opportunity to reduce the size of the

[10]This information is taken from Stanley Drabeck, "An Analysis of Provincial Cabinet Membership, 1949–1963," an unpublished paper prepared for Professor K. Grant Crawford at Queen's University, 1963–64, Appendix A.
[11]*Ibid.*

cabinet. Then, in 1963, the membership of the House was increased to 108 so that the ratio of executive members to legislative members was substantially changed, the cabinet including only 17.5 per cent of the MPPS. But even this put the cabinet in a strong position vis-à-vis the backbenchers on the floor of the House. In comparison the cabinet in Ottawa only claims 6.8 per cent of the MPs.[12] In the United Kingdom the cabinet only includes 3.6 per cent of the membership of the House of Commons, and even if the total ministry of 102 (which includes at least a dozen members of the House of Lords) is taken into account, this still only comes to 16.2 per cent of the total House of Commons.[13]

Furthermore, if the Government backbenchers are considered to be an instrument for controlling the executive – as they certainly should be, although their influence is more behind the scenes than in the formal institutions of government – then the size of the cabinet vis-à-vis the party caucus is of the utmost importance. With a large number of cabinet positions to be allotted, aspiring politicians are inclined to be rather tractable. And, if a majority of the caucus holds cabinet positions as is sometimes the case in provincial parliaments, then the role of the Government backbenchers in controlling the cabinet is greatly diminished, if not eliminated entirely. In Ontario the cabinet was always reasonably small in proportion to the Government caucus in the first fifty years of its history, never exceeding 20 per cent of the total. Then the United Farmers, with only 44 seats in the 111-seat House, created a cabinet with 11 members, or 25 per cent of the caucus. Relative to the size of the Government caucus, this was the largest cabinet in Ontario until 1943 when the Conservatives, with only 38 seats out of a House of 90, formed a cabinet of 10 giving executive authority to 26 per cent of their representatives in the House. In 1948 a 16-man cabinet was constituted, including 30 per cent of the 53 Conservative MPPs. Finally, in 1950, the cabinet of 17 set an all-time record, including as it did nearly one-third of the Government caucus. The imagination need not be stretched in order to see that a cabinet of these proportions would be in a very strong position if ever there were any opposition from the caucus.

Representation in the Cabinet

Since the cabinet is the centre of all government activity in Ontario, it is inevitable that it be not only large in relation to the Assembly and the

[12]As of February 1, 1965.
[13]These figures are based on the original Labour Ministry announced on October 27, 1964.

party caucus but also fairly representative of the social, economic, and political complexion of the province. The most obvious illustration of this is the nice balance that is maintained between rural and urban representation in the cabinet. Since the second world war there has been a direct correlation between the percentage of members of the Assembly representing rural seats and the percentage of the cabinet ministers representing rural seats. Table 4 illustrates this correlation, and while it leaves the impression that the rural areas are usually under-represented in the cabinet, this is certainly not the case. The reason for this false belief is that the rural areas are substantially over-represented in the legislature: until the partial redistribution in 1963 the rural seats formed a majority in the Legislative Assembly, but this did not reflect the true numerical significance of the rural population. In fact, when viewed strictly in terms of population, rather than in terms of seats, the rural areas are still greatly over-represented in the cabinet, in spite of the 1963 redistribution. The 1961 census gives Ontario's urban population as 4,823,529, or over 77 per cent of the total,[14] and even if one limits the "urban" classification to persons living in communities of over 30,000, it still comes to 57 per cent of the provincial population. Nevertheless only 9 out of 19, or 47 per cent, of the cabinet ministers in the first session following the 1963 election were from predominantly urban seats. No doubt as the task of redistribution continues the rural areas will lose some of their representation in the Assembly, and the prime ministers will have the opportunity to correct the balance in the cabinet. In the meantime it is significant to note the consistency with which the cabinet has been divided between the urban and rural seats.

It is also interesting to see how consistently certain areas and economic interests in the province find representation in the cabinet. Not only does the prime minister need to listen to the demands of industrial centres like Toronto; ministers must be chosen from every section of the province, and the major industries and other economic interests expect to have at least one minister in the cabinet knowledgeable about, and sympathetic towards, their activities. Not infrequently a minister affiliated with a particular industry will have responsibility for the portfolio concerned with that industry and will also represent an area in which it is concentrated. A classic example of this in the early years of the province was the case of R. W. Scott, who was elected speaker of the House under Sandfield Macdonald. He had acted as the legal representative of the lumber interests and was charged with being their "paid agent" in the Assembly. Nevertheless, following a scene between Scott and Macdonald, Edward Blake

[14]Canada, Dominion Bureau of Statistics, *Canada Year Book*, 1962, p. 1197.

TABLE 4

URBAN–RURAL REPRESENTATION IN THE LEGISLATIVE ASSEMBLY AND CABINET IN ONTARIO, 1949–63

Year	Total seats in the Assembly	Rural seats	Percentage of seats that are rural	Urban seats	Percentage of seats that are urban	Number of ministers	Ministers from rural seats	Percentage of ministers from rural seats	Ministers from urban seats	Percentage of ministers from urban seats
1949	90	60	67	30	33	15	8	53	7	47
1950	90	60	67	30	33	17	10	58	7	42
1951	90	60	67	30	33	18	10	55	8	45
1952	90	60	67	30	33	18	10	55	8	45
1953	90	60	67	30	33	19	10	53	9	47
1954	90	60	67	30	33	19	10	53	9	47
1955	98	53	54	45	46	18	9	50	9	50
1956	98	53	54	45	46	19	9	47	10	53
1957	98	53	54	45	46	19	9	47	10	53
1958	98	53	54	45	46	18	9	50	9	50
1959	98	53	54	45	46	21	11	52	10	48
1960	98	53	54	45	46	23	11	47	12	53
1961	98	53	54	45	46	21	9	43	12	57
1962	98	53	54	45	46	21	11	52	10	48
1963	108	53	49	55	51	19	10	53	9	47

SOURCE: Stanley Drabek, "An Analysis of Provincial Cabinet Membership, 1949–1963," an unpublished paper prepared for Professor K. Grant Crawford at Queen's University, 1963–64, Table B.

persuaded Scott to resign the speakership and join the new Liberal cabinet as commissioner of crown lands. Besides being entirely satisfactory to the lumber interests, Scott gave representation to an area hitherto neglected in the cabinet, namely, the Ottawa valley, a centre of the lumber industry.[15] In more modern times a typical example of this practice was Charles McCrea who, in the early thirties, was a leading figure in the mining industry in the province, a representative of Sudbury constituency (a mining centre), and minister of mines, all at the same time. Another illustration of this was the appointment of Stanley Randall, the managing director of a large manufacturing company, as minister of economics and development following his election in the Toronto constituency of Don Mills in 1963.

To illustrate how similar the geographical representation is in Ontario cabinets, it will suffice to compare two recent ministries: the Frost ministry, in office during the second session of the 26th Parliament, 1960–61, and the Robarts ministry, as it was during the first session of the 27th Parliament, 1963. The former was the largest cabinet in the history of the province and the latter was one of the smallest in recent years. In both there were two ministers from constituencies in Northern Ontario: that area lying north of the traditional dividing line following the Mattawa River, Lake Nipissing, and the French River. Six represented Southeastern Ontario in the Frost cabinet; this was reduced to five by Mr. Robarts. Four in the Robarts cabinet came from Southwestern Ontario, but there were five from this section in Frost's cabinet. The remaining nine in Mr. Frost's cabinet of twenty-two came from constituencies located in the Mississauga Conurbation, commonly known as the "Golden Horseshoe," around the western shore of Lake Ontario, where more than half of the manfacturing industry of the province is located and where a majority of the population lives. Four of the nine had seats in Metropolitan Toronto and one came from Hamilton. Mr. Robarts had room for only eight from the Mississauga Conurbation in his nineteen-man cabinet, but five of the eight had seats in Metro itself.[16] (*See also* Figure 6.)

[15]Adam Shortt and Arthur G. Doughty, *Canada and its Provinces: A History of the Canadian People and their Institutions by One Hundred Associates*, vol. 17 (Toronto and Glasgow: Brook, 1914), p. 129.

[16]The four geographic divisions used in this analysis correspond to the following economic regions defined by the Department of Economics and Development: "Northern Ontario" includes the Northeastern Ontario and the Lakehead–Northwestern Ontario regions; "Southeastern Ontario" includes the Eastern Ontario and Lake Ontario regions; "Southwestern Ontario" includes the Metropolitan, Niagara, Lake Erie, Lake St. Clair, Upper Grand River, and Georgian Bay regions, except for those constituencies in the counties of Lincoln, Wentworth, Halton, Peel, York, and Ontario, which constitute the Mississauga Conurbation. To delimit the "Mississauga

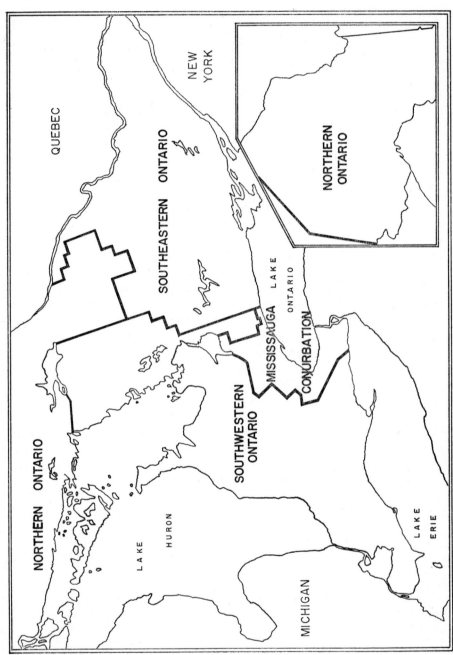

Fig. 6.   Areas represented in the Ontario cabinet.

Denominational representation in the cabinet is almost identical to that in the Legislative Assembly, but, as with urban-rural representation, the religious complexion of the House is not an accurate reflection of the total population. For example, although the Roman Catholic Church is the largest single denomination in Ontario, embracing 30 per cent of the population, only 10 per cent of the members of the Assembly list it as their religious affiliation.[17] This discrepancy between Roman Catholic strength in the total population and Roman Catholic representation in the Legislature is similar to the discrepancy between the proportion of urban voters and the proportion of members of the Assembly representing urban seats. As the 30 per cent of the population that is Roman Catholic is represented by only 10 per cent of the MPPs, so the 77 per cent of the population that is urban is represented by only 51 per cent of the MPPs. The connection between these two sets of data becomes evident when it is realized that 80 per cent of Ontario's Roman Catholics are urban dwellers whereas only 70 per cent of its Protestants are. Rural favouritism in the system of representation would therefore undoubtedly result in under-representation of the Roman Catholic element in the population. Of course, to explain fully why there are relatively few Roman Catholics in the House and in the cabinet would require an analysis of élites in Ontario to determine to what extent Roman Catholics have succeeded in infiltrating the traditional "Orange" establishment, as well as an extensive motivational research programme to find out how significant religious affiliation is as a determinant of voting behaviour – both of which are beyond the scope of this study.

If the Roman Catholics have been under-represented in the cabinet, the United Church of Canada has been grossly over-represented. The ten ministers who list this denomination as their church affiliation constitute 52.5 per cent of the cabinet, a substantially higher proportion than in either the House (37 per cent) or in the general population (26 per cent). The factors that have permitted, or created, this situation may be much the same as those that have resulted in the low proportion of Roman Catholics in government; only in this instance they have had the opposite effect. Aside from these two extremes the religious composition of the

---

Conurbation" I have generally taken the county and/or constituency boundaries which most closely approximate the boundaries commonly given to the area by geographers. See for example D. F. Putnam, "Mississauga," *Community Planning Review*, vol. IV, 1954, pp. 93–6; Norman Pearson, "Conurbation Canada," *Canadian Geographer*, vol. V, no. 4, Winter 1961, pp. 10–17.

[17]These figures are derived from the information supplied to the Clerk of the Legislative Assembly by the members elected in the general election of 1963.

TABLE 5

RELIGIOUS REPRESENTATION IN THE ONTARIO CABINET, 1949–63

Year	Number of cabinet ministers	Roman Catholic	United Church	Anglican	Presbyterian	Other
1949	15	1	7	6	1	1
1950	17	1	8	6	1	1
1951	18	1	8	7	1	1
1952	18	2	8	6	2	1
1953	19	2	8	6	3	1
1954	19	2	9	4	3	1
1955	18	2	8	4	3	1
1956	19	2	8	5	3	1
1957	19	2	8	5	3	1
1958	18	2	8	4	3	1
1959	21	3	9	4	3	2
1960	23	3	10	4	3	3
1961	21	2	11	3	3	2
1962	21	2	12	4	1	2
1963	19	2	10	4	1	2

SOURCE: Stanley Drabek: "An Analysis of Provincial Cabinet Membership, 1949–1963," Table D.

cabinet is a fairly accurate reflection of the composition of the Assembly and the total population.

What is perhaps most interesting for the purposes of this study is the consistency with which this pattern of religious representation has been followed in recent years. As the cabinet has grown in size, the representation of the major denominations has grown accordingly, so that each denomination has maintained almost exactly the same proportionate strength in the cabinet in each successive ministry. The faithfulness with which the over-all pattern has been adhered to in the last fifteen years is demonstrated in Table 5. Only two exceptions to the pattern merit mention. First, the Anglican Church, in the last decade particularly, has lost ground in the cabinet. This could very well be indicative of deep-rooted changes taking place in Ontario society as a result of postwar immigration, urbanization, and industrialization, manifested in a growing disenchantment with tradition, conservatism, and the British connection, all of which still form part of the popular image of the Anglican Church. The other phenomenon in cabinet representation to be noted is the increase in the "Other" category (see Table 5). This too mirrors a fundamental transformation of Ontario society and is indicative of the increasing heterogeneity of the population.

The final aspect of the representative nature of the cabinet which merits some mention is occupational representation. The result of investigation

TABLE 6

OCCUPATIONAL REPRESENTATION IN ONTARIO CABINET, 1963

Occupations	Percentage of the labour force	Percentage of the legislature	Percentage of the cabinet
Managerial	8.8	27.9	21.0
Professional and technical	9.9	38.0	47.0
Clerical	15.0	—	—
Sales	6.6	12.9	16.0
Service and recreation	12.3	3.7	—
Transport and communications	5.7	—	—
Farmers and farm workers	7.2	12.9	16.0
Loggers and related workers	0.5	—	—
Fishermen, trappers, hunters	0.075	—	—
Miners, quarrymen, and related workers	1.06	—	—
Craftsmen, production process, and related workers	25.9	4.6	—
Labourers (not elsewhere specified)	4.73	—	—
Occupation not stated	2.25	—	—
	100	100	100

SOURCE: Compiled from information supplied to the office of the Clerk of the Legislative Assembly by the Members elected in the general election of 1963 and the data found in the *Census of Canada, 1961*, III, Part 1, Table 17 (Catalogue: 94–511). The categories listed here are those used in the census.

is the expected one: the occupational breakdown of Ontario's cabinet is quite similar to that of the Ontario House, but it bears virtually no relation to the occupational patterns in the general population (*see* Table 6). The largest occupational category is the professional and technical, which includes nine ministers, or 47 per cent of the cabinet.[18] This category accounts for 38 per cent of the membership of the House but only 9.9 per cent of the population. The same tendency is evident in each of the four categories represented in the cabinet, although not to the same degree. The professional, sales, and farm occupations all have greater proportional representation in the cabinet than in the House; only the managerial occupations have proportionately more representatives in the House than in the cabinet. All four categories are among the numerically less significant groups in the total labour force, together amounting to only 32.5 per cent of the total. On the other hand, the large categories, such as the clerical, the service and recreation, and the craftsmen and production process occupations, which constitute a majority of the working population, are without representation in the cabinet and account for only 8.3 per cent of the members of the Legislative Assembly.

[18]Reference here is to the Robarts cabinet as it existed during the first session of the 27th Legislature, 1963.

On the basis of this evidence a number of tentative conclusions may be drawn. For instance, that most of the members of the cabinet come from occupations generally thought of as "middle class" is instructive. Conceivably this could be indicative of a middle-class orientation in the Progressive Conservative party, but any generalization here is impossible, because there has not been a cabinet formed for more than forty years that has had origins that were distinctly other than middle class. If a party that was firmly committed to either the farm population or the urban working class were to form a cabinet, occupational representativeness could be studied comparatively. Then, it would probably be possible to determine the connection between the class orientation of the party and the composition by occupation of the cabinet. However, enough data are already available to illustrate that class considerations, be they conscious and overt or merely subconscious, can only be of relatively minor importance in the final shaping of a cabinet. With extremely rare exceptions, Ontario's cabinet-makers have limited their search for ministers to the members elected in ordinary elections of the province. Furthermore, as illustrated in Table 6, the cabinet fairly accurately duplicates in microcosm the occupational composition of the House. So long as this is the case it follows that any favouritism or antipathy towards certain occupations in choosing cabinet members is to be explained by reference to either the desires of the people, as manifest in their votes, or to the operations of our electoral system which always distorts public opinion.

The results of behavioural research in Ontario are not adequate to explain exactly what motivates working-class voters to support middle-class candidates, but two tentative suggestions may be made. There is, first of all, the pervasive middle-class myth. The fact that Canada does have a relatively large middle class, coupled with a high degree of social mobility and a rising standard of living, has created a society oriented towards the middle class.[19] Many people who lack the economic, occupational, educational, cultural, and most other accoutrements of the middle class envisage themselves as belonging to that stratum. Another significant group see themselves as potential members of the middle class. Thus, while by most criteria these people are crossing class lines when voting for candidates from the managerial and professional occupations, psychologically the lines do not exist.[20] Secondly, even if voters do recognize that they

[19]John Porter, *The Vertical Mosaic* (Toronto: University of Toronto Press, 1965, pp. 4–6.

[20]Still the most convincing evidence of the limited significance of class considerations in Canadian voting behaviour is that compiled by Robert R. Alford in *Party and Society: The Anglo-American Democracies* (Chicago: Rand McNally, 1963), pp. 250–86.

are voting for people who represent socio-economic interests that differ from their own, there is a widespread belief that business or professional experience is an extremely valuable attribute for a politician, equipping him to conduct the province's affairs in a "business-like manner." Corroborative evidence for these popular beliefs and opinions is found in the mildness of the criticism of the occupational lopsidedness of the House and the cabinet; indeed, the most common criticisms are that there are too many farmers and too many lawyers in the House.

The over-representation of farmers in the Assembly is a result of the electoral system which favours the rural areas. Coupled with this is the fact that successful farmers on old, established farms find it easier to enter politics than do men in many other occupations and, as long as the sessions are limited to the winter months, serving in the House does not interfere greatly with their normal work. This over-representation is carried over into the cabinet and even enhanced. In part this is because once elected farmers seem able to hold their seats longer than urban members. Long political experience is an attribute that can bring a man into the cabinet even when his ability may be only moderate. The inclusion of a large number of farmers in the cabinet also stems from the Government's desire to embrace representatives of all the important occupational groups in the House in sufficient numbers to offset pressures from those groups. If the cabinet can control or at least forestall criticism from the major groups by including a large number of representatives of those groups within its own ranks, it will be in a very strong position vis-à-vis the less important pressure groups represented in the House.[21]

A high proportion of lawyers is a feature common to most modern parliaments.[22] In Ontario, following the 1963 election twenty-four members of the House and eight members of the cabinet were lawyers, or 22

[21]Another reason why farmers appear to have such strength in the cabinet may be that this occupation is often used as the Canadian equivalent of the British designation "gentleman." That is, politicians who give their occupations to be farmers are often not farmers in the real sense of the word at all but simply men of means who maintain residences in the country for political or aesthetic reasons—or simply to take advantage of the tax structure farmers enjoy.

[22]For example, the legal profession usually accounts for approximately one-third of the total membership of the Canadian House of Commons. Norman Ward, *The Canadian House of Commons: Representation* (2nd ed.; Toronto: University of Toronto Press, 1963), pp. 132–133; Allan Kornberg, *Canadian Legislative Behaviour: A Study of the Twenty-Fifth Parliament* (New York: Holt, Rinehart & Winston, 1967), pp. 43–44. For discussions of the place of lawyers in American political life see Joseph A. Schlesinger, "Lawyers and American Politics: A Clarified View," *Mid-West Journal of Political Science*, vol. I, no. 1, May 1957, pp. 26–39; and Heinz Eulau and John Sprague, *Lawyers in Politics: A Study of Professional Convergence* (Indianapolis: Bobbs Merrill, 1964).

per cent of the members and 42 per cent of the ministers came from the legal profession. The three most common explanations of this are: first, the legal profession is often chosen by individuals whose ultimate ambition is a political career; second, even if this were not their intention, their concern with the law becomes a natural stepping stone to a concern for the creation of law, which frequently leads them into politics; and third, the ease with which lawyers can arrange their affairs makes it much easier for them to enter upon a political career than is the case in most other professions. Once a large number of lawyers find their way into the Assembly it is inevitable – if the preceding analysis is correct – that they should be given due recognition in the cabinet.

As with all social institutions, growth in size and increase in responsibility have resulted in an elaboration of organization in the Ontario cabinet. Some indication of the extent of this organization may be had from a glance at Figure 7, to which reference will be made later. The chief administrative officer in the Department of the Prime Minister – the department responsible for administering the central machinery of the executive branch of government – is the secretary of the cabinet, and it will therefore be appropriate to begin this discussion of the organization of the executive branch with a description of this office.

Secretary of the Cabinet

It was not until after the second world war that the position commonly known as secretary of the cabinet began to take shape in Ontario. Prior to the war most of the functions now performed by a civil servant were the responsibility of the provincial secretary, who was a member of the cabinet. The degree of organization of cabinet business varied from ministry to ministry, depending upon the personality of the prime minister and the interest of the provincial secretary. At times some care has been taken in the conduct of cabinet business. For instance, when Sir William Hearst was premier, the Provincial Secretary, William D. McPherson, paid some attention to the organization of the work of the cabinet. In 1918 the gentleman who now holds the position of secretary of the cabinet, Mr. W. M. McIntyre, began his career as a civil servant in the provincial secretary's office. One of Mr. McIntyre's duties was to assist the provincial secretary in his work as secretary of the cabinet. This involved handling all recommendations to the executive council. An explanation of the content of each of these recommendations was provided in duplicate by the minister concerned. One copy of each was retained for Mr. McPherson's

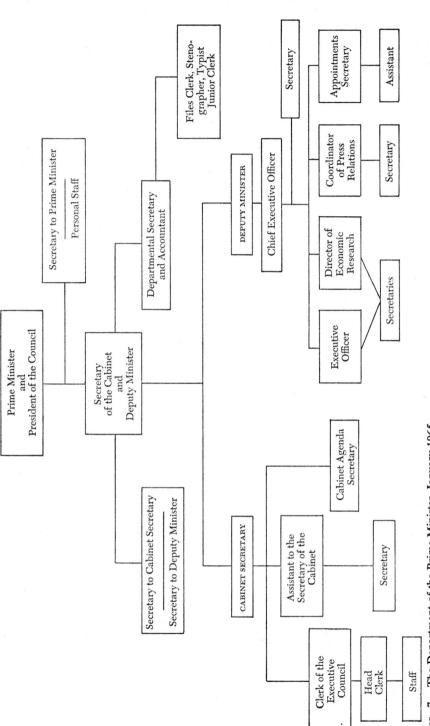

FIG. 7. **The Department of the Prime Minister, January 1965.**

files and the others were pasted onto a sheet under the name of the appropriate departments and ministers. This pasted sheet of recommendations then served as the agenda for the cabinet meeting.[23]

However, at other times cabinet procedures have been extremely disorderly. For instance, when the UFO came to power in 1919, none of the ministers had had any previous experience in office and procedures were developed on an *ad hoc* basis. Although the Prime Minister usually knew what matters the ministers wanted to raise, he never decided whether or not a subject could be discussed until the minister actually brought it up. In 1934, when Mitchell Hepburn took office, the officials who had served in the prime minister's office were let go and procedures fell into disarray once more.[24] Cabinet meetings were sporadic and disorganized and recourse was often had to what were termed "walking orders": orders in council that, instead of being passed by a quorum of the executive council at a regular meeting, were simply circulated by the Prime Minister to various members of the cabinet who signed the *pro forma* jacket of the order in the space usually used to indicate who was present at the meeting of the council at which the order was passed. By the use of this device the Premier could carry on the functions of government without the niceties of cabinet meetings, and he could insure the unopposed implementation of his will by the judicious selection of the ministers to whom he would send each walking order for signature.

When the pressure of government responsibilities began to build up in the late forties, it became apparent that regular procedures would have to be established for the conduct of cabinet business. One of those who was instrumental in bringing some order out of what had been akin to chaos was Roland D. Michener, who served as provincial secretary and secretary of the cabinet in the Drew administration before going into federal politics. When Michener assumed office in 1946, even the rudimentary procedures developed by McPherson during the first world war had lapsed. There was no agenda for cabinet meetings; on the morning of the day on which a meeting was to take place, the Clerk of the executive council would simply give the Secretary the bundle of recommendations to council that the various ministers had submitted, arranged in the order in which they had been received. These recommendations were the closest

---

23From an interview with Mr. W. M. McIntyre, January 29, 1965. It is interesting to note that in a sense Mr. McIntyre is performing now some of the same functions that he did forty-seven years ago, but with a trained staff using modern methods.

24From an interview with Mr. Ernest C. Drury, March 19, 1965. When Mr. Hepburn took office his secretary realised that it would be very useful to keep Drury's former Deputy, Mr. Wallace, in the Prime Minister's office. But when Mr. Drury broached the subject to Mr. Hepburn, the latter's answer was simply: "He's out!"

thing to a formal agenda that existed. The only record of what was done in the meetings consisted of the orders in council that were passed. To overcome these problems the Prime Minister asked Mr. Michener to study the British and Canadian precedents with a view to adapting them to the Ontario cabinet.[25] To assist him in developing better methods of operation Mr. Michener enlisted the services of a Windsor lawyer, Mr. Lorne R. McDonald, who was appointed assistant to the provincial secretary on August 1, 1946.[26] To gain the benefit of experience, Mr. McDonald consulted Sir Norman Brooke in the United Kingdom, where there had been a cabinet secretariat since the first world war[27] and Arnold Heeney in Ottawa, where a similar office had been established during the second world war.[28] Following the patterns suggested by these gentlemen, Mr. McDonald developed an agenda consisting primarily of a list of recommendations to the executive council. This was prepared on Mondays for meetings on Thursdays, but there was usually a supplementary agenda prepared to incorporate recommendations that were received too late to be included on the original. Political or general policy questions were not as a rule listed on the agenda, but it was quite common for the Prime Minister to circulate such items to the ministers in the form of a memorandum some time before the meeting. The agenda which Mr. McDonald prepared also served as a record of cabinet business; the items which were not agreed upon were clearly marked. Besides this record, the Clerk of the executive council kept copies of all recommendations to council and copies of all orders passed by the council. Thus the only items of business of which no permanent record was kept were those that did not entail any executive action. If the distinction between the executive council and the cabinet is maintained, it may be said that there were agendas and records maintained for the former but not for the latter.

[25]From a personal letter to the author from Mr. Roland Michener, then high commissioner for Canada in India, March 12, 1965.

[26]From an interview with Mr. Lorne R. McDonald, QC, February 16, 1965. Much of the following material on the early postwar years was provided by Mr. McDonald.

[27]On the manner in which Lloyd George took over the secretariat of the Committee of Imperial Defence and the early development of the office under Sir Maurice Hankey see Jennings, Cabinet Government, pp. 243–245. For a more extended treatment see J. P. Mackintosh, The British Cabinet (London: Stevens, 1962).

[28]For a discussion of the origins of the position in Canada see W. E. D. Halliday, "The Privy Council Office and Cabinet Secretariat in Relation to the Development of Cabinet Government," Canada Year Book, 1956, pp. 62–70; R. M. Dawson, The Government of Canada (4th ed. rev. by Norman Ward; Toronto: University of Toronto Press, 1963), pp. 248–9; also W. E. D. Halliday, "The Executive of the Government of Canada," in Canadian Public Administration, December 1959, pp. 229–41.

While the cabinet was ready to accept such innovations as agendas and even informal minutes to assist in following up cabinet business which was not recorded elsewhere, there was a good deal of opposition to the introduction into the cabinet of a stranger.[29] In order to install the system Mr. Michener had to continue to act as secretary of the cabinet for nearly a year, but eventually the opposition, led by Col. T. L. Kennedy, broke down, and Mr. McDonald was allowed to sit in on cabinet meetings. In the election of June 1948 Mr. Michener lost his seat, and Mr. McDonald was the first secretary of the cabinet appointed from outside the executive council. In October of that year Mr. Drew resigned office and was succeeded by Col. Kennedy, who headed the Government for some eight months. During this period the office of the secretary of the cabinet really began to flourish, although Mr. McDonald continued to perform some other functions as well: he was responsible for overseeing the King's Printer, Ontario House in London, the Ontario Northland Transportation Commission, and a number of other things that were not cared for by any service department and therefore fell under the jurisdiction of the Provincial Secretary's Department. The Hon. Leslie Frost became premier on May 4, 1949, and on June 2 Mr. McDonald was appointed "Deputy Minister to the Prime Minister and Secretary of the Cabinet."[30] Under Mr. Frost, he was able to make further refinements in cabinet procedures: for the first time in the history of the province, minutes of cabinet meetings were kept, consisting of handwritten notes taken by the Secretary; they were never transcribed and were turned over to the Premier in 1953 when Mr. McDonald left the Premier's office to become general counsel for the Hydro-Electric Power Commission of Ontario. No minutes were kept of executive functions that resulted in orders in council, so that in a sense the orders were really cabinet minutes, not executive council minutes. Methods of making recommendations to council were also improved. Not only did Mr. McDonald attempt to stop the use of walking orders, but he insisted that the formal recommendations submitted to the council be in proper form and that they include a statement of the statutory authority for the recommended order. To accomplish these reforms he was empowered by the Premier to reject those recommendations that did not comply with his specifications.

For some time after Mr. McDonald was appointed secretary of the cabinet and deputy minister to Premier Frost he continued to perform other duties. Most closely related to his job as secretary of the cabinet were his responsibilities as secretary of the Budget Committee and secre-

[29]From a letter from Mr. Roland Michener, March 12, 1965.
[30]In 1948 he had been appointed "Deputy Minister and Secretary of the Cabinet."

tary of the Treasury Board.[31] However, in the forties and early fifties these institutions did not have the volume of work that now flows to the Treasury Board: the Board did not even meet on a regular basis and only certain policy questions and the estimates were referred to it. On occasion the two groups met together. Mr. McDonald also often served as secretary for cabinet committees, although men from the departments most concerned would sometimes be chosen for this.

When Mr. McDonald left in 1953, the Premier selected Mr. W. M. McIntyre[32] to succeed him as secretary of the cabinet and deputy minister of the Department of Prime Minister.[33] Figure 7, which depicts the organization of the Department of Prime Minister in January 1965, illustrates to what extent the cabinet secretariat – to use a general term to cover the numerous offices under the supervision of Mr. McIntyre – has been expanded from the time the first secretary was appointed in 1948.[34] This expansion has gone hand in hand with a further refinement of procedures and an extension of functions.[35]

Still one of the primary functions of the secretary of the cabinet is to oversee the preparation of the agenda, which is done as follows. Ministers, including the prime minister, submit to the secretary the items they want considered by cabinet. These may be detailed recommendations for orders in council, reports of cabinet committees, policy proposals, or anything else that a minister feels important enough to warrant the attention of the cabinet. The secretary scrutinizes the formal recommendations to council to determine their validity, to see that they are in proper form and contain all the required information, and to ensure that there is no overlapping or contradiction in the recommendations made. In the event that a recommendation does fulfil the required standards, it is returned to the minister

[31]*Infra*, pp. 55–6 for descriptions of these bodies.

[32]Mr. McIntyre had left the government service when Mr. Hepburn became prime minister but had returned in July 1953 and had become executive assistant to Mr. Frost. In December of the same year he was appointed secretary of the cabinet.

[33]On November 1, 1960, Mr. McIntyre was given a third title: Director of the Executive Council Office. The fact that he has this title as well as that of secretary of the cabinet adds some credence to the distinction between executive council and cabinet, and this was even more the case when the executive council office was separate from the office of secretary of the cabinet. He had in fact been directing much of the work of the executive council office for some time prior to 1960, and the title was conferred after the death of Mr. Allan Stewart who was clerk of the executive council and served in that capacity under Mr. McIntyre.

[34]Figure 7 is on p. 43 above.

[35]The information about current procedures has been garnered chiefly through interviews with former Premier Leslie Frost and the Cabinet Secretary, Mr. McIntyre, but a number of others, including people at all levels of the civil service, have also provided useful material.

who submitted it. When all the items have been collected, they are listed on the agenda along with very brief descriptions of their nature and purpose. The agenda is organized under a number of headings, depending on the type of subject matter being raised at any particular meeting. A usual category is "routine matters" under which are listed, by department, the items of business which are thought to be of a routine or non-controversial nature but which nevertheless require executive council approval.[36] Recommendations of some significance are generally grouped under a separate heading, "special matters," and general questions of policy are listed under "policy matters." Occasionally items are submitted too late to be incorporated into the regular agenda and if there is some urgency these may be appended in the form of a supplementary agenda. The agenda thus arrived at is typed up by 2 PM Wednesday for the meeting at 10 AM the following day. Included in the agenda are copies of all recommendations, reports, or other documents submitted by the ministers. Copies of the agenda and all supporting documents are then delivered by hand to all ministers for their study and perusal before the meeting. The secretary of the cabinet is also responsible for issuing summons to special meetings of the cabinet and certain meetings of its committees.

In the cabinet meeting the secretary is assisted by an executive officer, who helps in obtaining necessary signatures, etc. The minutes that are taken serve simply as a reminder to the secretary, who must carry out certain decisions of the cabinet and inform the appropriate departments of others. They are not made available to anyone else, and there is no provision for their preservation in the Public Archives or elsewhere. However, as before, a copy of the agenda, with matters to be held over for another meeting clearly indicated, is kept and serves as a permanent record along with the recommendations and orders in council preserved by the clerk of the executive council.

The secretary of the cabinet acts as a continuing liaison between the cabinet and the operating departments to ensure that there is a full understanding of decisions of the cabinet, including if necessary the preparation of directives either for the signature of the premier or, with his concurrence, the signature of the secretary. He also acts as the liaison between the premier and the lieutenant governor on matters of Government concern. A person with long experience in such an office is in a unique position to counsel ministers on the proper execution of the duties of their offices. On occasion he can provide information to the premier or the cabinet

[36]"Routine matters" include such things as appointments and promotions which require orders in council.

that would not be available to anyone who was not so close to the centre of activity. An ideal opportunity to provide this service is in the meetings of the various cabinet committees. At one time Mr. McIntyre used to serve as secretary to a number of these, but the increase in cabinet business has made it necessary for him to assign these tasks to others in his Department. Occasionally someone from one of the other departments who is familiar with the subject matter of concern to a particular committee is named its secretary.

Another function that has been brought under the office of the secretary of the cabinet is the direction of the executive council office. The duties assigned to this office are: to process and maintain records of the formal recommendations to the executive council submitted by the various ministers; to receive "objections";[37] to have custody of all orders in council; to issue certified copies of orders in council as required; and to swear in ministers, members of commissions and special committees, and certain other officers appointed by the crown.[38] The clerk's office is thus a mine of information and is often asked to provide facts that are not readily available in any other form. The present Clerk of the Executive Council, Mr. J. J. Young, also acts as assistant clerk of the Legislative Assembly, but this function is quite distinct from his position in the executive council office. At one time the clerk of the executive council also held the title clerk of the crown in chancery, but that position no longer exists.

The cabinet does not meet much more frequently than it did twenty years ago. When the House is not in session it meets every Thursday morning; during the session it usually meets at least twice a week. Besides these meetings to discuss regular business, the cabinet receives approximately twenty delegations a year from some of the more important interest groups in the province. Most of these meetings also take place while the House is sitting, although attempts are made to schedule them at other times in the year. Less important groups seeking an audience with the premier or the cabinet have to be satisfied with an interview with a small group of ministers which, in effect, constitutes a committee of cabinet.

Usually the regular meetings of cabinet last about three hours but, as one minister of long experience put it, they can be interminable. The number and type of subjects raised varies from meeting to meeting. At

[37]Objections usually take the form of petitions to the lieutenant governor in council from groups of citizens aggrieved by decisions of the Ontario Municipal Board or the Highway Transportation Board, asking that the decisions in question be disallowed.

[38]From an interview with Mr. J. J. Young, clerk of the executive council, February 19, 1965.

some meetings a host of subjects will be discussed and decided upon, but on other occasions only one or two items may be discussed and perhaps no conclusions will be reached. In the latter event, the subject will be held over for a subsequent meeting; in the meantime a minister or a committee of cabinet may be asked to investigate the matter more fully. Sometimes the items listed on the agenda under the heading "routine matters" will be dispensed with in as little as fifteen minutes, but at other times some objections may be raised or questions asked about a certain order and a long discussion will take place. What was thought to be a routine item may turn out to be so important that it is held over for another meeting.

Proceedings in cabinet are entirely informal and completely under the control of the premier, who may choose which items on the agenda will be discussed and decided upon and which, if any, will be held over. Certain topics, such as the budget speech, are never formally raised at cabinet meetings.[39] No votes are ever taken; the premier simply "sums up" the discussion and the ministers then assume collective responsibility for the decision. Long presentations by individual ministers are unnecessary because they can circulate statements, explanations, reports, etc., as appendices to the agenda, but it is still sometimes necessary for a minister to take ten or fifteen minutes to explain a proposal. The usual decision-making process at the cabinet level on important matters is as follows. When a department of government has a clear proposal to make, it is presented to cabinet by the minister of the department. If the idea receives approval in principle, the department prepares a bill or an order. Assistance with the actual drafting is provided by the legislative counsel's office in the Department of the Attorney-General. When the draft is ready, it is taken again to cabinet for approval. If the bill is approved, it is then ready to be presented to the Assembly; if it is a recommendation for an order, it becomes an order in council immediately upon approval by the executive council and signature by the lieutenant governor. Less important items come before the cabinet only when they are ready for final approval. Walking orders are no longer used.

Officials, other than the cabinet secretary and his assistant, do not attend cabinet meetings on a regular basis. They may be called in to provide information on certain items but they are excused as soon as they have fulfilled this purpose. In meetings of cabinet committees the rule is not so stringent and officials will sometimes enter directly into the work of a committee. However, the need for officials is more obvious in the case of

[39]This was not always the case. During Mr. Drury's period of office the budget speech was fully discussed. From an interview with E. C. Drury, March 19, 1965.

committees, where detailed work is done, than it is with meetings of the cabinet as a whole, where the proposals submitted have, as far as possible, been fully investigated beforehand, and where most relevant information can be supplied in the form of a written statement. The general exclusion of officials from cabinet meetings, the care taken in the circulation of cabinet documents, and the absence of any printed minutes of cabinet proceedings – along with the oath of secrecy taken by all ministers and the secretary of the cabinet[40] – have generally been sufficient to keep cabinet business from reaching the public without the approval of the cabinet.[41]

In spite of the increasing burden that has been laid upon the cabinet there has been only a slight increase in the number and length of cabinet meetings. Five factors can be isolated which in large measure explain this accomplishment. The first is the improvement in the procedures for conducting the business of cabinet. The use of a formal agenda, the circulation well in advance of documents relevant to cabinet discussions, and the orderly liaison between the cabinet and the departments through the permanent secretary of the cabinet, who is the chief officer of the executive council, have streamlined operations considerably. Secondly, much more formal consultation is carried on between meetings of the cabinet than there used to be. Normally all proposals for increased expenditures go to the Treasury Board before going to cabinet, and succeeding premiers have made it clear that all questions affecting more than one department should be submitted to all of the departments concerned before being brought before cabinet for final approval. Along with this has been the tendency for the premier to consult certain senior or influential ministers before raising large or controversial issues with the full cabinet, but doubtless this was the practice even in the early years. Thirdly, a great many more decisions are left to individual ministers than was the case in the days when there were fewer decisions to make. Fourthly, and related to this, has been the increased delegation of authority to various boards and commissions. More will be said of this later.[42] The fifth factor is the development of the committee system. Committees of cabinet were used in the United Kingdom early in the nineteenth century,[43] but they were first organized on a really systematic basis during the second world war

[40]See Appendix A.
[41]A number of illustrations of the rigidity of cabinet secrecy could be cited, but one may suffice. The whole issue of a metropolitan form of government for the city of Toronto and its suburbs was thrashed out for weeks before the final proposal was made public and there were never any leaks.
[42]See chap. 7.
[43]Jennings, *Cabinet Government*, p. 255.

in order to meet the heavy demands then made on the cabinet.[44] In Canada as well it was the war that brought about the proliferation of committees and some degree of organization.[45]

The same pattern may be seen in Ontario. There were committees of cabinet before the war, but they were usually of an *ad hoc* nature and quite informal.[46] During the Frost administration they became an integral part of cabinet organization. In the late forties and early fifties there was an attempt to organize the committees on a systematic basis, and a list of standing committees was drawn up by the Secretary of the Cabinet. However, this organizational effort proved abortive: some committees never met and there were meetings of others that were not formally constituted. Since 1953 there have been no permanent committees other than the Treasury Board, of which more will be said later. However, some committees have continued to exist and function for extended periods of time and are in fact permanent committees of cabinet in all but name.[47] Aside from the Treasury Board and a few of these "quasi-permanent" committees, the committees of the Ontario cabinet are purely *ad hoc* in nature, appointed by the premier for a particular purpose and dissolved when that purpose has either been achieved or abandoned. Anywhere from three to a dozen committees may exist at one time, and there is very little formal organization such as exists in Britain or at Ottawa. With the exception of the Treasury Board, no executive authority is ever delegated to a committee as is done in the United Kingdom, although the cabinet may provide for a department to take action on the recommendation of a committee.

The committees meet when necessary or convenient and have as secretaries either someone from the Department of the Prime Minister – if the prime minister is particularly interested in the outcome of the committee's deliberations – or from one of the departments which has some connection with the subject matter of the committee. Occasionally the secretary of the cabinet will serve a committee himself in order to facilitate action.

[44]For an excellent discussion of the increased use of committees and the way in which they are organized in the United Kingdom see Lord Morrison of Lambeth, *Government and Parliament: A Survey from the Inside* (2nd ed.; London: Oxford University Press, 1959), pp. 16–27.

[45]For a statement on the origin of committees in Canada see James Eayrs, *The Art of the Possible: Government and Foreign Policy in Canada* (Toronto: University of Toronto Press, 1961), p. 12. For general discussions of cabinet committees in Canada see Dawson, *The Government of Canada*, pp. 245–246 and Halliday, "The Executive of the Government of Canada," pp. 240–1.

[46]No cabinet committees were used during the Drury administration. From an interview with Mr. E. C. Drury March 19, 1965.

[47]The best illustration of this quasi-permanent type of committee is the Mining and Access Roads Committee, which has existed now for a number of years.

Committees usually enlist the support of other officials who sit and work with the ministers as well. When the committees are ready to report they give a copy of the report to the secretary of the cabinet who puts the item down on the agenda and attaches copies of the report to the agendas circulated to the ministers. Sometimes, if the report is not very long or involved it will be given verbally, but this practice is becoming less and less common.

Cabinet committees serve a number of purposes. Fundamentally, they are created to make the cabinet more efficient and they contribute to this end in various ways. In the first place they simply relieve the cabinet as a whole of some work: for example, a committee of cabinet will meet delegations on behalf of the Government. Committees also reduce the time spent in cabinet on any one item of business. Occasionally the cabinet can simply adopt a committee's report as it is presented, but even if this is not feasible the report at least will have prepared the ground for discussion. A good illustration of this was when the Ontario Government was planning for the creation of the Municipality of Metropolitan Toronto. For at least a year preceding the introduction of the required legislation, Mr. Frost had been working out details with a small group of his colleagues in the cabinet. Other ministers were approached only about specific problems related to their areas of responsibility: the Attorney General about police services; and the Ministers of Health, Public Works, and others about sewage disposal and sundry related services. Only when most of the problems associated with the new Municipality had been dealt with was the project laid before the cabinet.

Committees reduce the demands placed on individual ministers. To consider a proposal thoroughly entails far more than just attending the cabinet meeting when it is discussed. If no committees were used, every minister would supposedly be equally responsible for investigating the feasibility of every recommendation to council, and no doubt the result would confirm the law of administration that states that when everyone is given responsibility for the same job no one will do it properly. When committees are used, it is possible for those ministers who are interested in a subject to devote themselves to it, while the other members of the cabinet are freed from that responsibility so that they may concentrate on other matters more to their liking. A good example of how this principle operates was the committee on the suppression of crime. Naturally all ministers were concerned with the object of this committee's work, but only certain ministers either administered departments whose jurisdictions touched on the subject or had special talents to apply to the problem.

Hence, a committee was set up which utilized the best resources available and at the same time allowed the other ministers to employ themselves in other ways.

A further purpose of committees, and one which is directly related to the preceding point, is to permit more detailed examination of certain problems than would be possible in regular cabinet meetings. Those ministers who are chosen to sit on a particular committee are expected "to find out every damn thing about the subject and report back to cabinet."[48] Clearly, a committee is ideal for such an assignment and the cabinet is made more efficient through the use of such devices.

But committees of cabinet have a wider utility than simply improving the efficiency of the cabinet: they also serve to co-ordinate the work of the government as a whole. There are many specific objects of government concern which do not fall under the aegis of any one department and one way to prevent duplication of effort is to assign the subject to a committee. Before the Department of Transport was set up and given responsibility for highway safety (among other things), there was a committee of cabinet which served as co-ordinator of the programmes aimed at promoting highway safety which the various departments sponsored. Another good illustration of a committee co-ordinating government services was the work of the drainage committee. The Departments of Agriculture, Public Works, Energy Resources, and Highways all had programmes to cope with this problem and the ministers of these departments formed a committee on the subject. The result was the Drainage Act, 1962–63, which ran to forty-one pages and repealed five acts which had previously dealt with the subject.[49]

Committees can also be used to isolate and resolve interdepartmental conflicts. When there is a dispute between two departments over the responsibilities of administering a particular act or handling a particular problem, a committee will be set up, usually composed of the ministers from the departments concerned and a strong mediator. If the dispute is politically dangerous, the Prime Minister may sit on the committee or at least see to it that someone from his department serves as secretary of the committee so that he will be kept fully informed of all proceedings.

Committees can also serve as a forum for the confrontation of conflicting interests or the co-operation of like interests. Ministers of the departments whose operations are under pressure from groups outside government which have vested interests in the same question – whether the interests be antithetical or synthetical is immaterial – may form a

[48]From an interview with the Hon. Leslie M. Frost, January 27, 1965.
[49]*Statutes of Ontario* (*SO*), 1962–63, c. 39, s. 89.

committee on the subject to ensure that all points of view are considered during the formulation of policy. A good case in point was the milk crisis which plagued the province off and on for a number of years following the end of the war. The "Milk Committee" was constituted in such a way that the producers, truckers, processors, and retailers all had ministers representing their interests in one capacity or another.

Finally, committees of the cabinet can be used to deal with issues that no individual minister feels inclined to tackle. A perfect illustration of such an issue was the question of whether or not the Government should encourage the fluoridation of water supplies. Although it might have been logical to dump the problem in the lap of the Minister of Health, it would hardly have been fair, since the issue had become so controversial and so replete with emotional overtones; hence, the whole question was referred to a committee which could advise the cabinet without jeopardizing the career of any one minister.

The Treasury Board

The one permanent committee of the executive council – and one which warrants some special attention in this study, because it was established as a direct result of the growth in government functions, and because it is close to the tangential point of legislative-executive relations – is the Treasury Board. Before the Treasury Board was reconstituted and given greatly expanded functions and powers in 1954,[50] the tendency was to make expenditure decisions piecemeal. The individual minister would go to the treasurer and the prime minister and ask for the money to finance a proposal. If successful at this initial stage of his endeavours, he next took the matter to cabinet, where discussions would invariably centre on the merits of that particular proposal. At best the matter would be discussed in the light of the existing state of the budget. There could be little or no intelligent examination of the proposal, because there was no responsible organization with the authority to carry out continuous analysis of the aggregate spending policies of government. The inadequacies of such a system for controlling government expenditures were not so apparent before 1939, because there were strong external pressures to reduce both expenditures and taxes. The few proposals for disbursements that did get through the cabinet were usually quite easily accommodated by the budget and the provincial economy. The advent of the positive state, however, made it necessary to institute more elaborate procedures for controlling

[50]*SO*, 1954, c. 30, s. 2–5.

and directing expenditures. As usual, the necessary adaptations took place not in the legislative branch but in the executive branch, and the result was a strengthened Treasury Board.

The Treasury Board was first created in 1886 by the Act to Provide for the Better Auditing of the Public Accounts of the Province.[51] In 1908 this statute was re-enacted as the Audit Act.[52] However the provisions of the Audit Act were not adequate to achieve the desired end: the Treasury Board had few powers aside from its formal role in the procedure for passing Treasury Board orders and special warrants, it met sporadically, and it had no permanent staff. As a step towards rectifying this situation Walter L. Gordon, of Woods, Gordon & Company, suggested new legislation[53] which was passed in 1954 as the Financial Administration Act.[54] In September 1955 the Treasury Board began to hold regular meetings entirely separate from the meetings of the cabinet.[55] Improvements in the organization and staff of the Treasury Board since 1955 will be discussed later, but something must be said now of the composition and functions of the Board itself.

The Treasury Board consists of the treasurer, as chairman, and from four to seven other ministers, as designated by the lieutenant governor in council.[56] The powers and duties of the Treasury Board are set forth in the Financial Administration Act: the Board acts as a committee of the executive council on "all matters relating to finance, revenues, estimates, expenditures and financial commitments and on any other matter concerning general administrative policy in the public service that is referred to the Board by the Executive Council or on which the Board considers it desirable to report to the Executive Council." It may require any public officer or any agent of the crown to produce any document or information that it considers necessary for the performance of its duties. And, subject to the approval of the lieutenant governor in council, it may make regulations for the collection, management, and administration of public money and for any purposes necessary for the efficient administration of the public service.[57]

[51]*SO*, 1886, c. 4, s. 1.
[52]*SO*, 1908, c. 9.
[53]Ontario, Legislative Assembly, *Debates*, February 1, 1960, p. 81.
[54]*SO*, 1954, c. 30. By this Act sections 1, 8, 13 (3), 17, 20, 23, 28, and 30 of the Audit Act, the Consolidated Revenue Fund Act, the Public Revenue Act, the Provincial Loans Act, the Provincial Loans Amendment Act, 1951, and the Provincial Loans Amendment Act, 1952, were all repealed.
[55]From an interview with Mr. H. H. Walker, associate deputy minister, Treasury Department, March 2, 1965.
[56]*RSO*, 1960, c. 142, s. 2.
[57]*RSO*, 1960, c. 142, s. 3, 4, and 5.

There are a number of matters which the executive council requires to be referred to the Treasury Board, perhaps the most important being the necessity to submit all proposed expenditures to the Board. Besides the annual and supplementary estimates there are three special forms of expenditure proposals which entail Treasury Board action. First, under section 29 of the Financial Administration Act, applications for special warrants must be referred to the Board which then estimates the amount of expenditure required and reports back to the executive council. Upon receipt of this report, the statement of the treasurer that there is no appropriation for the expenditure, and the recommendation of the minister concerned, the lieutenant governor in council may order a special warrant to be prepared for the signature of the lieutenant governor authorizing the payment of the amount estimated. A special warrant thus creates a new appropriation to cover some expenditure which was unforeseen but which is urgently required for the public good. Secondly, applications for Treasury Board orders must of course go to the Treasury Board. The main distinction between a special warrant and a Treasury Board order is that the former creates a new appropriation while the latter simply increases an existing one. Two further distinctions may be made: while a special warrant requires approval by the lieutenant governor in council, the Treasury Board alone authorizes Treasury Board orders, and, while a special warrant may only be issued when the Legislature is not in session, a Treasury Board order may be issued at any time.[58] Thirdly, a request for an authorization for commitment must go to the Board. Such requests are made in the same circumstances as requests for Treasury Board orders, except that the amount of the over-expenditure is quite uncertain; hence the actual Treasury Board order is delayed.

Matters other than proposed expenditures which must be referred to the Treasury Board include: proposed regulations having a financial implication; recommendations to council where there is a financial implication, but excluding those appointments to staff and salary increases for which funds are available and which are within the approved complement; proposals to construct or purchase buildings, purchase land (except for a highway right-of-way), or lease property; proposed changes in federal-provincial financial relations; proposed changes which will affect future expenditure or revenue; proposed legislation affecting revenue or expenditure; proposed changes in complement; Treasury Board certificates

[58]C. E. Brannan, "The Treasury Board of Ontario," a statement submitted to the Public Accounts Committee of the Ontario legislature, February 28, 1964, pp. 8 and 9. The statutory provision for Treasury Board orders is to be found in the Financial Administration Act, s. 30 as amended in 1962. *SO*, 1961–62, c. 43, s. 3.

(Department of Highways only) and grant authorizations (Hospital Services Commission only).[59] It is also common practice for the executive council to refer to the Board important matters of concern to two or more departments and all questions of general administrative policy in the public service.

Even this brief list of the functions of the Treasury Board is sufficient to indicate both the amount of work of which it relieves the cabinet and the power of its position in the governmental process. It analyses the estimates to determine whether the proposed extensions of existing services or the creation of new programmes are in keeping with over-all goals of Government policy and, if the proposed programmes are consistent with these goals, whether they will accomplish their purpose in the most efficient manner possible and whether the present and projected revenues will be adequate to support them. On top of this general overseeing of expenditures, the Board gives continuous attention to financial developments throughout the year in the ways suggested in the preceding paragraph and by reviewing monthly statements from the departments showing total actual revenues and expenditures against those which have been estimated. When problems are revealed in these statements, the Board attempts to find out the causes of any discrepancies between actual and forecast expenditures in order to suggest alternative solutions to the departments concerned. In the decade following its reorganization in 1954, the Treasury Board held more than six hundred meetings, an average of five or six meetings each month.[60]

In keeping with the growth of its functions, the Treasury Board has provided itself with a fairly large permanent staff, and it is instructive to note the manner in which this was accomplished. From the very beginning, the person holding the office of treasurer of Ontario has sought advice and assistance from senior officials in his own and other departments to more effectively administer the finances of the province. Eventually this practice became more or less formalized through the creation of what was called the "Budget Committee."[61] This was an informal committee of civil servants who worked with the treasurer and one or two other ministers who were generally also members of the Treasury Board. On occasion the two groups would sit together.[62] When the Financial Administration Act was passed in 1954, this *ad hoc* committee was given statutory recognition by section 19 which provided: "There shall be a committee to be

[59]Brannan, "The Treasury Board of Ontario," pp. 2–3.
[60]From an interview with Mr. H. H. Walker, March 2, 1965.
[61]From an interview with Mr. L. R. McDonald, March 3, 1965.
[62]From an interview with Mr. W. M. McIntyre, January 29, 1965.

called the Budget Committee composed of such officers of the Treasury Department and of any other department as the Lieutenant-Governor in Council may designate from time to time."[63] The Act authorized the committee to appoint its own chairman and secretary and to determine its own rules of procedure. Under the direction of the Treasury Board, the Budget Committee had mandatory responsibilities: to examine, advise upon, and compile the estimates; to advise upon the expenditures and revenues of each department, investigate all matters relating to the receipt, disbursement, and payment of public money; to make suggestions generally with a view to promoting efficiency and economy in any department; and to "perform such other services as the Treasury Board may assign to it."[64]

Although the Act of 1954 gave the Budget Committee legal status, it did not change its real nature, so that it continued to be composed of officials who had other positions and who were therefore able to give only intermittent attention to the duties assigned to it by the Treasury Board under the terms of the Act. The Committee appointed as secretary the official who had previously performed this function, the Comptroller of Accounts, Mr. H. H. Walker. The secretary of the Treasury Board was supposed to be the deputy provincial treasurer, or in his absence, the secretary of the budget committee. Since the deputy provincial treasurer was seldom able to serve in this capacity, Mr. Walker became, in effect, the secretary for both bodies. In 1956, the section of the Financial Administration Act relating to the secretary of the Treasury Board was amended to read: "The Treasury Board shall have a secretary who shall be designated by the Board."[65] In practice this amendment did not affect the Board, because it simply appointed Mr. Walker who had already been performing the duties of secretary. At this time the Budget Committee and the Treasury Board were still meeting together as a matter of convenience, because they had a joint secretary and all requests for additional money had to go to the Budget Committee before going to the Treasury Board anyway. Besides, the personnel of the two bodies usually completely overlapped: the Budget Committee usually met with those ministers who formed the Treasury Board and the Treasury Board used as its staff the members of the Budget Committee.

On June 12, 1958, an order in council was passed creating a "Committee on the Organization of Government in Ontario" to be chaired by Mr. Walter L. Gordon. In its report the Committee concluded that there

[63]SO, 1954, c. 30, s. 19.
[64]SO, 1954, c. 30, s. 19 (3).
[65]SO, 1956, c. 21, s. 1.

was a need for early and continuous liaison between the departments and the Treasury Board as programmes were formulated, but that the Budget Committee, because of its composition, could not adequately perform the functions of a secretariat for the Board. The Committee therefore recommended that "the duties now assigned by statute to the Budget Committee be re-assigned to a full-time staff directly attached to the Treasury Board."[66] At the same time the Gordon Committee suggested that the Budget Committee be retained to act in a purely advisory capacity to the Treasury Board and to the provincial treasurer in his capacity as chairman of the Board.

The Government accepted the recommendation for a permanent secretariat and engaged Woods, Gordon & Company to conduct a study and make recommendations.[67] This firm recommended that the Treasury Board staff consist of two branches, the Secretariat Branch and the Organization and Methods Services Branch. They suggested that the Secretariat Branch be assigned those duties previously carried out by the Budget Committee and in addition be made responsible for reviewing the expenditures of the departments against estimated expenditures on a month by month basis. The Organization and Methods Services Branch would act in a purely advisory capacity to departments, boards, and commissions.

As has already been indicated, these suggestions were accepted and the two branches were created in 1961. On April 18, 1962, royal assent was given to Bill 115 which amended the Financial Administration Act so as to discontinue the Budget Committee and transfer its former powers to the staff of the Treasury Board.[68] The section dealing with the secretary of the Treasury Board was again amended, this time to provide staff for the Board: "The Treasurer shall designate an officer of the Treasury Department to be the secretary of the Treasury Board and the Treasurer shall, from among the persons employed in the Treasury Department, provide the Board with such staff as is necessary for the proper conduct of the business of the Board." Having finally provided the Board with its own permanent staff, the Legislative Assembly went on to repeal section 18 of the Financial Administration Act, which had provided for the com-

[66]Ontario, Committee on the Organization of Government in Ontario, *Report*, W. L. Gordon, Chairman (Toronto, 1959), p. 37. (Hereinafter referred to as the Gordon Committee *Report*.)

[67]Memorandum to the Select Committee of the House appointed on the 4th day of April, 1960, to Examine into and to Study the Administrative and Executive Problems of the Government of Ontario, submitted on June 7, 1960. Hereinafter referred to as the Select Committee on Administrative and Executive Problems.

[68]*SO*, 1961–62, c. 43.

position and duties of the Budget Committee. And, finally, section 30 of the Act was amended, removing the necessity to refer applications for Treasury Board orders to the Budget Committee. Once again, Mr. Walker, who was now associate deputy minister, was appointed secretary of the Treasury Board. However, in October 1963 Mr. C. E. Brannan was given that position, becoming the first full-time secretary of the Board.[69]

In organizing the work of the Treasury Board secretariat the principle of departmental specialization has been followed: "Each analyst is assigned a number of related departments and any matters requiring Treasury Board approval are reviewed by the analyst responsible."[70] In this way, each analyst is put in a position in which he can become quite familiar with the operations of a few departments, and ready contact between the Secretariat and the departments is maintained.

The Organization and Methods Services Branch is, in the words of its Director, Mr. J. G. O'Neill, "a captive management consulting firm."[71] The function of the Branch is to make recommendations; it is up to line management to decide whether, and to what extent, these proposals will be implemented. The Branch has completed many projects, the scope and complexity of which have varied from a study of filing systems and equipment for a branch to a broad organization and methods study of a department. In addition, the Branch has conducted training courses in co-operation with the Training and Development Branch of the Department of Civil Service[72] and has prepared the *Manual of Administration*, a constantly updated guide to the public service in Ontario.[73]

Executive Instruments

In this discussion of the instruments of executive authority, no attempt will be made to relate the use of executive power to the constitutional principle of the supremacy of parliament.[74] Instead, the political fact of

[69]From an interview with Mr. H. H. Walker, March 9, 1965.

[70]Brannan, "The Treasury Board of Ontario," p. 14.

[71]J. G. O'Neill, "Organization and Methods Analysis: An Aid to Management." A lecture delivered to the 1963 Senior Officers' Conference, May 20, 1963, p. 1.

[72]Brannan, "The Treasury Board of Ontario," pp. 14–15.

[73]From an interview with Mr. E. F. Strauss, Organization and Methods Services Branch, March 4, 1965.

[74]Still the best statement of the principle is that by A. V. Dicey in his *Introduction to the Study of the Law of the Constitution*, the first edition of which appeared in 1885. The rise of disciplined political parties has rendered obsolete the idea of the

cabinet supremacy is accepted and attention is turned to the means chosen by the executive for giving effect to its authority. By this approach, the somewhat artificial distinction that is sometimes made between the supposed delegation of powers to the executive council and delegation to subordinate agencies will be avoided. Instead of viewing the powers delegated to boards, commissions, and other agencies of government as something entirely separate from the powers vested in the executive council, they will be viewed simply as one other means of exercising executive powers. There are, of course, exceptions to this pattern, and relationships between individual agencies and the executive council and Legislative Assembly differ markedly: some tend to be entirely dominated by the cabinet; a few are regulated, to a certain extent at least, by the House; some are relatively free from interference from either of the two politically responsible bodies; and others fall under intermediate degrees of control from either, or both, of the two bodies. More will be said of these subordinate agencies after the more direct instruments of executive power have been described.

One of the most direct means available to the executive for controlling the affairs of the province is the order in council. From the very beginning orders in council have been far more numerous than the statutes by which they have been authorized, and, as illustrated in Figure 8, they have increased in volume far more rapidly than have the provincial statutes.[75] In 1960 there were only slightly more than twice as many statutes passed as had been passed in the first full year of the Province's existence, but the number of orders in council was more than twenty-seven times the number that had been passed in the Province's first year. And the number of orders in council would have been even greater in recent years were it not for three developments: first, a great many more decisions are left to individual ministers now than used to be the case; secondly, many routine recommendations, such as those for appointments, are now consolidated into a few omnibus orders in council instead of a number of individual orders; and, thirdly, whole fields of jurisdiction have been transferred to boards, commissions, and other bodies that have been given power to pass

cabinet as merely a "committee of the legislative body," the phrase used by Walter Bagehot in 1867, exercising only those limited powers delegated to it by a sovereign parliament. However, the principle of the supremacy of parliament still holds true at the provincial level today in the sense that an act of the Legislative Assembly is superior to all other forms of law passed in the province. But, in practice, this has had nearly the opposite effect from the original intent of the principle for it means that if a cabinet has a majority behind it in the House its powers are unlimited, except by the general precepts of the constitution.

[75]*SO* for the years concerned, and information provided by the Clerk of the Executive Council.

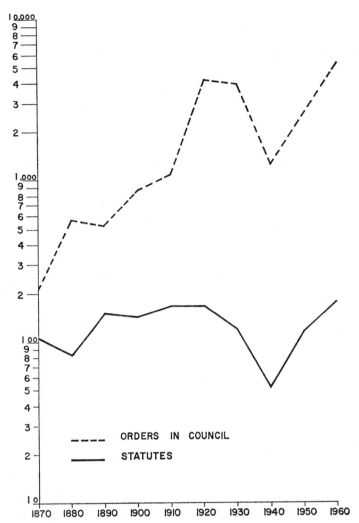

FIG. 8. Statutes and orders in council passed in Ontario in selected years, 1870–1960.

regulations, rules, orders, or by-laws on subjects that would require orders in council if left in the hands of the executive council.[76]

Factors such as these have led to the charge of "government by order in council" in Ontario. While it cannot be denied that the cabinet dominates the whole of government operations, there are few grounds for this

[76]From an interview with Mr. McIntyre, January 29, 1965.

specific charge. In the first place, only a fraction of the orders passed by council are of a legislative nature. An order in council which is of a legislative nature is defined as a "regulation": "a regulation, rule, order or by-law of a legislative nature made or approved under an Act of the Legislature by the Lieutenant Governor in Council, a minister of the Crown, an official of the government or a board or commission all the members of which are appointed by the Lieutenant in Council. . . ."[77]

With certain exceptions, all regulations must be filed in duplicate with the registrar of regulations and published in the *Ontario Gazette*. The only regulations that are not filed and published are specifically excluded by statute from the application of the Regulations Act. In general, the exceptions have been made where there is some other machinery that ensures the regulations are available to the public, where the subject matter is not of general public application, or where it is not primarily of a legislative nature but there is a possible doubt.[78] It is with these regulations "of a legislative nature," which are filed with the registrar of regulations, that one is primarily concerned when investigating the charge of "government by order in council," but they only make up a fraction of the total number of orders in council. The total number of regulations filed under the Regulations Act for the years 1945 to 1964 is compared with the total number of bills passed by the House in the same years in Figure 9. The result is quite different from the comparison between the number of bills and *all*

FIG. 9. Statutes and regulations passed, 1945–64.

[77]The term was first given a statutory definition in an Act to provide for the Central Filing and Publication of Regulations, 1944. The definition quoted here is from the Regulations Act, *RSO*, 1960, c. 349, s. 1. (*d*).

[78]These exceptions are listed in the Regulations Act, *RSO*, 1960, c. 349, s. 1 (*d*), (*i*)–(*v*).

orders in council passed in those years, as was depicted in Figure 8. In 1960, for instance, there were 176 statutes enacted by the legislature, and there were 345 regulations and 5,438 orders in council passed.[79] Although there were still nearly twice as many regulations as there were statutes in that year, the number of orders in council exceeded the number of statutes thirty times over. Indeed, when compared with most of the indices of the growth of government responsibilities (*see* chap. 2), the increase in the number of regulations since the end of the war does not appear to have been out of proportion at all. Furthermore, while the regulations made or approved by the lieutenant governor in council make up the large majority of all regulations, there are also regulations approved by a minister[80] or a board or a commission of which all the members are appointed by the lieutenant governor in council.[81] Of course, the fact that regulations are made by ministers or by public servants appointed by the cabinet does not in any way reduce the extent to which the executive branch dominates the governmental process, but it does illustrate the specific point that orders in council are not the only, nor even the most significant, means by which the executive exercises its control. Only some orders in council are important in this respect, and there are other instruments which may be equally significant.

Sometimes the charge of "government by order in council" is made in a manner which implies that this type of legislation is somehow illegal. The only way in which such a situation could develop would be for the executive council to go beyond the powers delegated to it by the Legislative Assembly, and there is certainly no need for the cabinet to do this, for the simple reason that it can use its majority support in the House to get any powers it requests.[82] Hence, the Registrar of Regulations could say

[79]*SO* for the years concerned, and information provided by the Registrar of Regulations.

[80]A. N. Stone, then assistant registrar of regulations, in a memorandum submitted to the members of the Select Committee on the Organization of Government on September 19, 1960, listed twenty-seven cases in which a minister could make regulations without the approval of the executive council.

[81]*Ibid.* The only notable instances of regulations made by boards and commissions without further approval are those made by the Farm Products Marketing Board and the Milk Industry Board.

[82]The submission of the Board of Trade of Metropolitan Toronto to the Gordon Committee on November 6, 1958, for instance, was highly critical of the tendency in Ontario legislation to confer much broader powers on ministers, officials, and agencies than is required. The submission listed the following instances in which extremely broad powers and/or summary procedures were conferred, and which thus protected governmental officials from attack for exceeding their powers: The Highway Improvement Act, *SO*, 1957, c. 43, s. 4 and 33; The Housing Development Act, *RSO*, 1950, c. 174, s. 6(*a*); The Labour Relations Act, *RSO*, 1950, c. 194, s. 58; and The Ontario Municipal Board Act, *RSO*, 1950, c. 262, s. 48(*a*).

in 1961 that there were no complaints of Ontario regulations being without authority and that he knew of no instance in the previous ten years where a regulation had been found by a court to be invalid for lack of authority.[83]

Far from being instruments by which the cabinet legislates in place of the Assembly, a great many orders in council are used to curb the tendency of ministers and officials to give legislative effect to their desires by resort to regulations of one form or another. The alternative to an order in council would be, in many instances, to leave the decision up to the individual minister, to a subordinate executive agency, or even to an extra-departmental agency. The purpose in having these decisions authorized by the executive council is to control irresponsible action rather than to encourage it. This being the case, instead of seeking a reduction in the number of orders in council passed each year, those who fear the abuse of executive powers ought to promote their use, at least until the Assembly either assumes responsibility for passing sufficiently detailed legislation to obviate the need for delegated legislation or else develops its own machinery for controlling the use of delegated powers.

Another use to which orders in council are still sometimes put is even less deserving of the charge of executive abuse. Under this category fall the routine matters which seldom, if ever, extend the influence or apply the powers of the cabinet but which nevertheless require formal action on the part of the executive council. For example, until it was revised in 1953,[84] the Mortmain and Charitable Uses Act made it necessary for an order in council to be passed in order to grant licenses in Mortmain.[85] There has been a conscious effort to remove such routine matters from the purview of the executive council by leaving them to the responsible minister or subordinate authority,[86] but they still account for a significant portion of the orders in council issued.

Before leaving the subject of orders in council it is interesting to look in more detail at those passed in the three years from 1955 to 1957, typical postwar years both in regard to the total number of orders in council passed and the over-all rate of increase in their use. Table 7 lists separately two of the most important types of orders in council: those relating to the staff of the public service, because they account for more than half of the total, and those which are filed as regulations because of

[83]A. N. Stone, submission to the Legal Bills Committee, February 22, 1961.
[84]*SO*, 1953, c. 68, s. 2.
[85]*RSO*, 1950, c. 241, s. 3. This particular illustration was suggested by Mr. W. M. McIntyre in an interview on September 9, 1964.
[86]Compare, for instance, the provisions of the Corporations Act (*SO*, 1953, c. 19) with those of the Companies Act (*RSO*, 1950, c. 59), which it replaced.

TABLE 7
Origins of Orders in Council, 1955–57

Departments, boards, and commissions	1955 Types of Orders in Council				1956 Types of Orders in Council				1957 Types of Orders in Council			
	Staff	Regu-lations	Other	Total	Staff	Regu-lations	Other	Total	Staff	Regu-lations	Other	Total
Prime Minister	8	—	30	38	13	—	25	38	11	—	22	33
Provincial Treasurer	61	4	43	108	86	7	53	146	97	14	322	433
Provincial Secretary	33	4	39	76	54	5	35	94	55	11	39	105
Liquor Control Board	53	—	2	55	61	2	18	81	62	1	27	90
Labour	27	22	6	55	57	25	8	90	52	21	11	84
Agriculture	137	24	45	206	111	22	45	178	206	26	41	273
Public Works	80	—	42	122	80	—	37	117	91	—	54	145
Public Welfare	57	5	158	220	55	13	153	221	61	17	180	258
Health	395	41	65	501	285	40	31	356	424	35	75	534
Reform Institutions	189	—	12	201	162	—	21	183	185	—	19	204
Education	102	12	25	139	91	13	17	121	125	13	13	151
Mines	35	2	46	83	42	4	28	74	40	3	33	76
Municipal Affairs	19	—	54	73	38	—	102	140	26	—	97	123
Lands and Forests	128	13	113	254	127	23	94	244	121	34	127	282
Highways	143	41	189	373	171	44	141	356	462	42	416	920
Planning and Development	44	—	86	130	75	—	100	175	58	—	139	197
Attorney General	241	17	261	519	239	17	322	578	305	27	312	644
Travel and Publicity	23	1	—	24	29	—	—	29	30	—	1	31
Ontario Hydro	—	4	23	27	—	2	20	22	—	2	29	31
TOTALS	1775	190	1239	3204	1776	217	1250	3243	2411	246	1957	4614

SOURCE: Compiled from detailed information provided by the executive council office of Ontario.

their peculiar significance in a discussion of legislative-executive relations. Lumped together with a number of minor fields under "other" origins or purposes of orders in council are some fields of jurisdiction which account for significant proportions of the total output of orders. Numerically, some of the most important are the following, all of which required at least fifty orders in council in one year alone: mothers' allowances; crown timber licenses; highways and roads; coroners and justices of the peace; police magistrates, sheriffs, judges, crown attorneys, and probation officers; the Ontario Municipal Improvement Corporation; conservation authorities; and the sale of lands.

From the data provided in Table 7 certain conclusions may be drawn. The 44 per cent increase in the number of orders in council passed in these three years may be accounted for by reference to three factors: the increase in staff appointments of 35 per cent, the increase in the number of orders dealing with highway matters, particularly roads, of 100 per cent, and the nineteen-fold increase in the number of Ontario Municipal Improvement Corporation debentures under both the Department of Municipal Affairs and the Department of the Treasurer. Although the number of regulations did increase nearly 30 per cent, this rate of increase was less than that of the over-all increase in the use of orders in council, demonstrating again that the greatest expansion in the use of orders in council has been for routine and regulatory matters rather than for matters falling in the legislative category.

Aside from orders in council, the only other direct means in the hands of the cabinet for controlling the affairs of the province are its powers to authorize special warrants, Treasury Board orders, and commitments. These instruments of executive power have already been described,[87] and the degree of discretion allowed the executive council in the use of them will be discussed later.[88] As in the case of orders in council there is at least the possibility of legislative review of these instruments, since they are passed only by responsible ministers who must face criticism from Her Majesty's Loyal Opposition.

However, there are other means by which the province is governed which are not subject to legislative review in any direct sense and, in some cases, are supposedly not even under the direction of the cabinet. To end this chapter on the executive branch, something must be said about the use of these special bodies, variously termed commissions, boards, authorities, committees, corporations, foundations, and councils.[89]

[87]See p. 57.   [88]See chap. 7.
[89]The terms "board" and "commission" are most common in Ontario, but the other designations are used. For example: the Ontario Telephone *Authority*, the

Semi-independent Agencies

Exactly what type of governmental agency we are discussing here will become apparent only as the general characteristics of this form of organization are described. The number of generic terms applied to this type of administrative body almost equals the variety of names given to the specific organizations that fall within the general category. Harvey and Bather called them "quasi-government" or "special" bodies.[90] Sometimes they are called "administrative tribunals," but in the United Kingdom this term is generally reserved for those "citizen courts" which are charged with quasi-judicial functions. There are very few such bodies in Ontario. Canadian political scientists usually refer to all government agencies outside the regular departments as "semi-independent agencies," but they are also called "non-departmental enterprises" or simply "boards" or "commissions."[91] R. E. Cushman used the designation, "independent regulatory commission," which he defined as "any Commission, board, or authority which lies outside the regular executive departments and which has for its major job the exercise of some form of restrictive or disciplinary control over private conduct or private property" in the United States.[92]

For the purposes of this study the commonly accepted term, "semi-independent agency," is generally used. By this is meant any public (i.e., governmental) body which has the following characteristics: (a) it exists outside the regular departmental structure, (b) its officers are appointed, not elected, and usually they do not fall under the regulations governing the officers of the ordinary civil service, (c) it comes under some form of public control but at the same time has a greater degree of independence than is customarily enjoyed by branches or divisions of government departments, and (d) it makes, or assists in making, policy in a fairly strictly defined area of government responsibility. With the infinite degree of variation found in the constitutions of modern semi-independent agencies, it would no doubt be possible to find some agencies which belonged to this category but which did not fit this general description, or vice versa. How-

Milk Industry Advisory *Committee* of Ontario, the Ontario Telephone Development *Corporation*, the Alcoholism Research *Foundation*, and the *Council* of Nursing.

[90]J. Harvey and L. Bather, *The British Constitution* (London: Macmillan, 1963), p. 305.

[91]Dawson, *The Government of Canada*, pp. 263–4.

[92]R. E. Cushman, *The Independent Regulatory Commission* (New York: Oxford University Press, 1941), p. 4, as quoted in J. Gould and W. L. Kolb, *A Dictionary of the Social Sciences*, compiled under the auspices of the United Nations Educational, Scientific, and Cultural Organization (London: Tavistock Publications, 1964), p. 105.

ever, the four characteristics which have been listed are common to most of the semi-independent agencies listed in the Gordon Committee *Report*[93] or dealt with in this chapter; any exceptions will be noted as they arise.

British legal historians trace the origins of semi-independent agencies back as far as the sixteenth century and the time of Henry VIII, in whose reign commissioners of sewers were appointed. In 1563 a statute of England required the justices of the various areas to meet and fix the wages to be paid locally to labourers.[94] The use of such agencies was fairly common in Upper Canada: by a statute of 1825 the legislature required the justices in each town to fix the price of bread for a two-week period and to meet on the first and third Saturday of each month for this purpose. In 1838 the collectors of customs in Ontario and the justices of the peace were authorized to inspect steamboat and factory machinery and were given statutory power to direct that necessary guards be erected.[95] The number of these agencies has increased considerably, particularly since the end of the second world war, reaching a total of nearly a hundred in 1963.[96]

The general reasons given for creating semi-independent agencies instead of using regular departmental structures are given here. First, semi-independent agencies may be set up to deal with a certain subject matter so as to remove it from the field of political controversy. By taking jurisdiction over the matter away from the department, the citizens concerned are less likely to feel that decisions which adversely affect them stem from political bias, and, by the same token, the politicians are freed from political pressures and cabinet ministers from political responsibilities. It must be added that this supposed independence from politics may be more apparent than real, but in political life appearances are important. A second justification is that this form of organization is more "business-like" and therefore more efficient. This is a moot point but, if it is true, it is a sad commentary on ordinary civil services. The more logical solution, as one senior Ontario public servant has pointed out, would be to correct the woeful situation existing in the departments instead of accepting it as inevitable and circumventing the regular departmental organization.[97] A third argument used is that they find it easier to recruit

[93]Gordon Committee *Report*, pp. 465–7.

[94]From the brief to the Gordon Committee filed by the Ontario section of the Canadian Bar Association, January 6, 1959, p. 1.

[95]*Loc. cit.*

[96]*Canadian Forum*, July, 1964, p. 84. The Gordon Committee listed eighty-eight in 1957.

[97]G. E. Gathercole, in an unpublished manuscript entitled "Outline of a Basis for Discussion by the Select Committee on Administrative and Executive Problems," p. 2.

staff. Again, if indeed this is true, it is an unfortunate state of affairs and should be remedied by adjusting salary scales and other aspects of civil service employment instead of setting up competing organizations which would make it even more difficult to recruit good personnel for the ordinary departments. A fourth reason why extra-departmental bodies are set up is to provide the government with expert outside advice. While it is certainly possible for the civil service to acquire its own experts, it is sometimes advantageous to hear the opinions of those who have not been subjected to the conditioning process that results from long affiliation with a highly integrated department. Besides, in some cases it is more economical to enlist the part-time aid of qualified persons outside of the service than it is to hire the same people on a permanent basis. Nevertheless, if this argument were applied generally, it would seriously undermine any attempts to recruit a professional civil service, because the status and prestige of its personnel would certainly diminish.

The Gordon Committee *Report* added to the justifications for semi-independent agencies by listing four specific reasons: (*a*) "It may be desirable to create a separate board or other agency where the Government is taking on a new function the limits or requirements of which cannot be fully defined or anticipated."[98] The Committee suggested that in such a case an agency could initially be given fairly wide discretionary powers and then, as the situation became clarified, the Government and the House could define its responsibilities and powers more precisely. As an illustration of such a development, the Committee listed the Hospital Services Commission of Ontario. While there might be some reason for laying down fairly flexible terms of reference for new enterprises, such as a hospital insurance scheme, this is not a sufficient explanation of why the agency charged with the task of developing and administering the scheme should be separate from the Department of Health. It has been suggested, for instance, that it was a desire to establish a separate financial identity and "to placate the Medical, Hospital and Insurance interests that led to the use of this device" in this case.[99] May it not also have been a device used by the Government to allow it the freedom to experiment without having to answer for its actions as it would have had to, had it administered the scheme through the appropriate department?

(*b*) "A board or commission might be set up where the function is of a judicial nature and where either some special expertise is involved or the avoidance of delays and expenses are in themselves important elements in

[98]Gordon Committee *Report*, p. 49.

[99]William D. Chambers, "The Independent Commission in Ontario," April, 1962, an unpublished paper prepared for the Select Committtee on Administrative and Executive Problems, p. 87.

the dispensing of justice."[100] Given as examples of agencies in this category were the Ontario Securities Commission, the Labour Relations Board, and the Workmen's Compensation Board. There is certainly much more cogency to this second argument in favour of semi-independent agencies than there was to the first, but as a general principle it is not sufficient to explain why these particular functions were turned over to boards or commissions, while roughly equivalent functions, also judicial in nature, have been left to the departments. Was it because, in the instances cited, there existed influential interest groups which were able to demand a more powerful voice in the bodies given responsibility for these functions than they would have had if regular departmental divisions had been used?[101] Perhaps too, the Government felt that by using this administrative technique it could maintain a sufficient degree of control over the performance of these functions without incurring direct political responsibility for the results of any control it might choose to exercise.

(c) "Where the function is of a commercial or industrial type, a corporate form, perhaps under the general direction of a board or commission, may be adopted. . . .[102] This reason for the use of a semi-independent agency is almost identical to the general argument already discussed, namely, that this form of organization is more "business-like" and therefore more efficient. The Gordon Committee used as illustrations of this type of agency the Ontario Northland Transportation Commission, the Food Terminal Board, the Hydro-Electric Power Commission of Ontario, and the Liquor Control Board. Unless one is willing to subscribe to the belief that civil servants are incapable of making decisions quickly, adjusting operations to meet changing conditions, keeping secret certain plans of action, and costing and pricing with a view to making an enterprise pay for itself – all reasons given by the Committee for resorting to a public corporation form of organization – then it is difficult to accept this argument. In particular, it is hard to imagine that the functions exercised by such an organization as the Liquor Control Board are more efficiently performed because that organization is not under the direct supervision of a minister of a department. Surely political considerations – such as the desire of ministers to avoid responsibility for the detailed administration of that section of the Liquor Control Act that relates to the regulation and control of the sale of liquor through the government-operated stores – must have been just as important in choosing this form of organization. In

[100]Gordon Committee *Report*, p. 49.
[101]This suggestion was made in Chambers, "The Independent Commission in Ontario."
[102]Gordon Committee *Report*, p. 49.

other cases, it is likely that the Government set up semi-independent agencies of this corporate type simply because the pressure groups concerned would accept nothing else. The Food Terminal Board, for instance, permits a degree of government control through its chairman, who is also the commissioner of the Markets Branch of the Department of Agriculture and yet satisfies both the wholesalers and the producers whose representatives constitute the remainder of the Board. By the use of this semi-independent agency, the dealers and suppliers are able to do with public authority what they had been unable to do without this authority, namely, regulate themselves. Although the Government could have achieved its ends – order and control – through regulations enforced by the Department of Agriculture, to ensure the support of the people concerned it was expedient to set up a semi-independent agency in which these people would share responsibility with a representative of the Government.

(*d*) "Lastly, when the function cuts across single jurisdictions or areas of responsibility, a committee or corporate form of organization may be used. . . ."[103] The examples of this type of organization given by the Gordon Committee were: the Lake of the Woods Control Board, which brings together the interests of the federal government and those of Manitoba and Ontario; the Junior Farmer Establishment Loan Corporation and the Co-operative Loans Board, both of which combine the interests of the Departments of Agriculture and the Treasury. While it is understandable that special organizations would have to be created in order to co-ordinate intergovernmental or interdepartmental enterprises, it is doubtful that these bodies should be placed in the category of semi-independent agencies. Certainly the three illustrations of this type of organization given by the Gordon Committee do not fit the definition of the semi-independent agency that has been put forward in this chapter, since none of them possesses any "greater degree of independence than is customarily enjoyed by the branches and divisions of government departments." The Lake of the Woods Control Board is a case unto itself, and the other two agencies are as responsible to the Government and the Assembly – in policy and operational matters – as are the regular departments. In view of this, they do not merit any special attention here.

In the preceding paragraphs the customary arguments in favour of semi-independent agencies have been shown to be less than adequate justifications for their use in many instances and it has been intimated that motives other than those of a purely administrative nature may have been behind their creation. The Gordon Committee – whose discussion of the reasons for the use of these agencies has just been criticized as being too

[103]*Ibid.*, p. 50.

narrow – recognized that "they [the subordinate agencies] might be resorted to indiscriminately – to circumvent public service regulations, to evade direct responsibility, perhaps even carelessly. . . ."[104] Certainly one of two alternatives is the case: either the semi-independent agencies are in fact free from control by the Government or the legislature – in which case they are "Governments in Miniature,"[105] irresponsible executive bodies, making and administering policy in their assigned spheres – or they are governed directly or indirectly by the cabinet. In either case it is evident that, for the purposes of this study at least, these special bodies merit inclusion in the executive branch of government. Whether or not they are simply one other instrument through which the cabinet governs the province remains to be examined.

Theoretically, many of the semi-independent agencies in Ontario are free from any supervision by the cabinet or the legislature. An examination of the statutes establishing these agencies shows that in many instances the legislature has neither retained the policy-making function nor delegated it to a responsible minister. It has instead delegated that function to an extradepartmental agency which is ostensibly independent, having no stated policy to administer. Traditionally the delegation of power has been understood to be vertical in nature: the legislature was thought to delegate power to the executive council or to departmental officials who were responsible to the legislature through their ministers. In such a case the principle of ministerial responsibility would be operative, ensuring that the decisions made and the deeds done by these officials would ultimately coincide with the wishes of the cabinet; hence they would meet with the approval of a majority in the Legislative Assembly. However, when powers are delegated to an extradepartmental agency the whole relationship is changed, and the traditional devices for guaranteeing that the delegated powers will be exercised in conformity with the wishes of the cabinet or the Assembly may become irrelevant. In this case there is a horizontal delegation of powers, but the traditional devices of control generally only apply in cases of vertical delegation.[106]

Two instances of this type of delegation may be cited.[107] The Ontario

[104]*Ibid.*, p. 48.

[105]The designation used by Professor John Willis in "The Relevance of the Franks Report to the Ontario Situation," a memorandum to the Select Committee on Administrative and Executive Problems, May 6, 1960, p. 1.

[106]This distinction between vertical and horizontal delegation of powers in Ontario was explored by Chambers, "The Independent Commission in Ontario," pp. 76 ff.

[107]These two cases were singled out by the Ontario section of the Canadian Bar Association in their brief to the Gordon Committee (January 6, 1959, pp. 12–13) as being illustrative of the degree of independence enjoyed by certain boards and commissions.

Fuel Board Act, 1954, delegated to the Fuel Board the power to "control and regulate the production, storage, transmission, distribution, sale, disposal, supply and use of natural gas in Ontario" and to make orders with respect thereto.[108] Without restricting the generality of the foregoing, section 16 of the Act required that rates, meter rentals, and other charges to be paid by the ultimate consumers of natural gas be fixed by the Board, but no basis for fixing such rates was suggested. There was not a word in the Act about matters such as what return on invested capital should be permitted, how to determine uniform rate areas, and what were the allowable differentials between classes of consumers or between quantities consumed. Other sections of the Act provided for the granting or approving of monopolies, without any statement as to exactly how this power was to be exercised. A second illustration of the degree of discretion allowed semi-independent agencies is to be found in certain provisions concerning the Ontario Municipal Board. Section 14 of the Municipal Act provides that the Board may amalgamate or annex to any municipality in Ontario the whole or any part of another municipality.[109] But, again, no guidelines as to what policy should be followed in executing these powers are laid down.

If the semi-independent agencies are in fact as unrestricted in the discharge of their functions as some legislative provisions suggest, then there is some validity to the charge that they are irresponsible miniature governments. However, while the statute law of the province may leave them relatively unfettered, the political realities are such that most of them must surely be subject to the dictates of the cabinet. When no directions for the use of their powers are to be found in the Acts conferring these powers upon them, it would be a great cause of wonderment if the semi-independent agencies did not rely upon the cabinet for guidance in policy matters. And, more significantly, in view of its dominant position vis-à-vis the agencies by virtue of its ultimate control over their personnel and funds, it would be rather unlikely that the cabinet would forego the opportunity to intervene in their affairs. It was this situation which moved John Wintermeyer, a former leader of the opposition, to charge that "In many instances Boards and Commissions have become adjuncts to Departments of Government wherein Government has determined 'policy', without responsibility for such policy."[110]

It would be a difficult task – and one far beyond the scope of this chapter – to trace the degree to which the extradepartmental agencies are

[108]*SO*, 1954, c. 63, s. 15.   [109]*RSO*, 1960, c. 249, s. 14.
[110]John J. Wintermeyer, "Brief to the Committee on the Organization of Government in Ontario," January 1959, p. 4.

subject to the wishes of the cabinet, but the main techniques available to the cabinet, should it desire to dictate to the agencies, may be briefly described.

In addition to the fact that in most cases the cabinet is the final arbiter of the amount of funds to be made available to the agencies – the consequences of which hardly need elaboration – the provisions for staffing and management generally leave ample scope for manipulation by the cabinet. An examination of the organizations of forty-four of the more significant outside agencies revealed the following information about the statutory provisions for their composition: [111]

Types of provisions re size of agency	Number of agencies of each type
(a) Size of agency fixed	9
(b) Maximum specified, no minimum	7
(c) Minimum specified, no maximum	13
(d) Maximum and minimum specified	10
(e) No provision in the statute	5
TOTAL	44

A fixed figure for the size of a board is usually considered an attempt to isolate the agency from Government pressure; failure to even specify a maximum size is generally thought to reflect the opposite tendency. Nevertheless, of the nine agencies having fixed sizes, only five are seriously intended to be in any real sense independent, while, on the other hand, some of those which are most open to being "swamped" – those with no specified maximum – are in fact among the most independent from the cabinet, e.g., the advisory boards based on representation from strong, organized pressure groups.

Equally important for the independence of an agency is the type of tenure its officials possess. In half of the forty-four agencies studied by Mr. Chambers there was no reference to tenure whatsoever, and in most of the other cases tenure was "at pleasure," i.e., at the pleasure of the lieutenant governor in council.[112] It would not be unreasonable to expect agency members who did not possess tenure during good behaviour to act in a manner that would guarantee their continued employment, particularly if the job were a full-time one.

In most cases the responsibility for appointing members of an agency lies with the lieutenant governor in council, although sometimes it is given

[111]Chambers, "The Independent Commission in Ontario," p. 136.
[112]*Ibid.*, p. 139.

to one minister, to the organized groups affected by the agency, or to the body which is senior to the agency. It is worth noting that, although appointment by the executive council or by an individual minister is perhaps the most obvious method the cabinet has of influencing the operations of an agency,[113] formal appointment by other public bodies or even outside organizations does not rule out cabinet control. The agency or organization which actually makes the appointment may be under the control of the cabinet, or at least be amenable to cabinet suggestions.

A final variable that must be investigated in order to assess the true relationship between a semi-independent agency and the cabinet is the provision for the management of the agency itself. In other words, who has effective control over the scope and direction of the agency's activities? In his study of forty-four agencies, Mr. Chambers found six patterns of management control.[114] There was no reference to management whatsoever in the legislation establishing eighteen of the agencies, including the Ontario Hospital Services Commission, the Ontario Water Resources Commission, and the Ontario Stockyards Board. In four instances the lieutenant governor in council was to make regulations regarding the "powers and details" of the agency. In thirteen cases the legislation specified that the board was to exercise the management function. Some of those that fell in this category were what the Gordon Committee called "departmental agencies": "organizations made up of individual officials, authorities and other bodies that sometimes are included in compilations of the boards and commissions in Ontario, but which . . . should properly be considered as a part of the departmental organization that is responsible for them."[115] The Co-operative Loans Board is an example of a depart-

---

[113]A good illustration of the way in which executive council appointments can be used to carry out government policy occurred during the Drury government. When it became apparent that the radial railway project was a failure, the Government repealed all railway legislation except that concerned with the line west of Toronto, where some money had already been spent. The municipalities concerned with this particular line were allowed a vote on the matter. In those days, Adam Beck, the chairman of the Hydro-Electric Power Commission, had spent Hydro money lavishly in municipal elections. Since Beck was in favour of the radial railway legislation, Mr. Drury wanted to ensure that no Hydro money would be spent in the election. To ensure this, and so defeat the radial railways legislation, Mr. Drury promoted one member of the Commission, Mr. Lucas, to a better-paying job as legal adviser of the Commission, and then appointed in his stead a man named Miller. Mr. Miller was appointed on the distinct understanding that the matter of aid in the election would be killed in the Commission. From an interview with Mr. E. C. Drury, March 19, 1965. Tapes of this interview have been deposited with the Ontario Public Archives and the Toronto Archives of the Canadian Broadcasting Corporation.

[114]Chambers, "The Independent Commission in Ontario," pp. 143–4.

[115]Gordon Committee *Report*, p. 53.

mental agency which is empowered to regulate itself within the terms laid down in the statutes relating to it. However, insofar as such agencies are really only adjuncts of the departmental structures, it seems reasonable to conclude that their management is fairly well integrated into the over-all departmental operations. On the other hand, some agencies that manage their own operations are quite separate from the departments. Perhaps the best illustration of this pattern would be the Workmen's Compensation Board. The fourth pattern of management control isolated by Chambers is that in which the responsibility is assigned to the senior executive officer of the agency or to the senior body under which the agency functions. It may be seen, then, that in a large number of cases the management of the agencies is either directly controlled by the executive council or by a minister exercising his control through departmental channels.

The whole problem of the relationship between the semi-independent agencies – which are relatively recent accretions to the administrative machinery of the state – and the traditional institutions of government is still very open. In Ontario the diversity in the relationships between the agencies and the Cabinet is such that no simple conclusions may be given. Nevertheless two quite opposite tendencies should be noted, both of which have real significance for a study of legislative-executive relations.

First, some agencies have been granted, by statute and/or convention, a large measure of independence from the cabinet. As has already been pointed out, agencies which are quite independent should be understood to exercise horizontally delegated powers. They do not form a part of the pyramid of delegated powers which characterizes the regular civil service and which has its apex in the executive council. Rather, they are more or less isolated public bodies exercising jurisdiction in a fairly strictly defined segment of public concern, and are responsible only to the legislature which created them and assigned their respective spheres of operation. They may rightly be considered independent executive bodies. This being the case it is unrealistic to expect the cabinet to assume responsibility for their actions. Indeed, to require the principle of ministerial responsibility to operate in them would, in many cases at least, deny the whole rationale behind their creation: the desire to remove the subject matter of their jurisdictions from all taint of "political" intervention.[116]

[116]The failure to recognize this fact probably accounts for a basic contradiction in the Gordon Committee *Report*. On the one hand the Committee claimed that certain agencies "must have a high degree of independence and be free from political considerations or pressures" (p. 49) and, on the other hand, it maintained that "ministerial responsibility should invariably be preserved" (p. 66). Ultimately the two ideals are completely irreconcilable.

Obviously, if the legislative branch of governments is to be the final source of authority in the governmental system, it must maintain some control over the operations of these extradepartmental, quasi-governments; but, unless the Legislative Assembly is willing to jeopardize the independence of the agencies in their day-to-day activities, it cannot use for this purpose stratagems contrived for controlling vertically delegated powers. More will be said in succeeding chapters about the mechanisms of control that would be appropriate in cases of horizontal delegation.

The second, and opposite, tendency is for agencies to fall completely under the sway of the cabinet. Clearly, if the executive council or a minister of the crown appoints its members, if these members only hold office "during pleasure," if the executive council has the sole right to make regulations regarding its powers and responsibilities, and if it is dependent on the whims of the cabinet for its budget, then it is inconceivable that an agency could have any real independence. And, when the omnipotent position of the cabinet in nearly every facet of the governmental process in Ontario is considered, it is obvious that it is not necessary for the cabinet to have all of the statutory powers just listed in order to wield very considerable influence over the conduct of the extradepartmental agencies.

This being the case, it might well be asked why these agencies were set up in the first place, in lieu of ordinary departmental divisions. In some instances it may be that the formation of extradepartmental bodies has stemmed from a desire on the part of the cabinet to have control over particular spheres of activity without having to accept on the floor of the House responsibility for their actions. By means of the formal and informal instruments at its disposal the cabinet could manipulate the affairs of certain agencies and still refuse to take responsibility for the results, on the grounds that the agencies were constituted for the very purpose that they should be free from political interference.

While it might be possible to find some evidence to support this thesis, it seems likely that the reasons for using the institution of the semi-independent agency in Ontario lie much deeper than this. In the final analysis, the increase in the use of this form of public administration since the second world war has resulted from the difficulty of adapting our liberal-democratic institutions to the demands of the positive state in a collectivist society. Classical liberal-democratic theory and the liberal institutions it created were both based on the assumption that the functions of the state should be strictly curtailed. Their aim was to maximize individual freedom – conceived as the absence of restraint – and the separation of powers was the means to that end. By setting up institutions to check the executive and by giving those institutions powers suited to their task, the liberals sought to divide and so to limit the over-all power of the state.[117] Institutions devised to put into practice such a limited concept of the legitimate role of the state would hardly be suitable for governing a social welfare state, although the experience of New Zealand indicates that it is possible for a dynamic Government to use the old institutions for this new purpose.[118] Rather than attempt to use these institutions for an assignment for which they were not intended, the usual tendency in Ontario has been to graft on to them new institutions more suited to the task. It comes as no surprise that almost invariably these new institutions violate the principle of the separation of powers, in that a given agency will usually perform legislative and executive – and sometimes judicial – functions, often without any system of appeal to the major legislative, executive, or judicial institutions of government.

In Ontario particularly, the politicians who have held office since the end of the war seem to have been unable to adjust their liberal philosophies to the demands for a welfare state that have been forced upon them. Wanting to maintain a façade of limited government and yet compelled to intervene in more and more areas of public concern in order to survive, they have resorted to extradepartmental agencies as a compromise solution to their dilemma. This expedient salves their own liberal consciences and also meets the demands of the organized pressure groups that want the kind of control over their operations that can be achieved only through public authority but that nevertheless fear direct government supervision of their activities – no doubt because they too were nurtured on the principles of classical liberalism.

But, regardless of why the semi-independent agencies have been created, the fact remains that they exist. And, if the goal of responsible executive government is to be achieved, some mechanism for controlling their operations, either indirectly through the cabinet or directly through legislative procedures, must be devised. What success has accompanied efforts in this direction will be discussed in the remaining chapters.

[117]It need hardly be pointed out that even in a parliamentary democracy, with its union of legislative and executive powers, there is still a definite separation of total powers, both through the provision of an independent judiciary and through the institution of Her Majesty's Loyal Opposition, which has traditionally been equipped with certain powers to restrain the executive. If some powers are given to the body charged with restraining the executive then it is correct to say that the powers of the state are divided.

[118]See, for example, the discussion of "the remarkably wide range of activity supervised in the name of the Crown by ordinary departments rather than by public corporations" in New Zealand in Alexander Brady, *Democracy in the Dominions* (3rd ed.; Toronto: University of Toronto Press, 1958), p. 290.

THE LEGISLATIVE
BRANCH

4

IN A PARLIAMENTARY SYSTEM of government any institutional methods of controlling the powers of the executive which may be devised will in all probability centre around the legislative branch. In Ontario this has always been the Legislative Assembly since, in contrast to the other original members of the Federation, it was given a unicameral constitution at the very outset of its existence as a province.[1] In July 1866, at the last session of the legislature of pre-Confederation Canada, Sir John A. Macdonald tabled the resolutions on the constitutions of the future provinces. In answer to criticism from J. S. Macdonald that the resolutions were not sufficiently detailed, he said that, as they had already determined the principles of the confederal constitution, now they were called upon to settle the general principles of the local constitutions. He was of the opinion that this task would not be onerous in Lower Canada, since the existing constitution of Canada had simply been adopted, with the exception of a nominated rather than an elected upper house. In Upper Canada there was to be a greater innovation: the adoption of a single-chamber legislature. "This then was the great question to discuss in these resolutions, and the other was whether they should or should not have Responsible Government in conjunction with a single chamber."[2]

[1]Of the five provinces that have had legislative councils during their existences as provinces, only Quebec still maintains an upper house. The other four dispensed with theirs as follows: Manitoba in 1876, New Brunswick in 1892, Prince Edward Island in 1893, and Nova Scotia in 1928.

[2]Report of the debates of the Legislative Assembly of Canada on July 27, 1866 in Canada, Parliament, House of Commons, *Debates, 1866–1870*, microfilm of newspaper accounts reported by the *Ottawa Times*, Toronto *Globe*, and Toronto *Mail* in the Library of Parliament, filmed by the Canadian Library Association (hereafter referred to as the *Scrapbook Hansard*).

The resolution calling for a single-chamber legislature of eighty-two members for Canada West and an Assembly of sixty-five, plus a Legislative Council of twenty-four for Canada East,[3] reflected the differing attitudes towards the future role of provincial governments. Those who sought a large field for government activity were apparently convinced that a bicameral legislature would be a greater bulwark against federal encroachment than would a unicameral one. *Le Canada* reasoned: "Plus on simplifiera la législature locale plus on amoindrira son importance et plus on courra risque de la voir absorber par la législature fédérale. Naturellement, le Haut-Canada, qui préférerait une Union législative, ne redoute guère cette absorption."[4] Whether or not an upper house really strengthens the position of its province vis-à-vis the central government is a moot point, but the converse reasoning – that a subordinate legislative body has no need of a second chamber – was eminently obvious to the other group, which sought more of a legislative union. As Macdonald put it: "Were this a sovereign legislature there might be two chambers, but for a subordinate legislature one was enough."[5] Two days later he reiterated the point, leaving no doubt as to his view of the place of provincial governments in the forthcoming union: "For a subordinate Legislature acting under authority of a general government, having in fact something the character of a Municipal body, one chamber had been considered sufficient."[6]

However, the unicameralists had some positive points in their favour, not the least of which was the fact that considerable saving would follow the elimination of the upper house. George Brown, who frankly disliked having responsible governments at the local level at all, was quite happy to do away with one more conceivable check on the executive and at the same time reduce the cost of provincial administration. He argued:

Undoubtedly the mode in which the local government shall be constructed will very much affect the cost of the whole scheme; but if we adopt (as I earnestly hope we will) simple and inexpensive machinery for local purposes, I am quite satisfied that there will be a reduction to the people of Canada in the amount they now contribute.[7]

---

[3]Eschewing the ten-year-old Canadian precedent of an elective upper house, the legislative councillors of Quebec were to be appointed for life by the crown. See P. B. Waite, *The Life and Times of Confederation, 1864–1867: Politics, Newspapers, and the Union of British North America* (Toronto: University of Toronto Press, 1962), pp. 129, 284.

[4]*Le Canada*, Ottawa, 17 juillet, 1866. *Ibid.*, p. 285.

[5]Toronto *Leader*, July 14, 1866. *Ibid.*

[6]Report of the debates of the Legislative Assembly of Canada on July 15, 1866, in the *Scrapbook Hansard*.

[7]Quoted in Charles Clarke, *The Member's Manual of Practice and Procedure in the Legislative Assembly of the Province of Ontario, with Decisions of Mr. Speaker,*

Mr. M. C. Cameron, opposing the suggestion of a bicameral legislature for Upper Canada, said:

One argument had been urged by the Attorney-General West in favour of a single chamber, which appeared to have escaped that hon. gentleman's [Mr. J. H. Cameron's] attention, the consideration of expense. The cost of an Upper Chamber to Upper Canada would be serious, after all the ordinary sources of revenue had been handed over to the General Government. He regarded it as a farce, a mere mockery of the British Constitution, to give an Upper Chamber to a Legislature which would be nothing better than a large municipal body.[8]

George-Etienne Cartier assumed that economy was the chief argument in favour of a unicameral legislature but was willing to undergo the expense in Canada East: "Ce n'est pas pour £15,000 à £20,000 que nous aurions voulu refuser de donner plus de respectabilité à tout notre système d'institutions."[9] The desire to decrease expenditures was the chief reason for the removal of the legislative councils in the other provinces as well. In Manitoba, the increase in 1875 in federal aid was granted with the understanding that the upper house would be abolished. No doubt as to the reason for this action was left in the title of the act which accomplished this end: An Act to Diminish the expenses of the Legislature for the Province of Manitoba.[10]

When, on August 2, 1866, concurrence was asked for the fifth of the Confederation Resolutions, the Hon. John Hillyard Cameron of Peel County moved an amendment calling for the traditional bicameral legislature. The amendment was seconded by a future lieutenant governor of Manitoba and subsequently a member of the Legislative Assembly of Ontario. Following an interesting if unexciting debate,[11] the House divided on the question; eighty-six opposed the amendment and only thirteen supported the proposal for a double chamber. Conspicuous amongst the advocates of a single chamber were five men destined to take an important

---

from 1867 to 1893: Rules of the House and Miscellaneous Information (Toronto, 1893), p. 6.

[8]Report of the debates of the Legislative Assembly of Canada on August 2, 1866, in the *Scrapbook Hansard*.

[9]*La Minerve*, Montreal, 17 juillet 1866, reporting debates for July 13. Quoted in Waite, *The Life and Times*, p. 286.

[10]*Statutes of Manitoba*, 39 Vict., c. 28.

[11]The attitude towards debating the details of the local constitutions may be illustrated by the remark made by Mr. Brown in reply to the Hon. William Macdougall, who had criticized him for "sending it forth before the country that a better scheme might have been devised if more talent and patriotism had been devoted to its consideration" and at the same time refusing to put forward any alternative plans. Mr. Brown's only reply was that, "since it was the general feeling of this House to give the constitutions provided by these resolutions a fair trial, there was no need of putting two schemes before the country to create useless discussion." (Report of the debates of August 2, 1866, in the *Scrapbook Hansard*).

part in the deliberations of the first Legislative Assembly of Ontario: John Sandfield Macdonald, Mathew Crooks Cameron, John Carling, and Edmund Burke Wood became members of the first Ontario cabinet, and Archibald McKellar became the leader of the first Ontario Opposition.

Once the experiment in unicameralism was launched, its advocates found their position entirely justified. After three years experience, the first Premier of the province, the Honourable John Sandfield Macdonald, could say: "I am sincerely attached to a single chamber, for it has been proved that it can manage satisfactorily the affairs of two millions of people without a second chamber, consisting of members appointed for life, and who, once elected, do not care for anybody."[12] By 1893 the second Clerk of the Legislative Assembly of Ontario, Mr. Charles Clarke, had discovered a number of advantages to the system. He eulogized:

In every succeeding Legislature the one chamber has proved itself to be even a greater success than was anticipated when it was first proposed. It cheapens the cost of legislation; facilitates the passage of needed laws; removes the delay which, under the double system, checks the completion if not the introduction of measures embodying salutary reforms; is quickly responsive to the touch of public opinion; and gives opportunity for prompt correction of legislative errors should such ever find entrance to the statute book.[13]

While many of the politicians from Canada West were quite content to see the status of the future provinces played down and considered the whole question of provincial constitutions somewhat of a bore, there was a more significant reason for this attitude than the unrelenting climate of Ottawa in July and August. The fact was that a majority of the politicians who decided the constitutional fate of the new provinces was aspiring to "wider fields of service" in the new federal Parliament. To become a member of a provincial legislature would clearly be a step down the ladder of power and prestige. In the end a majority of the members of the legislature of the Province of Canada did become members of the new federal Parliament, although, until the practice was outlawed in 1872, some of these men held seats in both the provincial and the federal legislatures. The assumed inferiority of the provincial position was dramatically revealed when Edward Blake, faced with making a choice between the two political arenas, renounced the premiership of Ontario and chose a seat in the Opposition benches of the House of Commons.

However, when the provincial politicians realized that they would probably gain no larger stage for the display of their talents and as the full scope of provincial powers was revealed through experience and judicial

[12]Quoted in Clarke, *The Member's Manual*, p. 6.
[13]*Ibid.*, p. 7.

interpretation, they began to take greater pride in their provincial institution. A running battle developed between the leaders of the Ontario government and the federal government, sparked by the attempts of provincial leaders to win for Ontario symbols commensurate with their concept of its juristic position. Three issues may be singled out as examples of this struggle which undoubtedly stemmed from a collective inferiority complex but which on occasion had repercussions of constitutional significance.

There was, first of all, the question of the name to be used when referring to the legislative body of the province. Section 69 of the British North America Act provides that "There shall be a Legislature for Ontario consisting of the Lieutenant Governor and of One House, styled the Legislative Assembly of Ontario." But, when this Legislative Assembly meets, is it a "legislature" or a "parliament" as at Ottawa? Probably from force of habit, but perhaps from design, the first session of the new provincial legislative body was termed "The First Session of the First Parliament" in the *Journals*. But in 1879 the less imposing heading, "The Fourth Session of the Third Legislature," was adopted. This lapse in patriotism was corrected in 1952 and the original terminology is now used. Lest this be dismissed as simply a problem of semantics, it should be noted that during the second year of the province's existence the federal government disallowed an act giving the Ontario Assembly the same parliamentary privileges, immunities, and powers as the federal Parliament had claimed for itself earlier in the same year and which were equal to those enjoyed by the House of Commons of the United Kingdom.[14] The federal government held that since the legislature was not a parliament the power to give itself privileges did not inhere in it by virtue of its status; it had only those powers expressly granted to it by the BNA Act, and this Act made no provision for parliamentary privileges at the provincial level.[15] In 1876,

[14]*Statutes of Ontario (SO)*, 1868–69, c. 3, assented to on December 19, 1868, and *Statutes of Canada*, 1868, c. 23, s. 1, assented to on May 22, 1868.

[15]See W. E. Hodgins, *Correspondence, reports of the Minister of Justice and orders in council upon the subject of Dominion and Provincial Legislation, 1867–1895,* compiled under the direction of the Hon. the Minister of Justice (Ottawa: Government Printing Office, 1896), p. 83. In this report John A. Macdonald went on to point out that if the province did have the right to legislate on the matter it seemed to follow that "while the general Parliament can under the 18th clause, confer no greater privileges than those enjoyed by the Imperial House of Commons, the provincial legislature being bound by no such limitation, might, if it were so disposed, confer upon itself and its members privileges in excess of those belonging to the House of Commons of England." Although the issue has not been raised officially since 1876, this seems to be the existing state of affairs.

It is also interesting to note that the very year in which the *Journals* began calling the Legislative Assembly a "legislature" rather than a "parliament," Fennings Taylor, deputy clerk and clerk assistant of the Senate, published a book entitled, *Are Legislatures Parliaments?* His conclusion was that "the assumption . . . by Provincial

however, the legislature passed a new act[16] claiming these same rights and privileges, and this legislation has remained in force without interference by the federal government.[17] Today, the *Directory and Guide to the Services of the Government of Ontario* notes that the legislature in Ontario has "full authority to make such laws as it sees fit with respect to its rights and privileges and to legislate within its jurisdiction as fully as can the Imperial Parliament itself."[18]

A related and more narrowly semantic a question was whether the term "House" should be applied to the provincial Assembly. A select committee appointed on April 4, 1946, to study the rules and make recommendations for their improvement changed all references to the "House" to "Legislative Assembly," apparently in the belief that the former term should be reserved for denoting the House of Commons. The report was never adopted and the Assembly is generally referred to as the House.[19]

A second problem of nomenclature had to do with the members themselves. Before Confederation, members of the Assembly of the Province of Canada were designated by the initials MPP, "Member of the Provincial Parliament." After Confederation it was suggested that, since the British North America Act provided for provincial legislative assemblies, members of those bodies should have the initials "MLA" after their names to identify them as "Members of the Legislative Assembly." Opponents of this proposal claimed that it would be the equivalent to designating members of the House of Commons by the initials "MHC," ignoring the fact that the Act specified that there was to be "One Parliament for Canada" and that the term parliament was never applied to the provincial constitution.[20] Finally, to end the debate between the "centralists," who wanted

---

legislatures of the 'privileges, immunities and powers' that belong to Parliaments is an assumption for which no authority can be found in the acts under which those legislatures were established, and from whence all their authority is derived." Fennings Taylor, *Are Legislatures Parliaments? A Study and Review* (Montreal: John Lovell, 1879), p. 18.   [16]*SO*, 1875–76, c. 9.

[17]W. E. Grasham, "Provincial Government," an unpublished manuscript, being an expanded version of a speech delivered to the Third Senior Officers' Conference at Guelph, Ontario, Summer 1963, pp. 37, 38.

[18]Ontario, Department of Tourism and Information, *Directory and Guide to the Services of the Ontario Government*, Spring 1965, p. 271.

[19]Mr. Roderick Lewis, the clerk of the Legislative Assembly, has argued that adopting the terminology recommended by the select committee would have hamstrung the rules, because the term "Legislative Assembly" necessarily includes all 108 members of the Assembly, whereas the designation "House" need only include the Prime Minister and a quorum of the Assembly.

[20]Compare sections 17 and 19 of the British North America Act. A more plausible argument, raised by Mr. Lewis, is that the Legislative Assembly is the counterpart of the House of Commons and that, while both of these bodies come and go with the exigencies of politics, in both cases an abstract entity, parliament continues to exist.

to play down the significance of the provincial governments, and the "provincialists," who sought to add one more symbol to the myth of the equality of the local units with the centre, the Legislative Assembly made "MPP" the official abbreviation on April 7, 1938.[21]

The third illustration of the struggle over symbols also had real constitutional overtones. As already indicated, section 69 of the BNA Act provided for a provincial legislature consisting of the lieutenant governor and the Assembly. Section 17, however, provided the federal government with a Parliament "consisting of the Queen, an Upper House styled the Senate, and the House of Commons."[22] In spite of the obvious import of these sections, Ontario immediately asserted the inclusion of the Queen in the legislature by adopting the enacting clause: "Her Majesty, by and with the advice and consent of the Legislative Assembly of the Province of Ontario enacts as follows."[23] Inevitably there arose a controversy between the federal government and the province as to whether or not the Queen did in fact form part of the legislature, but the federal government never succeeded in its attempts to get the province to use some other enacting formula.

Although this struggle for recognition on the part of the provincial legislature was primarily aimed at asserting its power as opposed to that of the central government, it had significance within the provincial structure as well. It must be remembered that many influential leaders were opposed to any form of legislative control over the provincial executives. Mention has already been made of George Brown who advocated making the heads of departments responsible to the lieutenant governor, not to the legislature. A similar plan was put forward in Canada East by the *Courrier du Canada*.[24] That responsible men of affairs could take such an attitude was indicative of the general tendency to disparage the role of provincial legislatures. Four years later, when the politically and economically immature province of Manitoba was admitted to the union, this opposition to the trappings of responsible government took more concrete form. Professor M. S. Donnelly found that the first two lieutenant governors "organized and ran the provincial government for the first six years of its existence and in addition performed a number of other exceptional duties. . . ."[25] In Ontario the struggle for the achievement and

---

[21]Ontario, Legislative Assembly, *Journals*, 1937–38, p. 136.

[22]This point is raised in Grasham, "Provincial Government," pp. 37–8.

[23]The Statutory authority for the use of this clause was given in the first section of the first act in the first volume of Ontario statutes and read: "The following words may be inserted in the Preambles of Statutes and shall indicate the authority by virtue of which they are passed: 'Her Majesty, by and with the advice and consent of the Legislative Assembly of the Province of Ontario, enacts as follows:'" *SO*, 1867, c. 1, s. 1.   [24]Waite, *The Life and Times*, pp. 286–7.

[25]Murray S. Donnelly, *The Government of Manitoba* (Toronto: University of

recognition of what has since come to be the accepted status of the provincial governments in the federation helped to counteract the inclination to belittle the functions and prestige of the Legislative Assembly. Enhancing the provincial legislature vis-à-vis the federal Parliament resulted in an augmentation of the influence of the Legislative Assembly in relation to its own executive. Before going on to investigate the nature of this relationship, some further details as to the composition and powers of the Legislative Assembly ought to be noticed.

Section 85 of the BNA Act provided that "Every Legislative Assembly of Ontario . . . shall continue for Four years from the Day of the Return of the Writs for choosing the same . . . and no longer."[26] This limitation on the duration of the legislature was carried over in precise language into the Legislative Assembly Act of Ontario as it was enacted and re-enacted from time to time until 1930, when the term was extended to a maximum of five years.[27] In 1942, by the Legislative Assembly Extension Act, the life of the then present Assembly was extended to October 19 of the following year.[28] A similar act was passed in 1943 to extend the duration of the Assembly to October 19, 1944,[29] but advantage was not taken of this statute and the Assembly was dissolved by the lieutenant governor in July 1943. The stipulation in section 86 of the BNA Act that "There shall be a session of the Legislature of Ontario . . . once at least in every Year, so that Twelve Months shall not intervene between the last Sitting of the Legislature . . . in one Session and its first Sitting in the next Session" has been transferred almost verbatim into the Legislative Assembly Act.[30]

According to Sir John A. Macdonald, representation in the new province of Ontario was to be based on population and territory,[31] a principle which is still followed to a large extent, despite the objections of residents of the urban centres who feel that they ought to have representation in proportion to their population. Section 89 of the BNA Act required that elections for the Legislative Assembly of Ontario should take place at the same time and in the same places as the elections for members for the House of Commons of Canada; thus the first Assembly

Toronto Press, 1963), p. 109. For his discussion of the development of responsible government in Manitoba see pp. 14–15.

[26]George Brown was of the opinion that four years was too long and advocated limiting provincial parliaments to three years. See the report of debates for August 2, 1866, in the *Scrapbook Hansard*.

[27]*SO*, 1930, c. 4, s. 2. The Legislatures of all ten Canadian provinces now have five-year terms.

[28]*SO*, 1942, c. 24, s. 1.

[29]*SO*, 1943, c. 12.

[30]*Revised Statutes of Ontario (RSO)*, 1950, c. 202, s. 4.

[31]Report of the debates for July 13, 1866, in the *Scrapbook Hansard*.

was composed of eighty-two members. But the legislature of each province was empowered to alter its own electoral districts following the initial election.[32] In Ontario, because the populations of certain constituencies grew more rapidly than others, they were sometimes given more than one member instead of being divided into two or more constituencies. This preserved the idea of representation of communities rather than of collections of individuals and at the same time made some allowance for variations in populations. The constant need to adjust representation in the Assembly to the needs of Ontario's growing population resulted in a steady increase in the number of members. Provision was made for 88 in 1874,[33] 90 in 1885,[34] 91 in 1889,[35] 94 in 1894,[36] 98 in 1902,[37] 106 in 1908,[38] and 111 in 1914.[39] The Representation Act of 1925 divided the province into 112 electoral districts and stipulated that "for each of such electoral districts one member shall be returned to the Assembly."[40] Since that date there have not been any multiple-member constituencies, even when the total number of constituencies was reduced to the 1885 level during the depression.[41] The number was raised again to 98 members in 1955[42] and to 108 in 1963 following the first report of the new redistribution commission.[43] The quorum of the House was set at 20 members, including the speaker, by sections 87 and 48 of the BNA Act and was carried over into the *Rules, Orders and Forms of Proceedings*, adopted on January 15, 1878, and into the Legislative Assembly Act. Table 8 shows how Ontario compared with the other provinces in these matters in 1963.

Until 1963 the task of redrafting constituency boundaries in Ontario was performed by the Legislative Assembly, with varied attempts on the part of the Government to gerrymander the results. The new practice is to have the boundaries delineated by the Commission that was appointed by the House on April 18, 1962. The usual procedure in other jurisdictions that have set up redistribution commissions is to establish boundaries by statutory enactment, e.g., New Zealand in 1887, Australia in 1902, the

[32]See Quebec Resolution number 24 in Canada, Legislature, *Parliamentary Debates on the subject of the Confederation of the British North American Provinces*, 3rd session, 8th Provincial Parliament of Canada, p. 3.

[33]*SO*, 1874, c. 2. In 1874 the eighty-eight members were from eighty-two districts, but in 1877 provision was made for eighty-eight districts each electing one member (*RSO*, 1877, c. 8).

[34]*SO*, 1885, c. 2. Toronto returned three members.

[35]*SO*, 1889, c. 2. The temporary judicial district of Nipissing was given one seat.

[36]*SO*, 1894, c. 2. Ottawa returned two members.

[37]*SO*, 1902, c. 4. The Act provided for ninety-seven electoral districts.

[38]*SO*, 1908, c. 2. The Act provided for 102 electoral districts.

[39]*SO*, 1914, c. 4. The Act provided for 107 electoral districts.

[40]*SO*, 1925, c. 7, s. 4.   [41]*SO*, 1933, c. 56.

[42]*SO*, 1954, c. 84.   [43]*SO*, 1962–63, c. 125.

TABLE 8

THE LEGISLATURES OF THE CANADIAN PROVINCES: NUMBER OF MEMBERS, NUMBER
OF CONSTITUENCIES, AND SIZE OF QUORUMS, 1963

Province	Members of Legislative Assembly	Single member constituencies	Multiple member constituencies	Quorum	Percentage of membership required for a quorum
Newfoundland	28	22	3 2-member	10	35
Prince Edward Island	30	0	15 2-member	12*	40
Nova Scotia	37	27	5 2-member	15*	40
New Brunswick	52	0	6 2-member	14*	27
			5 3-member		
			5 4-member		
			1 5-member		
Quebec	95	95		15	16
Ontario	108	108		20	19
Manitoba	57	57		10	17
Saskatchewan	55	48	1 3-member	11	20
			2 2-member		
Alberta	65	52	1 7-member	20	30
			1 6-member		
British Columbia	48	36	3 2-member	10	20
			2 3-member		

*In these provinces the quorum is fixed by the rules of the Legislative Assembly; in
the other provinces it is fixed by provincial statute. In Ontario both the rules and the
Legislative Assembly Act set the quorum.

United Kingdom in 1944, and Manitoba in 1955. It is also common to
have some detailed statutory criteria for the commission to follow in the
performance of its task. For example, the Act that created the Electoral
Divisions Boundaries Commission in Manitoba not only provided for the
personnel of the Commission, by listing the official positions from which
the commissioners would be chosen rather than by listing the names of
the commissioners, but also stipulated that the fifty-seven seats in the
legislature were to be divided between urban and rural constituencies in
the ratio of seven to four, and that in setting the new boundaries due consideration should be given to such things as community of interest, means
of communication, and physical features in the area.[44] In Ontario an
altogether different procedure has been followed.

In the first place the Ontario Redistribution Commission was not
established by statute but by an order of the House, thus avoiding the
usual three readings and consideration in committee and, hence, evading
the possibility of a number of debates. This also means that the next time
redistribution is necessary another commission will have to be appointed.
Secondly, the commissioners were named in the order. By doing this

[44]*Statutes of Manitoba*, 1955, c. 17. See Donnelly, *The Government of Manitoba*,
pp. 78–80.

instead of listing certain offices, the current holders of which would then act as commissioners, the Government laid itself open to the charge of stacking the Commission in favour of the party in power. However, the accusation was never made, mainly because of the high regard in which the personnel of the Commission were held. The members were: Mr. Justice E. A. Richardson, a member of the Supreme Court of Ontario; Professor K. Grant Crawford, director of the Institute of Local Government at Queen's University; and Mr. Roderick Lewis, QC, chief electoral officer for the province. The third and most important distinctive feature of the Ontario procedure was that the Commission was given a completely free hand with respect to such fundamental questions as the maximum size of the Legislative Assembly and the ratio of urban and rural constituency populations. When the Leader of the New Democratic party, Donald C. MacDonald, contended that at least the maximum size of the Assembly ought to be determined by the House and included in the instructions to the Commission, the Premier replied that the same end would be accomplished, because the Commission would make its recommendations to the House, which could then decide whether or not it would accept them. To the further objection of Mr. MacDonald – that rejecting a suggested maximum at that late stage would render useless all of the Commission's detailed work of revision – Mr. Robarts replied: "I can only say that the procedure was designed to remove this matter from the field of politics."[45]

As has been suggested previously, such attempts to remove political questions from the field of politics are not out of keeping with the style of government which has developed in Ontario. The actual terms of the order were: "That a Commission be appointed to inquire into the distribution of electoral districts in the Province and to recommend to this House the number, area and boundaries of such electoral districts, to be defined in the schedule forming a part of a new Representation Act. . . ."[46] It also directed that the Commission, in making its inquiry and investigation, was to give consideration to things such as the concentration of population in various areas of the province, the "varying conditions and requirements regarding representation as between rural and urban electoral districts," the traditional constituency boundaries, community or diversity of interests of population, the means of communication between the various parts of each electoral district, and the general physical features of the districts. Special emphasis was put on the desirability of including the whole of any one municipality in one electoral district in the rural areas. The Commis-

[45]Ontario, Legislative Assembly, *Debates*, April 18, 1962, p. 2529.
[46]Ontario, Legislative Assembly, *Journals*, 1961–62, p. 171.

sion was given the powers usually conferred upon royal commissions, including "full power and authority to call for persons, papers and things and to examine witnesses under oath."

In their first report, which was tabled in the House on December 17, 1962, the commissioners set forth the terms of reference that they had laid down to guide their own deliberations. First, they concluded that a reasonable maximum size for the Legislative Assembly would be approximately 120 members. Secondly, they accepted the principle that the constituencies should be classified into three groups: those that were substantially urban in nature, those that were substantially rural in nature, and those which were partly urban and partly rural. Thirdly, they proceeded on the basis that a reasonable relationship of population for such classes of constituencies would be as follows: for urban constituencies a population of 60,000 to 75,000; for rural constituencies a population of 25,000 to 50,000; and for urban-rural constituencies a population of 50,000 to 60,000.[47] The report also made the specific proposal that ten more seats be given to those portions of Metropolitan Toronto outside the City of Toronto itself. This report was adopted by the House and An Act to Amend the Representation Act was passed and came into effect on August 16, 1963, upon the dissolution of the 26th Parliament.[48] By this Act, the size of the Legislative Assembly was increased to 108 members.

The second report of the Redistribution Commission was laid before the House on February 3, 1965. It dealt with the City of Toronto proper and with the balance of the province outside Metropolitan Toronto. For southern Ontario the commissioners proposed a net increase of six seats, mainly in the urban areas where the greatest population growth had taken place. In northern Ontario, the main task had been one of relocating boundaries to even up the population of electoral districts, but three new seats were also added. The commissioners thus proposed a House of 117 members. As far as the relationship between the populations of the urban and rural seats was concerned, the commissioners found that it was unnecessary to go to either of the extremes they had laid down in their first report, which would have allowed urban seats to be three times the population of the smallest rural seats. Instead, the populations of their proposed electoral districts ranged from a high of approximately 66,653 to a low of approximately 32,728.[49] Nevertheless, this still left the largest urban seat with more than twice the population of the least populous rural seat.

When the report was tabled in the House, members of all parties

[47]Ontario, Legislative Assembly, Commission on Redistribution, *Interim Report*, December 17, 1962 (Sessional Paper 60).

[48]*SO*, 1962–63, c. 125.　　　　　　　　　[49]*Debates*, February 3, 1965, p. 238.

raised specific objections to it as it affected their own constituencies and requested that it be referred to the Standing Committee on Privileges and Elections. This was done, and in its report the Committee recommended that the Redistribution Commission's report should be referred back to the Commission, "in order that the Commission may give consideration to submissions relating to the electoral district boundaries made by interested persons," and that the Commission should report back to the Legislative Assembly not later than the next regular session.[50] The Committee's report was adopted and a revised report by the Commission – which proposed a number of boundary changes but no change in the total number of seats – was then accepted by the House.

The franchise for Ontario provincial elections has gradually been extended from a male suffrage based on property in 1867 to complete adult suffrage, achieved in 1954. The first provincial statute governing this subject was the Election Act of 1868,[51] which gave the vote to males who were at least twenty-one years of age and subjects of the Queen and who owned, rented, or occupied real property of the value of $400 in cities, $300 in towns, or $200 in incorporated villages or townships. The latter qualification was supplemented in 1874 with the provision that adult male British subjects with an income of at least $400 per year from some trade, calling, office, or profession could also vote. By the same statute "enfranchised Indians" were allowed to vote, provided that they met the other qualifications set forth in the Act.[52] Three years later significant changes in the franchise were introduced: the vote was extended to farmers' sons and to unenfranchised Indians not living among Indians, subject to the same qualifications as other voters, and the income requirement was lowered from $400 to $250 per year.[53]

A few minor changes were made during the following decade, but the next real landmark was the Manhood Suffrage Act passed in 1888.[54] By this Act, the franchise was extended to all adult male British subjects, except unenfranchised Indians living on reservations. Unenfranchised Indians who did not live among Indians were still subject to the same property qualifications as had been set out in the 1877 legislation. In 1892 the property qualifications for unenfranchised Indians living off the reservations were set at $200 in cities and towns and $100 in villages and townships,[55] and in 1908 these property qualifications were finally removed.[56]

[50]*Debates*, April 29, 1965, p. 2379.   [51]*SO*, 1868–69, c. 21, s. 2–5.
[52]An "enfranchised Indian" meant an Indian who had by letters patent received a grant in fee simple of a portion of a reserve. See J. E. C. Munro, *The Constitution of Canada* (Cambridge: Cambridge University Press, 1889), p. 56.
[53]*SO*, 1877, c. 9; *RSO*, 1877, c. 10.   [54]*SO*, 1888, c. 4.
[55]*SO*, 1892, c. 3, s. 7 (*c*).   [56]*SO*, 1908, c. 3, s. 18.

The largest single increase in the electorate came in 1917 when, for the first time, women were given the right to vote "in the same manner and upon the same qualifications" as men.[57] In spite of the terms of this Act, the women of the province did not achieve absolute voting equality with men until about 1935, mainly because of peculiarities in the law governing citizenship, which in some cases even made it necessary for women to obtain a judge's certificate to prove that they were citizens.

The last major change in the franchise was made in 1954.[58] The chief purpose of the Act passed in that year was to give Indians the same voting privileges as other citizens resident in Ontario; this was accomplished by simply repealing all of the sections of previous acts which stipulated special qualifications for Indians. Another accomplishment of the Act was the removal of the clause prohibiting persons living in charitable institutions from voting. With these changes, the franchise in Ontario became virtually universal, excluding only people living in penal and mental institutions and certain individuals, such as judges, magistrates, and election clerks, who are expected to remain aloof from politics.[59]

One peculiar aspect of the Legislative Assembly of Ontario for the first forty years of its existence was that while there were a number of restrictions on the right to vote for members of the Assembly, there were practically no restrictions on the right to stand for election to the Assembly. And, while the limitations on who might enjoy the franchise have been gradually removed, exactly the opposite trend regarding who might be elected to the House has developed. Instead of removing restrictions on those eligible for election, acts have been passed for the purpose of specifying restrictions or, in two instances, clarifying what were not to be considered restrictions.

Section 84 of the BNA Act required that, until the legislature of Ontario otherwise provided, the laws in force at the time of Union, relative to the qualifications and disqualifications of persons to be elected to the Assembly, were to apply to the elections of Ontario. This meant that every candidate for election, if requested by any other candidate, had to declare that he was "duly seized at law or in equity as of freehold, for my own use and benefit, of lands or tenements held in free and common soccage . . . of the value of Five Hundred Pounds, of sterling money of Great Britain. . . ."[60] However, before any elections were held under

[57]SO, 1917, c. 6, s. 3; see also c. 5, s. 4. For a discussion of the struggle for the franchise for women in Ontario see Catherine Lyle Cleverdon, *The Woman Suffrage Movement in Canada* (Toronto: University of Toronto Press, 1950), pp. 19–45.

[58]SO, 1954, c. 25.

[59]For a list of those classes of persons who may not vote in Ontario, see *RSO*, 1960, c. 118, s. 14–16.

[60]*Consolidated Statutes of Canada*, 1859, c. 6, s. 36.

provincial law, this property qualification was removed. Thus the original provincial statute governing the qualifications of candidates for the seats in the Assembly was permissive in nature, enacting that "no qualification in real estate shall be required of any candidate for a seat in the Legislative Assembly of Ontario. . . ."[61] No other requirements were prescribed, although there were the usual classes of people that were declared ineligible for election because of the nature of their offices, e.g., those holding any "Office, Commission or employment . . . at the nomination of the Lieutenant Governor, to which an annual salary, or any fee, allowance, emolument, or profit of any kind or amount whatever from the Province is attached. . . ."[62] Not until two decades after manhood suffrage had been achieved were any general qualifications required of candidates, and these were simply that he must be a male, of the full age of twenty-one years, a British subject, and a resident of Ontario.[63] The next statute dealing with qualifications was also permissive in that it allowed women to stand for election.[64] Since 1919 there have been no substantial changes in the required qualifications of candidates, although the rules have been elaborated to prevent specific classes of people from running.[65]

Having already discussed the results which the electoral process has produced – as far as geographical, religious, and occupational representation in the House are concerned – in connection with representation in the cabinet,[66] it is now necessary to turn to the question of how the legislative branch of the Ontario government has equipped itself for performing its chosen functions and, in particular, its function of controlling the executive. In general, the discussion of this subject will fall under two topics: the organization of the House itself, and the provisions that have been made to ensure that members are able to get the information they require and the services they need in order to put this information to use. Both aspects of the subject will be considered in later chapters so that here the discussion will be limited to the committee system, under the first topic, and to specific items, such as remuneration, research facilities, and secretarial services, under the second topic.

Committees of the Legislature

While a body containing many members may be used for the discussion of principles, it is inappropriate for the examination of details. Not only are details often too inconsequential to warrant the attention of a large

[61]*SO*, 1869, c. 4, s. 2. [62]British North America Act, 1867, s. 83.
[63]*SO*, 1908, c. 3, s. 11. [64]*SO*, 1919, c. 8.
[65]For the current requirements, see *RSO*, 1960, c. 208, s. 6–16.
[66]*Supra*, pp. 32–42.

number of people, but in many cases they are often of such a technical nature that only a few members of the large body are qualified to consider them. The usual course, therefore, in parliaments as in other human institutions, is to form a committee of a few members who can discuss the details of proposals and then report their recommendations back to the full body. "The essence of a committee is," according to Professor Wheare, "that it is a body to which some task has been referred or committed by some other person or body." He continues: "It may be asked or required or permitted to carry out this task. But that is not all. The notion of a committee carries with it the idea of a body being in some manner or degree responsible or subordinate or answerable in the last resort to the body or person who set it up or committed a power or duty to it."[67]

One committee that is common to all parliaments that have been closely modelled after the "mother of parliaments" originated for a quite different reason than those just suggested. The Committee of the Whole House was originally constituted for the sole purpose of providing greater freedom of debate, especially in matters affecting the king. As the name implies, this Committee is comprised of all members of the House who happen to be present at any time it is constituted, and it differs from a regular sitting of the House only in the fact that the speaker, originally the king's representative, is not in the chair; hence, the debates are less formal. In Ontario the Committee of the Whole House considers all bills after they have received second reading; it also deals with the financial resolutions associated with money bills.[68] Under the name "Committee of Supply" it deals with the estimates of the moneys required for the next ensuing fiscal year,[69] and, as the "Committee of Ways and Means," it passes the resolutions appropriating out of the consolidated revenue fund the money voted by the Committee of Supply.

Usually "parliamentary committees" refer to the smaller bodies appointed by the House – the standing and select committees – and, since the various uses made of the Committee of the Whole are discussed in some detail later, the analysis offered here will be limited to them.

The standing committees are the most numerous of the smaller committees and are distinguished by the fact that they are set up at the beginning of each session for the consideration of all subjects of a particular class which may arise in the course of the session and be referred to them. Technically the standing committees are select, both in the sense

[67]K. C. Wheare, *Government by Committee: An Essay on the British Constitution* (Oxford: Clarendon Press, 1955), pp. 5–6.
[68]*Infra*, p. 163.
[69]*Infra*, pp. 203–4, 240–48.

of consisting of less than the total membership of the House and in the sense of being confined to selected areas of activity. It was for this reason that until 1951 the annual motion authorizing their establishment usually referred to them as "select standing" or "select" committees. However, the term "select" has now come to be reserved for those special committees established *ad hoc* to carry out specific inquiries, and the usual sessional committees are simply called "standing committees."[70] The usage of the term "select standing committee" prior to 1951 was similar to that of the term "select sessional committee" that is still used in the United Kingdom to refer to committees, such as the Public Accounts Committee, the Estimates Committee, and the Committee on Privileges, which would now be called "standing committees" in Ontario.

Professor Wheare attempted to classify all committees into six general types according to the function or the process which the committee carried out.[71] The committee system in the Ontario legislature has never provided any illustrations of committees "to negotiate" or "to administer," but Wheare's other four categories have been represented at one time or another. The Committee on Printing, until it was amalgamated with the Committee on Standing Orders, was basically a "committee to advise," since is sole function was to recommend what sessional papers should be published and what stationery allowance and free publications should be given to members. The Committee on Privileges and Elections usually functions as a "committee to inquire" and even its study of the Redistribution Commission's reports in recent sessions could be placed under this category. "Committees to scrutinize and control" would be represented in Ontario by the Public Accounts Committee[72] and the Committee on Government Commissions.[73] The rest of the committees would probably fall under Wheare's category of "committees to legislate." This is particularly true of the committees concerned with private legislation, because Government policy is seldom at stake and members are quite free to look at the merits of each bill. The only public bills that have reached committee stage in recent years have been Government bills and, with very few exceptions, these had already been approved in principle and thus could not be amended except in detail. Nevertheless, the committee stage is still part of the legislative process, and those committees that consider public bills may be referred to as "committees to legislate."

[70]Kenneth Bryden, "Committees of the Ontario Legislature," an unpublished paper prepared for a graduate seminar in public administration conducted by Professors M. Brownstone and W. E. Grasham, University of Toronto, April 15, 1965, p. 2.
[71]Wheare, *Government by Committee*, p. 2.
[72]*Infra*, pp. 250–57.
[73]*Infra*, pp. 237.

In spite of the fact that the principle of a bill has usually been approved before the bill ever gets before one of the standing committees, the committee stage can still be a very useful legislative device. In the first place, even though the Opposition cannot modify the basic intention of a bill that is referred to a committee, they can sometimes amend its specific provisions.[74] This willingness on the part of ministers to allow the Opposition to make amendments to Government bills in committee leaves members of the Opposition in a peculiar dilemma: on the one hand, they want to see that the best possible laws are put on the statute books but, on the other hand, the more assistance they give the Government in this respect, the harder it will be for them to convince the electorate that a change of Government is necessary. However, if they use the privilege of offering amendments for such purposes as defining delegated powers more clearly, making provisions for the review of executive decisions, clarifying the lines of responsibility, providing for appeals from administrative decisions, and, where possible, curtailing excessive delegation, the standing committees can play a significant role in controlling the executive.

Secondly, even if amendments were never allowed, committees would still be useful instruments for criticizing the Government because they permit freer debate than is possible on the floor of the House. In parliaments like that of the United Kingdom, where the pressures of time mean that regular debate has to be strictly curtailed, committees are beneficial not only because they allow unhindered debate, but simply because they allow more debate. However, in Ontario the parliamentary timetable has not yet reached that predicament, and the value of committees lies not in extending debate but in allowing more spontaneity and direct exchange during debate. There is no restriction on the number of times a member may speak in committee so that it is possible to proceed on a question-answer basis or according to a proposal-rebuttal format. In this way specific points of contention can be pursued to some kind of satisfactory conclusion instead of being passed over when the control of the floor passes to someone else, as happens so often in regular House sittings.

Thirdly, committees make for a more efficient use of members' time and encourage them to become more expert in their chosen fields of interest. Only those who are interested in the work of a committee need attend its meetings, and if members take advantage of the opportunities that the committee presents they can become well-informed on the subject matter of its deliberations and thus be in a stronger position to criticize and so control the executive.

[74]From an interview with Mr. John White (PC: London South), chief government whip, May 13, 1965.

However, it is agreed by members of all parties that the standing committees find their greatest usefulness as vehicles for representations from the public. Indeed, gathering the opinions of interested parties has been given as their primary *raison d'être* by Premier Robarts, who once said: "Committees really, in my opinion, are designed to permit the general public to come and make representations."[75] Naturally the Government can benefit from such a system of organized feedback from the public, but if the Opposition can use the same forum for purposes of embarrassing the Government, perhaps even to the extent of forcing it not to proceed with a particular bill, then obviously the standing committee is a serviceable instrument for controlling the executive. A good case in point was the Operating Engineers Act which the Government introduced in the 1964 session. When the tradesmen who were affected by the proposed bill were informed of its contents – by the Opposition, needless to say – they organized demonstrations and appeared before the Standing Committee on Labour, Legal and Municipal Bills to which the bill had been referred. The number attending was so large that the Committee had to adjourn to the floor of the House. As a result, the Government let the bill die on the order paper and introduced a modified version the following session. It is not known whether the Government hesitates to refer bills to committees for fear of similar rebuffs or simply because the Premier desires to keep the consideration of legislation on the floor of the House as much as possible,[76] but the fact remains that less than half of the bills dealt with by the House are referred to its standing committees. In the 1964 session only 57 out of 135 bills were referred to committees. In some cases it may be that a bill would be referred to a committee if an appropriate one existed, but with only ten committees it is difficult to cover all fields.[77]

A fundamental principle underlying the whole committee system is that both the powers and the duties of committees must be defined by the House. In Ontario this principle is pushed as far as it can be and, by general agreement, may even be violated. Although the standing committees cannot be given powers greater than those possessed by the House, the powers they do receive are not significantly less than those of the

[75]*Debates*, January 16, 1964, pp. 82–3.

[76]"I think perhaps we have referred too many things to committees which should be dealt with here. Why take a subject and refer it to a small group of this Legislature when we have the means here to debate it fully with everyone present?" – Premier John Robarts, *Debates*, January 16, 1964, p. 82.

[77]Kenneth Bryden has given as a possible example of this the fact that the new training schools legislation, introduced in the 1965 session, did not go before a committee to enable the many interested groups to make representations. None of the existing standing committees has responsibility for reform institutions. Bryden, "Committees of the Ontario Legislature," p. 16.

House. Certainly they have all the authority necessary for performing their normal functions, including the power to send for persons, papers, and records, but, as far as the duties of the committees are concerned, the situation is in no way clear. Aside from the names given to the various standing committees, which are intended to designate the general fields of activity within which they are to operate, no individual terms of reference are laid down for them. The exact wording of the motion authorizing the standing committees at the beginning of each session is simply that "said committees shall severally be empowered to examine and enquire into all such matters and things *as shall be referred to them by the House* and report from time to time their observations and opinions *thereon,* with power to send for persons, papers and records."[78] The conclusion to be drawn from this is that committees have no authorization to do anything not specifically referred to them by the House; this conclusion is corroborated by sections 58 and 59 of the Legislative Assembly Act.[79] Nevertheless, it is a well-established practice for some standing committees to meet without having any specific matter referred to them, and to deliberate on matters coming within the general scope of the subjects for which they were created. Since from a legal viewpoint the committees have no power to require anyone to do anything in such circumstances, progress must be made by voluntary co-operation alone.[80] However, the absence of legal authority has not hindered this aspect of committee work, and the custom has become so engrained in the committee system that members would probably feel that the committees were being robbed of a part of their proper functions if their activities were restricted to the terms set forth in the motion of appointment and in the Legislative Assembly Act.

According to rule 104, it is the responsibility of a special committee to prepare and report lists of members to compose the standing committees of the House. In fact, the role played by this committee, popularly known as the "Striking Committee," is purely formal, and the actual mechanics of arranging the membership of the committees to reflect the political composition of the House is worked out by the party whips. Ordinarily, the members indicate to their whips which committees they wish to serve on, and this information is forwarded to the Striking Committee, of which the whips are the key members. Unless a party has more members desiring to serve on a particular committee than it is entitled to, the members are assigned to the committees according to their expressed preferences. Any

[78]*Debates*, January 16, 1964, p. 79. Italics added.

[79]*RSO*, 1960, c. 208, s. 58 and 59.

[80]This point was made by Mr. L. R. MacTavish, QC, senior legislative counsel, in a letter to the Hon. M. C. Davies, speaker of the Legislative Assembly, February 24, 1953.

adjustments that need to be made are carried out by the whip of the party concerned, except in the Conservative party, where there is a deputy whip who has responsibility for correlating the wishes of the members of his party with the number of spaces available.

Neither the number of standing committees nor the size of each committee is limited by the rules. In the first session of the Ontario legislature there were five standing committees ranging in size from 9 to 34, for an average size of 25.8 members per committee. This meant that there were 129 committee positions to be distributed among 82 members, which resulted in an average of 1.6 positions per member. Until 1960 both the number and the size of the committees increased considerably, as is illustrated in Table 9, which is based on the data given in Appendix B.

By 1960 there were nearly four times as many committees as there had been in 1867 and more than twice as many as there had been at the turn of the century. The average size of the committees has remained fairly constant during the years included in the Table, but this is 73.3 per cent larger than the size of the original standing committees of the House.

TABLE 9

STANDING COMMITTEES, 1900–60, DECENNIAL YEARS ONLY

Year	Number of committees	Average size of committees	Total number of committee positions	Number of seats in the House	Number of committee positions per member*
1900	8	43.3	346	94	3.7
1910	10	42.9	429	106	4.1
1920	10	47.0	470	111	4.2
1930	11	49.3	542	112	4.8
1939–40	11	49.8	548	90	6.1
1950	12	36.3	436	90	4.8
1960	19	42.3	815	98	8.3
AVERAGES	11.6	44.4	512.3	100.1	5.1

SOURCE: Compiled from Ontario, Legislative Assembly, *Journals.*
*Cabinet ministers are included in these calculations, although they were not always assigned to the standing committees.

Probably the chief reason for the increase in the number of standing committees and, hence, in the number of committee positions, was the need on the part of the Government to find something for its very large majority to do. But just increasing the number of committees could not possibly satisfy this need, because there simply was not enough time available for so many committees to meet. Meetings could not be held on Friday mornings because the House sits then and they could not be held

[81]Ontario, Legislative Assembly, Select Committee on Administrative and Executive Problems of Government, *Minutes*, June 14, 1960.

on Monday mornings because members do not usually return from their weekend visits home in time for that. This left only three free mornings to be divided among nineteen committees. If the committees had met with any degree of regularity, it would have been virtually impossible for even the most diligent MPP to attend all of the meetings of the eight committees the average member belonged to in 1960. This impossible situation no doubt helped to account for the three features which have come to characterize the Ontario committee system.

The first of these is the relatively poor attendance at committee meetings. In his evidence before the Select Committee on Administrative and Executive Problems of Government, the Clerk of the Legislative Assembly put forward the view that a standing committee membership of sixty was not an unwieldly number, because the average attendance for such committees was only fifteen to twenty members.[81] Under rule 102, a quorum of a committee consists of a majority of the members unless otherwise ordered by the House and, since the attendance of more than half the members of a committee is rare, quorums are now specified for each committee. The smallness of the quorums in relation to the size of the standing committees (*see* Table 10) is indicative of the poor attendance records registered by these committees.

A second characteristic of the Ontario committee system which has been encouraged by the proliferation of committees is that they do not meet very frequently. Taking 1960 again, for purposes of illustration the 19 standing committees met a total of 105 times, an average of 5.5 times each. This figure does not give the complete picture, however, because some of the committees, such as those on mining, and printing and standing orders, only met once or twice in a perfunctory manner, while others, namely those on education, energy, and legal bills, each met ten times. Nevertheless, it can hardly be said, on the basis of these figures at least, that the committees are used to a very great extent.

The third feature of the committee system in the Ontario legislature which is, at the same time, both a result of the situation just described and a factor which helps to explain that situation, is that relatively few items of business are referred to the committees. In most cases, bills are the only items that are formally referred to the committees of a legislative nature but, as may be seen in Table 10, relatively few public bills ever go to the standing committees. If we omit the work done by the Private Bills Committee, which must consider all private bills, an average of seventy-two bills was referred to the standing committees in each of the five sessions from 1960 to 1964. This is slightly less than half of the average number of public bills which received third reading in those sessions. Here again,

TABLE 10

STANDING COMMITTEES IN THE 23RD LEGISLATURE

Committee	1960				1960–61				1961–62				1962–63			
	Size	Quorum	Number of meetings	Number of bills referred	Size	Quorum	Number of meetings	Number of bills referred	Size	Quorum	Number of meetings	Number of bills referred	Size	Quorum	Number of meetings[d]	Number of bills referred
Agriculture	50	7	5	4	49	7	4	—	50	7	5	7	50	7		13
Conservation	35	5	5	—	35	5	5	4	50[c]	7	2	—	51	7		—
Education	50	7	10	7	50	7	6	4	51	5	9	8	51	7		8
Energy	25	5	10	2	35	5	5	1	35	7	7	2	35	5		—
Game and fish	50	7	3	—	49	7	3	—	49	5	3	1	51	7		1
Government commissions	35	5	8	8	35	5	4	3	35	5	3	—	35	5		—
Health	50[a]	7	5	—	50	7	4	1	50	7	3	12	51	7		13
Highway safety	50[b]	7	9	1	50	7	4	—	50	7	1	1	50	7		2
Labour	35	5	8	5	35	5	2	3	35	5	2	3	35	5		10
Lands and forests	50	7	2	9	49	7	2	1	—[c]	—	—	—	—	—		—
Legal bills	25	5	10	42	25	5	7	28	25	5	4	39	25	5		29
Mining	35	5	1	—	34	5	1	—	34	5	1	1	35	5		—
Municipal law	50	7	4	5	50	7	3	5	50	7	6	10	50	7		11
Printing	25	5	1	—	25	5	1	—	25	5	1	—	25	5		—
Private bills	60	7	8	46	60	7	12	48	60	7	8	38	60	7		66
Privileges and elections	15	5	3	—	15	5	—	—	15	5	4	1	15	5		1
Public accounts	50	7	9	—	49	7	2	—	49	7	4	—	9	5		—
Standing orders	25	5	2	—	24	5	4	—	24	5	4	—	25	5		—
Travel and Publicity	50	7	2	—	50	7	2	—	50	7	1	—	50	7		—

SOURCE: Ontario, Legislative Assembly, *Journals*.

[a]The name of the Committee on Health was changed to the Committee on Health and Welfare in the 1960–61 session.

[b]The name of the Committee on Highway Safety was changed to the Committee on Highways and Highway Safety in the 1960–61 session.

[c]The Committee on Conservation was amalgamated with the Committee on Lands and Forests in the 1961–62 session.

[d]The Clerk of Committees was unable to provide this information.

however, average figures are somewhat misleading. From Table 10 it may also be seen that in each year there were some committees of a legislative type which did not have any bills referred to them, and nearly half of the bills that were referred went to the Committee on Legal Bills. It has already been pointed out that some of these committees have investigated subjects other than bills but usually this is done on their own initiative and not at the request of the House.

There are other reasons for the limited use that is made of standing committees in Ontario: many of the members maintain their outside employment during the session and find it necessary to devote their mornings to that, and others could attend but prefer to spend their time on activities that will bring them greater publicity or endear them to their constituents. Nevertheless, it is extremely difficult to make very extensive use of committees if there is a great deal of overlapping in their memberships and there are only three mornings a week available for meetings.

A number of suggestions has been made, and some steps have been taken to correct this situation. The select committee set up in 1946 to study the rules recommended that standing committees should be reduced in size to not more than thirty members per committee.[82] The Gordon Committee made a similar recommendation and pointed out that an incidental advantage of smaller committees was that members could "specialize" within a narrower range of subjects.[83] On the other hand, the Select Committee on Administrative and Executive Problems appointed in 1960 opposed reducing the size of the committees, arguing that a member should be allowed to interest himself in committee work on as wide a basis as he may choose.[84] It was supported in this by the Clerk of the Legislative Assembly who observed that if a small committee were needed for some particular task, a select committee could be created for that purpose or the House could specifically authorize a standing committee to appoint a small subcommittee to inquire into the matter.[85]

In the 1960 session a different solution was attempted. Ordinarily the standing committees cannot sit while the House is adjourned for a day or several days on which it ordinarily sits, but in that session the House adjourned from Tuesday to Thursday on six occasions for the express purpose of allowing the committees to meet throughout the day on

[82]*Journals*, 1947, p. 27.

[83]Ontario, Committee on the Organization of Government in Ontario, *Report*, W. L. Gordon, chairman (Toronto, 1959). Hereinafter referred to as the Gordon Committee *Report*, p. 22.

[84]Ontario, Legislative Assembly, Select Committee on Administrative and Executive Problems of Government, *Interim Report*, 1960, p. 17.

[85]*Minutes*, June 14, 1960; see also Roderick Lewis, Memorandum to the Select Committee on Administrative and Executive Problems of Government, p. 13.

Wednesday. When adopting the motions to adjourn the House gave the necessary leave to the committees to sit while it was adjourned. At the time this experiment was looked upon with some favour by the members, but it has not been repeated since. Looking back on the experiment Premier Robarts said: "Hon. members will recall that several years ago we reserved Wednesdays for committee days. In my opinion this proved to be highly unsatisfactory. It simply meant that everybody went home in the middle of the week. I did not notice that the committee functioned any more efficiently."[86]

During the 1964 session a second and more successful attempt was made to improve the committee system. Instead of attempting to reduce the size of the committees or provide more time for them to meet, the number of committees was simply reduced from eighteen in the 1962–63 session to ten. The average size of the committees was left about the same as it had been,[87] but fewer committees, coupled with the fact that the membership of the House had been increased to 108, meant that there were only 4.3 committee positions per member compared to 8.3 in the 1960 session.[88] The actual task of compressing the eighteen committees into ten was not so difficult, because there had previously been so much overlapping of personnel that in many instances it meant little more than taking a group of members who, under the previous system, would have met under two or three separate titles with different chairmen and secretaries and putting them under one broad title with one chairman and one secretary. This one committee could then embrace as many members, meet as many times, and do the same amount of work as the two or three committees had under the old system. Furthermore, this could be done without the confusion entailed in having three committees with their separate organizations and officers. The data for the standing committees in the 1964 session are given in Table 11.

Along with the reduction of the number of standing committees there was a new effort to organize their meetings.[89] The Chief Government Whip, John White, drew up a schedule of meetings before the members of

[86]*Debates*, January 16, 1964, p. 80.

[87]The Public Accounts Committee had been reduced from 49 to 9 members in the 1962–63 session and this size was maintained in the 1964 session. It was mainly this change that accounted for the reduction of the average size of the committees from 44.2 members in the 1961–62 session to 39.1 in the 1962–63 session and to 38.2 members in the 1964 session.

[88]F. A. Walden, "A Study of Standing Legislative Committees," an unpublished paper prepared for a course in public administration conducted by Professor W. E. Grasham, University of Toronto, May 7, 1965, p. 8.

[89]See Arthur Ford, "Political Splintering Bogs Down Commons," *London Free Press*, April 3, 1965. Despite its title, the burden of this article is to describe reorganization of the Ontario committee system under the direction of the chief government whip.

TABLE 11

STANDING COMMITTEES OF THE ONTARIO LEGISLATURE, 1964

Name	Size	Quorum	Number of meetings	Average attendance	Number of bills referred
Agriculture	50	7	3	27.7	4
Education, Health and Welfare	50	7	2	22.5	9
Government Commissions	35	5	6	19.2	2
Highways and Tourism	50	7	3	30.0	4
Labour, Legal and Municipal Bills	35	5	11	21.8	35
Natural Resources, Wildlife and Mining	50	7	4	24.5	3
Private Bills	60	9	9	37.1	31
Privileges and Elections	18	5	—	—	—
Public Accounts	9	5	14	7.0	—
Standing Orders and Printing	25	5	3	15.3	—

SOURCE: Compiled from the information provided in the *Journals* and from the minutes of meetings deposited in the office of the clerk of the Legislative Assembly.

the committees were selected, thus enabling the whips to avoid putting a member on committees with conflicting schedules. Furthermore, the chairmen and the vice-chairmen of the committees were designated well in advance of the session and, although they were not formally elected until the first meetings of their respective committees, they were able to begin preparing agendas and arranging for witnesses long before the committees actually met.

It is difficult to assess the results of the changes in the committee system that were made in 1964. It is true that the committees met more frequently than in the past – an average of 6 times each compared to an average of 5.5 times each in 1960 – but, theoretically, they probably should have met almost twice as many times because ten committees were supposed to do the work that had previously been done by nineteen. The average attendance of the committee members also improved somewhat: not counting the Public Accounts Committee, which had a membership of only 9, or the Committee on Privileges and Elections, which did not meet, the average attendance was 25, or 55.6 per cent, the average size of these committees being 44. On the other hand, they had fewer bills referred to them than had usually been the case in the previous four sessions: 42.9 per cent of the public bills that received third reading were referred to standing committees in 1964, compared to an average of 51.7 per cent for the sessions from 1960 to 1963. On the basis of evidence such as this it may be said that, while members certainly appreciated the administrative changes that were made, the fact remains that committees can be used to advantage only when they are given something to do. Once the mechanics of the committee system have been improved the responsibility for making more use of the opportunities it presents lies primarily with the Government and only secondarily with the members.

It has often been suggested that in order for specialized standing committees to become very effective there must be a high degree of continuity in their membership, with members remaining on the same committee or committees for the life of each parliament, if not longer. Such a suggestion was proffered in Ontario at least as early as 1880,[90] and the same reasoning was behind the recommendation in 1962 that a statutory public accounts committee should be created, the members of which would remain in office for the duration of a whole parliament.[91] However, lack of continuity in membership would not seem to be a hindrance to the efficient functioning of committees in Ontario. Since, with few exceptions, the present system allows members to serve on whatever committees they choose, the only way in which greater continuity of membership could be achieved would be to require members to serve on committees other than those they prefer. Whether forcing members to sit on committees that do not interest them would enhance the usefulness of those committees is extremely doubtful. Besides, the free choice system of making up committees already does result in a fairly high degree of continuity in committee membership. If the Conservation, Lands and Forests, and Public Accounts committees are left out of the calculation (the first two because they were amalgamated in the 1961–62 session, and the last because its membership was reduced from 49 to 9 in the 1962–63 session), an average of 78.3 per cent of the members of each committee remained on that committee for the duration of the 26th Parliament which lasted for four sessions. The degree of continuity for each committee is set out in Table 12.

The same degree of continuity does not exist for committee chairmanships. The practice is to rotate these positions fairly frequently among backbenchers of the majority party. This not only means that chairmen do not have that expertise in the committee's field of responsibility that can come only through longer tenure in office, but it often means that they do not even gain the experience necessary to master the art of conducting committee meetings. The Chief Government Whip has suggested that special instruction should be given to committee chairmen, and the Clerk of the Legislative Assembly has recommended that his office be given the necessary personnel to provide trained clerks for committees; neither of these recommendations has yet been acted upon.

[90]Charles Clarke, *Sixty Years in Upper Canada, with Autobiographical Recollections* (Toronto: William Briggs, 1908), p. 244.
[91]Select Committee on Administrative and Executive Problems of Government, *Second Interim Report*, March 19, 1962, p. 4.

TABLE 12

CONTINUITY IN THE MEMBERSHIP OF THE STANDING COMMITTEES OF THE
ONTARIO LEGISLATURE IN THE 26TH PARLIAMENT, FOUR SESSIONS, 1960–63

Name of committee	Percentage of members who remained on the committee for all four sessions
Agriculture	82
Education	76
Energy	80
Game and Fish	82
Government Commissions	71
Health and Welfare	86
Highway Safety	80
Labour	67
Legal Bills	80
Mining	74
Municipal Law	86
Printing	76
Private Bills	82
Privileges and Elections	73
Standing Orders	80
Travel and Publicity	78
AVERAGE	78

The provision of staff for standing committees has been modified in recent years and varies from committee to committee. Until the 1960 session, clerks for the committees were normally chosen from among the members of the press gallery. It was felt that it would be inappropriate to use officials from the government departments to staff legislative committees, and the members of the press gallery were the only personnel available who were not in the employ of the government. While this arrangement was quite satisfactory in some instances, in other cases it was decidedly inadequate. It was not unusual for these part-time secretaries to fail to attend the meetings of the committees they were supposed to clerk, and sometimes the clerk of the Legislative Assembly was left to write their reports for them. In any case, this rather peculiar relationship between the press gallery and the standing committees came to an end in 1960, when the gallery passed a resolution declining to supply secretaries for the committees on the grounds that such a practice appeared to compromise their cherished independence from the Government of the province.

Although some reporters were willing to continue to serve the committees and receive the extra pay, the Clerk of the Legislature decided to abide by the resolution and, therefore, found it necessary to borrow personnel from the various departments in order to staff the committees. This solution had already been suggested by the Gordon Committee[92] and

[92]Gordon Committee *Report*, p. 22.

was reiterated by the Select Committee on Administrative and Executive Problems,[93] but strong opposition to this was voiced by the Clerk, who felt that such a practice violated the principle of the separation of powers and feared that there could very easily be a conflict of interest between a clerk's duty to his department and his duty to the legislative committee which he served.[94] Alan Grossman, who later joined the cabinet, opposed the practice on more practical grounds, pointing out that recruiting the staff for the committees from wherever they happened to be available meant that the clerks were not adequately trained for arranging for the smooth operation of committees or for guiding their chairmen on points of procedure; often, too, they had to leave important work in their departments while they were serving the committees.[95] These and other protests notwithstanding, the practice of using departmental personnel seems firmly engrained in the Ontario committee system.

It should be added that there are committees that do have expert assistance in their work. Rule 123(1)(e) stipulates that it shall be the duty of the legislative council and law clerk of public bills "to act as Secretary of the Legal Committee and when the Municipal and Private Bills Committees are sitting at the same time, of the Private Bills Committee." In keeping with the spirit of this rule, officials from the legislative counsel's office provide both counsel and secretaries for the Private Bills Committee and the Labour, Legal and Municipal Bills Committee.[96] The Public Accounts Committee also has expert assistance from the provincial auditor or the assistant provincial auditor at all its meetings, except, of course, when it is drafting its report. And the Committee on Standing Orders and Printing is served by the clerk of the Legislative Assembly or by the clerk of committees. Only six of the ten committees do not have any kind of expert help, and even these can request the services of the legislative counsel's office if a special need arises. However, only the Committee on Labour, Legal and Municipal Bills and the Private Bills Committee have permanent secretaries; the others still labour under the disadvantages of having part-time secretaries from the departments serving them. With the number of committees reduced to ten and with careful scheduling of meetings, it would probably be possible for two full-time clerks to serve those committees which do not now have permanent secretaries. If the work that committees sometimes do without reference from the Assembly is to

[93]*Minutes*, October 18, 1960.

[94]Lewis, Memorandum to the Select Committee on Administrative and Executive Problems of Government, p. 14.

[95]Allan Grossman, Memorandum to the Select Committee on Administrative and Executive Problems of Government, June 20, 1960, p. 2.

[96]From an interview with Mr. L. R. MacTavish, August 5, 1965.

be considered legitimate, then there may also be need for qualified counsel to assist them with their deliberations. And, if the standing committees began to take either verbatim records or even fairly complete summaries of committee proceedings, trained assistance would be required. As it is, the secretaries or, more properly, the clerks of the committees, provide only limited services, such as calling the roll, recording divisions, recording amendments to bills, and assisting the chairmen with the preparation of agendas and the drafting of reports. The reports are usually very brief. Sometimes the members of a committee who disagree with the committee's report will refrain from signing it, and occasionally they will even be allowed to make a minority report, but this must be presented at the same time as the majority report and then only with the consent of the committee.[97]

In conclusion it may be said that, while some standing committees meet frequently, have adequate staff, and accomplish a good deal, other committees seldom meet, have no qualified staff, and make only a very modest contribution to the work of the legislature. The terms of reference for the committees are not clearly set out and, as a result, some committees go much further than others in their investigations of matters related to their areas of interest. The primary purpose of committees in Ontario is to serve as sounding boards for public opinion. By exploiting this opportunity to mobilize criticism of Government policy and by close examination of the bills referred to the committees, the Opposition is able to exercise some control over the Government through the committee system; but the chief tools available for this purpose are the Committee of Supply, the Committee on Government Commissions, and the Public Accounts Committee, which are discussed in the appropriate sections of later chapters.

Select committees are, in many respects, more useful bodies than standing committees, because they are called into existence to meet special needs and because their terms of reference are usually quite specific. They are normally provided with adequate staff and in recent years, at least, have been given permission to carry on their work between sessions. They are appointed by order of the House to consider a particular bill (or bills) or any other matter upon which the House desires information and assistance and which does not come within the ordinary work of any standing committee or which cannot be dealt with conveniently by any standing committee. The order, known as the "order of reference," specifies the purpose for which the committee is set up and the powers that the com-

[97]See the ruling by Mr. Speaker on April 1, 1926, in Alex Lewis, *Parliamentary Procedure in Ontario* (Toronto: King's Printer, 1940), p. 236.

mittee may exercise. Here, for example, is the order of reference setting up the Select Committee on Youth:

Ordered, That a Select Committee of this House be appointed to conduct a comprehensive inquiry into the report upon the special needs of youth, with particular reference to educational, cultural, recreational, and employment opportunities, as well as the health, welfare and sports facilities now available to youth, and the steps to be taken which in the opinion of the Committee would ensure a wider participation by youth in the life of the community;

To conduct hearings for the purpose of receiving representations from organizations and individuals engaged in youth activities and to hold meetings to study the experience of others in the youth field; and to engage the necessary staff to provide study papers and research materials.

And, That the Select Committee shall consist of fourteen members and shall have authority to sit during the interval between Sessions and have full power and authority to appoint or employ counsel and secretary and such other personnel as may be deemed advisable and to call for persons, papers and things and to examine witnesses under oath, and the Assembly doth command and compel attendance before the said Select Committee of such persons and the production of such papers and things as the Committee may deem necessary for any of its proceedings and deliberations, for which purpose the Honourable the Speaker may issue his Warrant or Warrants.

The membership of the Committee to be as follows:—

Mr. Apps (Chairman), Messrs. Brown, Butler, Ewen, Gaunt, Lewis (Scarborough West), McKeough, McNeil, Morningstar, Newman, Peck, Troy, Welch and Wells.[98]

Inasmuch as the chief function of the select committee is investigation, it may be considered the legislature's equivalent of the executive's royal commission.[99] However, the two institutions differ in many respects, the chief difference being in their personnel: members of select committees are, of course, members of the legislature and therefore they can devote only a portion of their time to committee work; royal commissioners, on the other hand, are usually able to devote nearly their full time to their commissions and thus can developed an expertness that rarely characterizes members of select committees. Part of this difference is eliminated in those cases where a select committee hires professional staff which then assumes many of the responsibilities ordinarily carried by members of royal commissions. Nevertheless, the select committee can never function quite like a royal commission because its members are first and foremost politicians; commissioners are usually chosen from the

[98]*Journals*, 1964, p. 163. Italics omitted.

[99]The term "royal commission" is used here to refer to any investigatory body set up under the Public Inquiries Act, even though the body may not include those words in its title.

bench or from some other form of employment supposedly remote from the political arena.

For this reason it is usually customary to leave investigations of a judicial nature to royal commissions and to assign to select committees responsibility for investigating matters concerned with public policy. However, this is just a tendency and in no sense a fixed demarcation of appropriate spheres; sometimes, for instance, an investigation by a committee will lead to an inquiry by a royal commission. An example of this occurred in 1959 when a royal commission inquiry into certain purchases by the Niagara Parks Commission was ordered as a result of a previous investigation by the Standing Committee on Privileges and Elections.[100] Very occasionally – in fact only once in the last twenty-five years – a select committee may be constituted for the specific purpose of inquiring into charges of irregularity or impropriety, the kind of investigation that is normally left to royal commissions.[101]

The fields of jurisdiction occupied by select committees and royal commissions more frequently overlap in matters of public policy. For example, in the 1940s a royal commission was set up to investigate highway transportation, but in the 1950s topics such as highway safety, toll roads, and the organization of the Department of Highways were referred to select committees. And, in 1960, a select committee on automobile insurance was established, but in 1963 the question of medical insurance was handed over to a body set up under the Public Inquiries Act. Apparently, the decision as to whether a matter should go to a select committee or a royal commission depends on whether the problem is of a judicial nature, whether it requires expert attention for an extended period of time, and whether the Government feels that its chances of emerging with a clean slate are better if members of the Opposition are not appointed to the body doing the investigation. Normally, if any one of these factors is a consideration, the task will be handed to a royal commission, but each case is considered on its own merits and probably the whim of the moment is as significant a factor as any when the Government decides whether or not to use a select committee.

Rule 101 of the Ontario Legislative Assembly stipulates that select

[100]This illustration was suggested by Allan Grossman (PC: St. Andrew) in his presentation to the Select Committee on Administrative and Executive Problems of Government, June 20, 1964.

[101]The only inquiry of such a nature since the second world war has been the one in 1954 relating to the Department of Highways. As a result of this investigation certain prosecutions were initiated, the Department was reorganized, and, belatedly, the responsible minister resigned. See Bryden, "Committees of the Ontario Legislature," p. 18.

committees are not to consist of more than fifteen members, and the average size over the last twenty years has been about ten members, always chosen to reflect the political complexion of the House as closely as possible. Since this number is so small, usually no special quorum is set, and the provision in rule 102(*a*) that a majority shall constitute a quorum applies. Ordinarily, the members of each select committee are named in the motion establishing the committee, and any subsequent changes in the composition of the committee must be made by special orders of the House. Sometimes, in order to expedite the business between sessions, the House has ordered, after naming a committee, "that in the event of a vacancy occurring in the membership of the committee the vacancy shall be filled by the appointment of a member on the recommendation of the leader of the party to which the former member belonged."[102] In most cases there is no duplication of membership among committees in existence at the same time. The chairman of a select committee, always a Government supporter, is usually formally "elected" by the committee, although he may already be designated in the motion setting up the committee. Occasionally a minister has been appointed a chairman or a member of a select committee. This has in the past given rise to the interesting situation where the minister, in his capacity as chairman, has had to assume some responsibility for the committee's report and then, in his role as a member of the Government, he has subsequently had to share responsibility for rejecting all or part of that same report. For example, many of the recommendations of the Select Committee on Administrative and Executive Problems appointed in 1960 and chaired by the Attorney General were not acted upon by the Government.

Few select committees were used in the immediate postwar years but they became more popular during the fifties, and in recent years there have usually been enough committees in existence at any one time to utilize the services of all private members of the House. Since 1945 there have been approximately as many select committees appointed as there have been royal commissions. These committees often afford excellent opportunities for members to become well-informed on particular subjects. With the majority party dominating the committees it is impossible to criticize the Government in the committee reports themselves, but the committee investigations sometimes provide the Opposition with information that can later be put to good use in debate.

In many respects the select committees point the way that standing

---

[102]As quoted in L. R. MacTavish, *Select Committee: A Summary of their Functions and Practices in the Legislative Assembly of the Province of Ontario* (Toronto: Queen's Printer, 1955), pp. 12–13.

committees must follow if they are to become either effective legislative bodies or useful tools for the control of the executive. In the first place it should be pointed out that much of the valuable work done by the select committees is accomplished during the periods between sessions. If they had to carry out their assigned functions while the House was sitting, it would be impossible for them to do the thorough job that they can perform at other times. An encouragement to MPPs to carry on their public responsibilities during the interval between sessions is provided in the form of certain allowances. These include: a *per diem* expense allowance of $30 ($35 in the case of chairmen) for every day during the time between sessions upon which a member attends a meeting of a committee or upon which he is absent from home and is engaged on the work of a committee, exclusive of days spent travelling to and from meetings of the committee; a travelling allowance of $20 for each day spent travelling to and from meetings of the committee, plus actual disbursements for berths, meals, and gratuities; and, while on an inspection tour, the *per diem* allowance plus actual out-of-pocket expenses for transportation and sleeping accommodation.[103]

Secondly, select committees are usually able to enlist the aid of counsel or some other qualified person, as well as a secretary. (The committee itself may not engage experts or others to assist it because it has no means within itself of ensuring that such persons will be compensated. The practice, therefore, is for the chairman to communicate the committee's desires in this respect to the provincial secretary, who then submits the matter to the lieutenant governor in council. If the executive council agrees, an order in council is passed authorizing the payment of the necessary amount. Although this practice violates the principle of the separation of powers, it is resorted to merely as a matter of convenience, because the House has no simple means of effecting the result desired by the committee.)[104] Of course, an expert staff of one or possibly two is still very small in relation to the magnitude of the inquiries that are sometimes undertaken by the select committees, but it is a very great improvement over the provisions that are made for the staff of most standing committees. Now that it is becoming customary for four or five select committees to be working during the summer months, the way seems open for a major change in the method of staffing committees. In the past, one of the reasons why the government has refused to provide either permanent secretaries or counsel for the standing committees has been the fact that they would have no duties to perform when the House was not in

[103]*RSO*, 1960, c. 208, s. 65.
[104]MacTavish, *Select Committees*, pp. 18–19.

session. At the same time it has been loathe to take professional staff from the departments to work with the committees because this would mean that their regular employment would be neglected. However, now that there are only ten standing committees meeting during the session and usually no more than five select committees working while the House is not sitting, it has become feasible to set up a small, well-trained staff of clerks and lawyers to service all committees on a year-round basis. Logically, such a staff would be placed in the office of the clerk of the Legislative Assembly, which would schedule meetings in such a manner that it would get the best possible service for each committee. Besides meeting the immediate needs of the committees, such an innovation would solve the constitutional and practical problem that now exists when civil servants are asked to serve committees of the legislature, which are often set up for the sole purpose of investigating Government activities.

A third feature of the select committee that could be copied by the standing committees, to the latter's distinct advantage, is the practice of keeping detailed minutes of proceedings. The completeness of their minutes varies from committee to committee, but generally speaking those kept by select committees are far more extensive than those kept by standing committees. For some time, the select committees kept tape recordings of their proceedings, using for this purpose the recorders discarded by the House when it began using its modern two-band equipment, but this practice is not commonly followed now. Failure to keep adequate records of their meetings often means that much valuable information provided to the committees is wasted. Absent members are unable to inform themselves of the deliberations of the committees and significant aspects of the history of the political affairs of the province are irretrievably lost. Information is perhaps the prime prerequisite to legislative control of the executive: the greater the fund of information built up through adequate records of investigatory bodies, the greater potential to impose checks on executive actions.

Although select committees are superior to standing committees in many respects, they also have their own peculiar limitations. They are still relatively few in number and they have no opportunities to initiate investigations of their own choosing. The subjects of their inquiries are selected by the Government, their terms of reference are defined by the Government, the funds they require are provided by the Government, and, by means of its control over a majority of the members of the committee, the Government is able to direct even their day-to-day activities. Nevertheless, select committees have performed excellent service on occasion and they remain a useful tool in the hands of the legislative branch.

Provisions for Members

Whatever instruments are devised by the Legislative Assembly to assist it in the performance of its functions, they can be used to full advantage only if certain preconditions are met. These range from the need for salaries for members to free them from extraparliamentary employment, to the need for independent research facilities to ensure that members have access to the information they require if they are to evaluate Government policy intelligently.

Serving as a member of the Ontario Legislative Assembly has never been considered a full-time occupation, and the indemnity paid to members has reflected this attitude. In the 1st Parliament of the provincial legislature, the indemnity paid to members was set at $450 per session plus ten cents per mile for a return trip from their homes to Toronto.[105] This has steadily been increased, the last change being made in the 1965 session. By Bill 80 of that session the indemnity was raised from $5,000 to $8,000, and the expense allowance was increased from $2,000 to $3,000 for members from Metropolitan Toronto, and from $2,000 to $4,000 for other members. In addition to this, members from outside the provincial capital are allowed ten cents per mile for fifteen trips per annum from their places of residence to Toronto.[106] Thus, a member from a riding in Toronto receives a total allowance of $11,000 per annum, $3,000 of which is non-taxable, and a member from a constituency as far away as Ottawa receives a total allowance of $12,000 per annum, $4,000 of which is tax free, plus $375 for travelling expenses.

The indemnity now paid to MPPs is generally considered adequate, and in private conversation some members admit to the opinion that a fairly large number of their colleagues are being paid much more than they deserve. Only one member voted against the increase and he happened to be one of the few members of the House who does not have regular employment outside the legislature. Mr. Bryden, the New Democratic party member for Woodbine who opposed the increase, suggested that the $500,000 the raise would cost should be given to pensioned teachers and teachers' widows.[107] Members of the Ontario legislature are now the third highest paid elected parliamentarians in Canada, following members of the federal Parliament and the members of the Quebec legislature. In 1963 Quebec MLAS were given a sessional indemnity of $10,000 plus a tax-free allowance of $5,000, and in 1965 this was raised to a $12,000

[105]Clarke, *Sixty Years in Upper Canada*, p. 149.
[106]*SO*, 1965, c. 56.   [107]*Globe and Mail*, March 31, 1965.

indemnity plus a $6,000 expense allowance for a total of $18,000, the same amount that is paid to the federal MPs.[108]

Office accommodations for members have also been improved recently but are still less than adequate for those members who attempt to perform their functions conscientiously and do not have private offices.[109] Until the 1965 session there was practically no office space available for private members, and even the central offices for the two opposition parties were inadequate. The Liberals had an area divided into three small rooms by frame and glass panels for their members and a separate office for the Leader of the party and his secretary. The New Democrats had one office for ordinary members and another for the Leader and his secretary. The members of the cabinet naturally had their own offices, but the back-benchers of the Conservative party fared no better than their *confrères* in the other parties, having only one room with one long table and three small offices to be used on a first-come, first-served basis.

The accommodations provided for the 1965 session were a substantial improvement over previous arrangements. For the first time, each member was given his own desk and telephone. Enough rooms were provided for the Liberals and Conservatives so that there was one large room for about every ten members, and the NDP was given three small rooms for its seven members to share. Each opposition party was also given a reception room and an office for the leader. This meant that each member had at least a desk where he could work and a place where he could leave his papers. There is still no suitable place for members to hold private consultations, and they have no private offices where they can work without disturbance.

Secretarial assistance for private members is another fairly recent innovation. Prior to 1956 only sessional help was available, but since then the Liberals have had two secretaries throughout the year, and the NDP one. Besides these, there are usually about twenty-five sessional stenographers employed during the period that the House is actually sitting. This means that there is one stenographer for every four or five members. Since some members have their own secretaries in the city, and hence do not require typists at the Parliament Buildings, and other members do not seem to have much work that requires typing, those who do need the services of the sessional stenographers seem to have prompt and adequate service.

In 1965 a new system for allocating funds to the opposition parties for

[108]*Ibid.*, August 6, 1965.
[109]The following information has been garnered mainly from interviews with members of the legislature and with the secretaries employed by the three parties.

secretarial services was devised under which each party was given an allowance based on a set formula. The formula and the amounts provided for each party in the 1965–66 fiscal year were as follows:

	Liberals	New Democrats
Basic yearly operation		
1. For secretarial and office services including temporary assistants:		
(*a*) $1,000 each for the first 15 members and $500 for each additional member	$19,000	$8,000
(*b*) $4,000 for the offices of the two leaders	4,000	4,000
2. Maintenance and supplies and services:		
$175 per member	4,025	1,400
Research		
$1,000 each for the first 15 members and $500 for each additional member	19,000	8,000
Sessional requirements		
1. Stenographic services: One stenographer for each four members at $14 per day	6,000	2,000
2. Sessional maintenance: $25 per member	575	200
TOTAL	$52,600	$23,600

Omitting the amount set aside for research, which was a completely new appropriation, the Liberals were provided with $33,600 and the NDP with $15,600 for servicing their members and maintaining their offices. How these provisions compared with those of former years may be seen by comparing the amount given the NDP in 1965–66 with the amounts it had received in previous years: $3,500 in 1959, $4,000 in 1960, $5,500 in 1962, $6,000 in 1963, and $11,000 in 1964. When it is said that the amount of money now provided for secretarial assistance is adequate, it must be remembered that the terms are being used in a very narrow sense. The provisions for research assistance and other services of this nature are an altogether different matter and are a part of the larger problem of how an MPP gets information.

The members of the legislative branch cannot be expected to examine, criticize, improve, and ultimately approve or find wanting the policies of the executive unless they have sufficient knowledge of the facts on which these policies are based. In Ontario MPPs have the usual sources of published information, such as the reports of departments and semi-independent agencies, the *Estimates*, the *Public Accounts*, and the reports of the legislative committees. They also have the opportunity to ask questions and to seek information from the ministers during the proceedings of the Committee of Supply. But they have only recently been granted any money to carry out the kind of independent research that is necessary if they are to do a thorough job of evaluating and controlling the executive. The need for this kind of research is obviously not so necessary for backbenchers of the majority party because they are not particularly concerned with checking the powers of the Government. Besides, they can always get any information they need, either through private conversations with the minister concerned or directly from the department officials.[110] Occasionally members of the opposition parties can elicit information from the departments if it is clearly of a non-political nature, but they enjoy no absolute right of access to the civil service. It is made quite clear that the public service is meant to serve the Government and not the Assembly as a whole. The Opposition in Ontario is usually in relatively greater need of assistance than the Opposition at Ottawa or Westminster, because it is generally much smaller in comparison to the Government majority than it is in those two parliaments and, hence, the responsibility for checking the executive is shared by far fewer members.

Members of the opposition parties in Ontario are expected to keep a critical eye on all aspects of public affairs in a province with a population and area exceeding those of European countries, such as Denmark, Finland, the Irish Republic, Norway, and Switzerland, but they received no research assistance whatsoever until 1965. The provision for research funds for the Official Opposition in the 1965–66 fiscal year, calculated on the basis of $1,000 for the first fifteen members and $500 for each member thereafter, came to only $19,000. This was less than the salaries paid to some deputy ministers and less than the combined salaries paid to the Premier's three executive officers. Even when the $8,000 provided for the New Democratic party is added to the $19,000 given to the Liberals, the total is picayune compared to the total expenditures of the Government, which the members of the Assembly are supposed to oversee.

With such limited resources available, the opposition parties were unable to acquire the calibre of researchers they required plus the public

110From interviews with Mr. Dalton Bales (PC: York Mills) May 17, 1965, and Mr. John White (PC: London South) May 13, 1965.

relations men they felt were necessary to counter the vast public relations organization maintained by the Government. They, therefore, used their research money to hire persons who had formerly been employed by newspapers, in the hope that persons of such experience might be able to combine the two functions. Whether or not the Government increases the size of the research grants made to the opposition parties will probably depend on the use that they make of the money. If they spend it on projects obviously intended to win them immediate political advantage instead of spending it on basic research designed to improve their over-all efficiency as legislators, it is quite likely that a negative response will come from the Government. Undoubtedly certain members of the cabinet have the ability to see beyond the immediate struggle for political power and recognize the need for an Opposition equipped to oppose, but it is difficult for them to convince their backbenchers, whose political careers are most vulnerable, that the benefits which would accrue to the province from an improved Opposition would outweigh the disadvantages which such improvements would bring to the majority party.

Before the Government initiated research grants to the opposition parties in 1965, members were left to their own devices to gather the information they wanted but they were assisted by two institutions which merit some mention: the Press Clipping Service and the Legislative Library.

Systematic press clipping was begun shortly after the turn of the century when the Premier of the Province recognized the need to keep informed of press reaction to Government policy.[111] In the twenties, the Clerk of the Legislative Assembly had the Service enlarged so that members would have some accessible record of proceedings in the legislature besides the official *Journals*. Following an investigation under the direction of the Attorney General, the individual departmental press clipping units were dispensed with in 1934, and the central services under the office of the clerk of the Legislative Assembly were again extended to provide the requirements of the departments. Ten years later, when *verbatim* records of debates first were kept, the Press Clipping Service was reorganized, and it has existed with essentially the same organization and terms of reference since that time. However, the output of the service has increased considerably in the last twenty years. In 1944 it was subscribing to fifteen dailies, five weekly newspapers, and two semi-weeklies, and in that year it received 140 requests for clippings involving 1,860 items. In 1960 it subscribed to thirty-nine dailies, twelve dailies from other provinces, and the

[111]The information concerning the Press Clipping Service has been taken mainly from interviews with Mr. A. W. Corner, director of the Service.

C.C.F. *News*, and sent out an estimated 170,754 clippings on request.[112]

The Press Clipping Service of the Ontario government is unique in at least two respects. It is the only centralized government-operated press clipping service of its size in North America that attempts to meet the needs of a multitude of departments and agencies of government.[113] During 1960 it supplied regular service to fifty-four departments, branches, and agencies.[114] It is the only press clipping bureau in North America that also attempts to maintain a record library of press clippings based on such a large volume of clipping material. The clippings for the period from 1905 to 1955 have all been microfilmed and deposited in the Ontario Public Archives, and the material from 1934 to 1949 has also been indexed; the material gathered since 1955 is on file with the Press Clipping Service, but it has not been either filmed or indexed.

All of these facilities provided by the Press Clipping Service are available to members of the Ontario legislature without charge. However, although some members with an historical bent might appreciate the historical material and others may be interested in public reaction to Government proposals or their own statements, there is really not very much information that the Press Clipping Service can supply that is not already available to the members. The fact that they have to request the particular pieces of information that they want the Service to provide them with indicates that the members must already be aware of the information before they make their requests. The members do make use of the Service during the sessions and it is undoubtedly a valuable aid to Government and Opposition members alike, but its chief value lies in the fact that it is a means of feeding back to them the press reaction to their initiatives. What the Opposition members require much more is original research which will enable them to take more forceful initiatives.

The other institution that has always been available to members seeking information is the Legislative Library. At the time of Confederation, the library of the Parliament of the Province of Canada was taken over by the federal government and $100,000 was given to Ontario as compensation and as a fund from which to create a new legislative library.[115] This Library was under the control of the speaker and a standing committee of

[112]*Globe and Mail*, December 10, 1960.

[113]National Press Checking Services Limited, "Proposal to: Clerk of the Ontario Legislative Assembly, Press Clipping Service Department, subject: Problem Analysis and Cost Estimates for Supplementing or Replacing Government Service," p. 3.

[114]A. W. Corner, Memorandum to the Select Committee on Administration and Executive Problems of Government, November 16, 1960, p. 1.

[115]Ontario, Legislative Assembly, "Report of the Select Committee appointed to Inquire into the Revision of the Rules of the Legislative Assembly," *Journals*, 1947, p. 29.

the Assembly, and its collection had grown to 110,000 volumes by 1909. A fire in the west wing of the Parliament Buildings destroyed all but some 10,000 volumes.[116] Following the fire, work was begun on new quarters for the Library in the north wing of the Parliament Buildings, and in 1912 the Library was moved into its new accommodations. In the fifty-three years between 1912 and 1965, when thorough renovations were begun, very little was spent on maintaining the Library's section of the Parliament Buildings.

In spite of some problems of accommodation, the Legislative Library's collection has continued to expand and at the same time has become more specialized. In the early twenties the Toronto Normal School Library was amalgamated with the Legislative Library and the combined facilities were placed under the jurisdiction of the Minister of Education.[117] By 1947 this collection had been built up to an estimated 175,000 volumes, 50,000 of which were from the Normal School Library.[118] In 1964 jurisdiction over the Library was transferred again, this time from the Department of Education to the Department of the Provincial Secretary. The services provided for teachers in the Ontario public school system were cut back and some duplicate copies were eliminated so that by 1965 the number of volumes just exceeded 140,000, valued at more than $1 million.[119] In the fiscal year that ended on March 31, 1964, expenditures for the Library amounted to $66,240, $52,797 of which was spent on salaries for the staff of about a dozen, including five qualified librarians.[120] With only five librarians to maintain 140,000 volumes and serve the civil service and the MPPs, it is obvious that the Library cannot be expected to do very much research for MPPs. Circulation in 1963 reached 6,240, but this represents only a small part of the work done by the Library. The staff also answered an average of 237 queries per week[121] and assisted an average of 97 people a month who were allowed access to the stacks of the Library.[122] Nevertheless, the staff of the Library is able to help members locate the information they need and sometimes they can give answers to

[116]From a brief concerning the renovation of the Legislative Library prepared by Miss Jean Kerfoot, legislative librarian, for presentation to Mr. J. S. Yoerger, deputy provincial secretary, November 6, 1964.

[117]*Minutes*, October 19, 1960.

[118]"Report of the Select Committee appointed to Inquire into the Revision of the Rules of the Legislative Assembly," *Journals*, 1947, p. 29.

[119]From interviews with Miss Jean Kerfoot on August 10 and 12, 1965.

[120]Ontario, Legislative Assembly, *Public Accounts*, 1963–64, p. E26.

[121]This figure is based on sample weeks selected over a seven-month period. The data were supplied by Miss Kerfoot.

[122]This figure is based on data covering a six-month period.

specific questions. They do not undertake research into large problems or prepare written briefs for the members.

But, even with new accommodation, it is unlikely that many of the members who live outside of Toronto could have very much time to use the Library. During the session, attendance at committee, caucus, and regular House meetings leaves little time for browsing in the Library and, since very few of the members have ever had any experience in serious research, any time spent in the Library might be used inefficiently. It was no wonder then that in 1960 the Chief Librarian estimated that less than a dozen members actually used the Library facilities.[123] However, in the last few years a renewed interest in the Library seems to have developed. In August 1965 the Library records revealed that fifty members were active users of the reference facilities and a number of others, mainly from outside the Metropolitan Toronto area, used the newspaper and periodical section on a regular basis.[124] Several factors account for this revived interest in the Legislative Library. The Gordon Committee Report, the work of the Select Committee on Administrative and Executive problems, and the whole new attitude of the Government towards the Opposition – reflected in increased provisions for accommodations, secretarial services, and research assistance – have undoubtedly impressed the members of the opposition parties and the Government backbenchers with their significance and reminded them of their responsibilities. But, in spite of this evidence of diligence on the part of the members, the limited time available during the period when the House is sitting and the limited research ability of many MPPs lead to the conclusion that the provision of library facilities is no substitute for trained research personnel. Until members either acquire trained researchers attached to their offices or gain access to a permanent staff of such people, it will be extremely difficult for them to develop the kind of independent basic knowledge that will enable them to assess and intelligently criticize the operations of the executive.

In this chapter the emphasis has thus far been placed on the facilities provided for members of the opposition parties; in succeeding chapters it will be seen that most of the institutions and procedures available to the legislative branch to assist it in its attempts to regulate the powers of the executive are used almost exclusively by them. The details about the use that is made of these devices by the various parties will be given later when the institutions themselves are discussed, but the over-all tendency is clearly depicted in Figures 10 and 11. In spite of the fact that they make

[123]*Minutes*, October 19, 1960.
[124]From an interview with Miss Jean Kerfoot August 12, 1965.

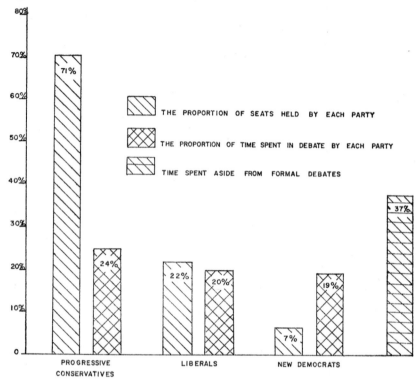

THE PROPORTION OF SEATS HELD BY EACH PARTY

THE PROPORTION OF TIME SPENT IN DEBATE BY EACH PARTY

TIME SPENT ASIDE FROM FORMAL DEBATES

FIG. 10. Proportion of time spent in debate by each party in the 1964 session.

up 71 per cent of the House, the members of the Government only accounted for 24 per cent of the time of the House in the 1964 session (Figure 10). The Government backbenchers in power only used 7 per cent of the time of the House, even though they constituted over 50 per cent of the membership (Figure 11). This substantiates the point already discussed in the Introduction: the realities of the party system are such that, for all practical purposes, the legislative branch is co-extensive with the opposition parties. However, outside of the constitutional arrangements, with which this study is primarily concerned, the Government backbenchers are able to exert considerable pressure on the executive and, to conclude this chapter, something must be said about this role in the governmental process.

As long as the party in power has a clear majority and is not dependent on any minority groups in the House, in the last analysis it is *only* the members of the majority party who can force the Government to do anything, because only they have the ultimate political weapon, namely,

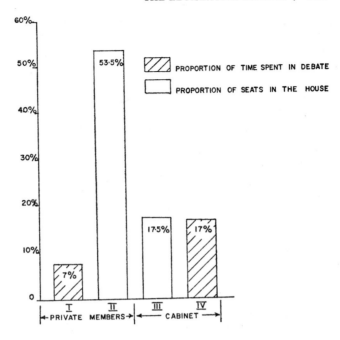

I PROPORTION OF TIME SPENT IN DEBATE BY BACKBENCHERS OF THE MAJORITY PARTY IN THE HOUSE

II PROPORTION OF SEATS OF THE HOUSE HELD BY BACKBENCHERS OF THE MAJORITY PARTY

III PROPORTION OF THE SEATS OF THE HOUSE HELD BY MEMBERS OF THE CABINET

IV PROPORTION OF TIME SPENT IN DEBATE BY MEMBERS OF THE CABINET

Fig. 11. Proportion of Government time taken up by members of the cabinet.

the power to defeat the Government and so bring about its downfall, as happened in Britain in 1886.[125] The chances of the Government party's backbenchers resorting to such drastic action in Ontario are remote, to say the least, but even open dissension in the ranks of the party is a sufficient source of embarrassment to the cabinet to encourage it to avoid displeasing its supporters. Hence, the wishes of the members of the majority party are given a great deal of weight by the cabinet. However,

[125]Sir Ivor Jennings, *Cabinet Government* (3rd ed.; Cambridge: Cambridge University Press, 1959), p. 480.

backbenchers must be careful of the way in which they make their wishes known. If they do so in public, they cause the Government some embarrassment, either by suggesting that the cabinet is incapable of recognizing certain needs itself or by bringing to light needs that the cabinet is unwilling to meet: "Lights must shine under bushels, if they are to illuminate anything at all. More exactly, they must shine in the parliamentary party caucus."[126]

As with many of the other aspects of government discussed in this chapter, 1964 marked the beginning of a new attitude towards the majority party caucus.[127] Although it is difficult to get accurate information about the operation of the caucus, because of the secrecy that surrounds the institution, it seems that the members took little interest in it and the cabinet paid it little heed in the years preceding the 1964 session. The Police Act incident of that session pointed out, to ministers and back-benchers alike, the dangers involved in allowing the caucus to shirk its traditional responsibilities. According to reports that circulated at the time, only ten members of the party were present at the caucus meeting where the Attorney General presented his eleven bills, one of which was to give rise to the greatest public outcry ever experienced by the then twenty-one-year-old Conservative Government.[128] Those members who were disturbed by the legislation when all of its implications were brought to light found that the proper place for them to raise their objections was in the party caucus, and the cabinet no doubt realized that it had much to benefit and little to lose from a diligent caucus. Since then the caucus has been better organized and more active than ever before.

The government caucus comprises all members of the Legislative Assembly who belong to the majority party, but nearly all of the deliberations undertaken are dominated by the private members because the ministers, having discussed matters in cabinet, are required by custom to support them, so that penetrating questions or expressions of dissent by them when Government policy is being reviewed by caucus would be inappropriate. The chairman of the caucus is now the chief government whip, but in the past it was customary to rotate the chairmanship among

[126]James Eayrs, *The Art of the Possible: Government and Foreign Policy in Canada* (Toronto: University of Toronto Press, 1961), p. 114.

[127]The information concerning the Progressive Conservative party caucus has been gathered through interviews with Mr. Dalton Bales, Mr. John White and through conversations with other members of the party.

[128]See Fred Schindeler, "Ontario," in John Saywell, ed., *Canadian Annual Review for 1964* (Toronto: University of Toronto Press, 1965), pp. 109–12. Section 14 of the original bill gave the Police Commission extraordinary powers to carry out its investigations into the extent of crime in the province and was amended in committee *before* being given second reading.

leading backbenchers. The chairman is elected by the caucus on the nomination of the premier.

In previous years the Conservative party caucus used to meet briefly between the lunch hour and the beginning of the day's sitting but, following the 1964 session, it began to meet regularly every Wednesday at 10 AM for two to three hours, as well as once or twice each week in the afternoon, usually at 1 PM on Tuesdays and Thursdays. In the fall of 1964 there was a special series of caucus meetings over a period of two days during which members made suggestions about possible legislation and discussed Government proposals. The agenda for caucus meetings is initiated by cabinet ministers who have bills to be discussed and by private members who wish to introduce other subjects for discussion.

Legislative proposals are brought before the caucus at various stages of readiness. Sometimes an idea will be discussed before any legislation has been drafted and at other times a minister will wait until he has a bill ready to introduce in the House, but eventually all bills go to the caucus for approval before being presented to the House. When a bill reaches the caucus it may be approved as it stands, amended, or on rare occasions, thrown out completely. Formal votes are taken, but ballots are not used and a consensus is usually obvious. Discussion generally proceeds on a question-answer basis. Now and then a member who has expert knowledge in the field concerned or who is affected more directly than others by the legislation will make a fairly lengthy speech, but most contributions to discussions are quite brief.

Committees of caucus are used quite frequently. They are set up to study major Government bills or other important matters. These committees have been instrumental in getting the Government to amend legislation. A more frequent benefit derived from the committee system is that members of the committees become well acquainted with the provisions and purposes of the bills referred to them and are thus in a position to explain the bills to other members and defend them on the floor of the House and in the standing committees of the House. No doubt many of the amendments forced upon the cabinet by its party caucus save the Government from a lot of opposition after the bills become public. Similarly, having informed members on the Government side no doubt facilitates the passage of Government bills through the House and its committees. The *quid pro quo* for this assistance to the Government is the right enjoyed by the backbenchers of the majority party to make their wishes and criticisms known to the ministers, either privately or in caucus, and so to exert considerable influence over the use that is made of executive powers.

This influence which the members of the governing party have over the executive comes from their position within that party and not from any particular right that they enjoy under the formal parliamentary institutions by which the province is governed. However, the burden of this study is to analyse these formal institutions to see how they maintain the balance between the legislative and executive branches of government. Of fundamental importance in this regard are the rules of procedure by which the Legislative Assembly is governed and this is the subject of the next chapter.

PARLIAMENTARY PROCEDURE: THE RULES, THE GENERAL DEBATES, AND THE FORMAL LEGISLATIVE PROCESS

5

IN SIR ERSKINE MAY'S classic treatise on parliamentary practice, procedures are divided into three groups: "the forms of proceeding used in either House, the machinery of direction and delegation established by each, and the rules which govern the working of the forms and machinery."[1] But, for our purposes, a more useful discussion of the nature of parliamentary procedure is that given by Lord Campion in *Parliament: A Survey*.[2] Taking as his theme the "democratization" of procedure – a process which has been described as "the converting of the comfortable old parliamentary coach into an up-to-date, streamlined legislative engine" – Lord Campion describes the traditional and modern components of the procedure followed in the British House of Commons. The traditional components, called the "practice of the House," include the body of rules which grew up, chiefly by precedent, during the early and middle period of Parliament, and may be likened to the common law. This aspect of parliamentary practice is roughly equivalent to May's "forms of proceeding" category, which includes many of the ancient rules that Campion lists as illustrations of the "practice of the House." For example, both use the illustration of procedure on bills which, with its three readings, was already in existence before 1547 when the House began to record its proceedings in its *Journals*. Since the practice of the House was formed, in the main, during that period of British history when the House was in

[1] Sir T. Erskine May, *Treatise on the Law, Privileges, Proceedings and Usage of Parliament*, edited by Sir Barnett Cocks (17th ed.; London: Butterworths, 1964), p. 221. (Hereinafter this work will be cited by its short title, *Parliamentary Practice*).
[2] Gilbert Campion, "Parliamentary Procedure, Old and New," in Lord Campion, L. S. Amery, *et al.*, *Parliament: A Survey* (London: George Allen & Unwin, 1955), pp. 141 ff.

chronic opposition to the monarch, it tended to give wide scope to the initiative of members and to afford no special facilities to the Government. Indeed, its purpose was rather to encourage opposition to the executive.

The standing orders are the modern components in Lord Campion's analysis. With the appearance of disciplined political parties, the rise of the cabinet to its position of pre-eminence, and the growth of government functions, the fundamental objective of the rules of procedure was not to promote opposition to the executive, but to limit it; not to encourage the expression of minority opinions but to curtail the rising flood of verbiage in order to allow the Government to get its business through the House. It was the advent of this democratic period that made it necessary to impose the standing orders upon the traditional practice of the House. Generally speaking, the standing orders and May's "rules of procedure" are one and the same. If the practice of the House is thought of as its common law, the standing orders may be considered its statute law. The relationship between the two in the British House of Commons was neatly described by Lord Campion: "It would be misleading to say that the standing orders are grafted on to the trunk of practice; they are more like shears pruning the overgrowth of leaves and branches. But either metaphor expresses an important fact . . . that the standing orders every-where presuppose practice. They are in no sense a code; they are amendments of the rules of practice.[3]

In Ontario also, parliamentary procedure includes both the practice of the House and the standing orders, although the latter term is not generally used in the province. However, the relationship between the two is quite different from the situation in the United Kingdom, primarily because Ontario, and Upper Canada before it, were created *de novo*; hence, the procedures of Parliament had to be set out in detail from the very beginning. Much of what existed in the United Kingdom by convention was written into the original rules of procedure adopted by the Legislative Assembly in Ontario. This is not to say that there has been no informal evolution of parliamentary procedure in Ontario, but that the changes which have come about by custom have necessarily been of such a nature as to amend or supplement the standing orders. In short, the relationship between the practice of the House and the standing orders of the House in Ontario is, in a sense, quite the opposite to their relationship in the United Kingdom: in Ontario custom modifies the written rules whereas in Britain the standing orders modify ancient practice. Of course, the situations in the two jurisdictions are not so neat as has so far been suggested here. The standing orders of the House of Commons in the

[3]*Ibid.*, p. 144.

United Kingdom are no doubt shaped by practice, and in Ontario there is a reliance upon ancient British practice.

In this study both the practice and the written rules of the House – but not what Sir Erskine May called the "machinery" of the House – are included in the discussion of parliamentary procedure. In Ontario, though, the 135 printed rules that form the core of procedure do not go by the usual name, "standing orders." Instead, they are known as the "Rules, Orders, and Forms of Procedure of the Legislative Assembly," a title which has the appearance of being far more inclusive than the name traditionally used. Nevertheless, they are no broader in scope than is customary for printed rules and, to avoid confusion, hereinafter they will be referred to as the "written rules" or simply as the "rules." There are also other sources of the rules under which the Ontario Assembly operates, including the British North America Act and its own statute, the Legislative Assembly Act,[4] and the provisions which flow from these sources must also be included in the discussion.[5] In his study of procedure in the Canadian House of Commons, Professor W. F. Dawson gives speakers' rulings as another source of rules,[6] but in Ontario the most significant rulings of the speaker are generally either interpretations of the written rules, applications of ancient practice (as defined by May) to the Ontario situation, or definitions of customs that have been developed in the Assembly itself,[7] and since the speakers' rulings seldom, if ever create new

[4]Procedure in the United Kingdom is based on statutes only to a small extent, since each House is in principle responsible for its own procedure. Nevertheless, certain British statutes do affect parliamentary procedure: Parliament Act, 1911, and the Statutory Orders (Special Procedure) Act, 1945. See Lord Campion and D. W. S. Lidderdale, *European Parliamentary Procedure* (London: George Allen & Unwin, 1953), p. 226.

[5]The four sources of rules given here correspond quite closely to the four types of rules listed by a select committee of the legislature appointed in 1946 to study the rules of the House with a view to their improvement. The committee reported: "The Legislature is governed primarily by the Imperial statute that created it, namely, the British North America Act, 1867; secondly by its own statute, the Legislative Assembly Act; thirdly, the standing, sessional and other orders adopted by the House; and fourthly, the usages and customs of the House established by practice." "Report of the Select Committee Appointed to Inquire into the Revision of the Rules of the Legislative Assembly," in Ontario, Legislative Assembly, *Journals*, 1947, p. 25. (Hereinafter only the short title, *Journals*, will be used to refer to the *Journals* of the Legislative Assembly of Ontario).

[6]W. F. Dawson, *Procedure in the Canadian House of Commons* (Toronto: University of Toronto Press, 1962), p. 6.

[7]Examples of these three types of rulings by the speaker may be found in the *Journals* for the following dates: on January 27, 1876, the Hon. R. M. Wells interpreted the rules regarding private bills; on February 18 and 19, 1879, Mr. Clarke, chairman of the Committee of the Whole, applied the long-standing practice of parliament concerning the reading of documents in the House; and on March 15,

rules, they are not considered to be a separate source of rules of procedure in this study.

The rules of parliamentary procedure perform a number of functions. In the first place, there is the plain necessity to bring some order to the proceedings of a large assembly of individuals, most of whom consider their opinions to be of some importance and many of whom have won their seats in that assembly by virtue of their natural propensities to loquacity. In the oft-quoted words of John Hatsell, the great clerk of the British House of Commons in the eighteenth century:

In these instances, and in every other of this sort, it is more material that there should be a rule to go by, than what that rule is: in order that there may be a uniformity of proceeding in the business of the House, not subject to the momentary caprice of the Speaker, or to the captious disputes of any of the Members. If the maxim "Stare super vias antiquas" has ever any weight, it is in these matters, where it is not so material, that the rule should be established on the foundation of sound reason and argument, as it is, that order, decency, and regularity, should be preserved in a large, a numerous and consequently sometimes tumultuous assembly.[8]

However, the rules of procedure are not devised solely to bring order out of what would otherwise be chaos; the order achieved itself serves the larger purpose of promoting the efficient functioning of the supreme legislative body of the province. With an ever-increasing amount of work to be accomplished it is imperative that the machinery of government make the best possible use of its time and resources. "Efficiency – economy and despatch – are required qualities of modern government" was the way that the Gordon Committee put it.[9] In seeking this end, the rules must be drafted to avoid not only the Scylla of unfinished business, but also the Charybdis of a muzzled opposition. While a rigidly controlled House would no doubt facilitate the speedy passing of important legislation, procedures must be fashioned in such a manner as to achieve efficiency in the long run. Measures passed against the objections of a minority and without sufficient time for debate may incite numerous delaying tactics both inside and outside the Government and may even result in the inconvenience of an election and the inefficiency which accompanies a change of Government. The purpose of the rules of procedure is to achieve the

---

1948, the Hon. James de Congalton Hepburn defined a custom of the Ontario Legislative Assembly, which superseded the written rule of the House, that orders be taken up according to precedence.

[8]Quoted in Eric Taylor, *The House of Commons at Work* (4th ed.; Middlesex: Penguin, 1961 [first published in 1951]), pp. 21–2.

[9]Ontario, Committee on the Organization of Government in Ontario, *Report* (Toronto, 1959), p. 9. Hereinafter cited as the Gordon Committee *Report*.

highest degree of efficiency consistent with the democratic process – a process which has never been noted for its immediate efficiency.

A third purpose of parliamentary procedure is to define and defend parliamentary privileges.[10] Parliamentary privilege has been defined by Sir Erskine May as "the sum of the peculiar rights enjoyed by each House collectively as a constituent part of the High Court of Parliament, and by members of each House individually, without which they could not discharge their functions, and which exceed those possessed by other bodies or individuals. Thus, privilege, though part of the law of the land, is to a certain extent an exemption from the ordinary law."[11] When May refers to privilege as being exempt from the ordinary law, he is alluding to the fact that the determination of breach of privilege rests entirely with the House, which also enjoys the right to punish offenders. The most important privileges that the provincial parliament has derived from Britain came into being in that country because both Houses, and particularly the House of Commons, found it necessary to uphold fundamental rights in their relationship with the sovereign. Today these ancient privileges are claimed by the speaker of the Ontario Legislative Assembly whenever a new parliament meets. Following his election and the return of the lieutenant governor – who had refused, upon his first entrance, "to declare the causes of the summoning of the present Legislature of this Province until a Speaker of this House shall have been chosen" – the speaker claims on behalf of the Assembly "all their undoubted rights and privileges, especially that they may have freedom of speech in their debates, access to your person at all seasonable times, and that their proceedings may receive from you the most favourable consideration." The lieutenant governor grants the requests.

The importance of the privileges granted to the legislators is that without them, as May has said, "they could not discharge their functions." Besides the three traditional privileges claimed by the speaker in his formal address at the beginning of each parliament, the most important privileges are the freedom of members from arrest, the right of the Legislative Assembly to provide for its own constitution, the right to regulate its own proceedings,[12] and the power to punish for breach of privilege or for contempt.[13]

[10]See the discussion of parliamentary privilege in Ontario in chap. 4.

[11]May, *Parliamentary Practice*, p. 42.

[12]Traditionally, parliaments assert this right by giving first reading to a fictitious bill at the commencement of every session *before* the debate on the address. In Ontario the tradition is maintained, except that an actual bill is used for the purpose; hence it eventually goes through the rest of the legislative process like any other bill.

[13]A list of the most important privileges claimed by the British Parliament is given in J. Harvey and L. Bather, *The British Constitution* (London: Macmillan, 1963), pp. 136–8.

But, perhaps, the basic function of parliamentary procedure, and certainly the most important for the purpose of this study of legislative-executive relations, is to define the respective responsibilities and powers of the Government and Her Majesty's Loyal Opposition. On the one hand, the rules must be constructed to enable the governing party to give effect to any mandate it may have received from the electorate. But, on the other hand, they must also provide the Opposition with whatever time and information are necessary to enable it to perform its constitutional functions.

To define the balance between these two desirable but somewhat contradictory goals, the rules of procedure must do at least three things. First they must allot the time of the House between the Government and the private members. The word "parliament" is derived from the French verb *parler* and apparently a large proportion of the members of modern parliaments are determined that the institution should live up to its name. In Ontario the written rules have tended to favour the private members, by providing them with certain days when their business is to take precedence before Government business, and by placing no time limit on their speeches, for example. However, the practice of the House has fundamentally altered the intent of the written rules and turned the control of the time of the House over to the prime minister. Whether or not the result has been detrimental to the Opposition is one of the important questions to be answered in this study. The second thing that the rules of procedure must do if they are to balance the needs of the Government against the demands of the Opposition is to ensure that the Opposition receives the information necessary to carry out its critical function in an intelligent fashion. There are many facets to this problem, and only a close investigation of procedures relating to topics such as questions, orders for returns, and the usual debates will begin to reveal whether or not the Opposition is sufficiently well supplied with information. However, even if the Opposition had all the information it desired and as much time as it could constructively utilize, it would not be able to perform its ultimate constitutional function unless it was given specific opportunities to overthrow the Government. It is the privilege of challenging the very existence of the Government that separates Her Majesty's Loyal Opposition from the numerous private groups which set themselves up in opposition to established authority, and unless the minority parties are provided with occasional opportunities to move "no confidence" motions of one form or another, they are hardly more significant in the over-all democratic process than the well-informed and articulate pressure groups. Thus, defining the number and kind of occasions available to the Opposition to force the

Government to defend itself against defeat on the floor of the House is the third function of the rules of procedure in regulating the struggle between the two perpetual antagonists. In this regard, too, the Ontario House has developed its own peculiar practices, and it must be determined how, and to what extent, these modifications of the Westminster model have affected legislative-executive relations in the province.

Before beginning a detailed analysis of parliamentary procedure in Ontario and its effect on legislative-executive relations, something must be said about the history of the written rules and how these have been modified in practice.

The Written Rules

On the second day of the first session of the first provincial parliament, the Prime Minister moved "That the Rules, Orders and Forms of Proceedings of the House of Commons of Canada, be, until altered, the Rules, Orders and Proceedings of this House, as far as practicable."[14] On January 14, 1868, a twelve-man select committee was appointed to frame regulations for the government of the House, and the rules of the House of Commons of Canada were referred to the committee for its guidance.[15] The very next day the committee reported that they had "carefully considered the subject referred to them, and now submit the result of their labor for the consideration of your Honourable House."[16] How carefully the committee considered the subject may be judged from the fact that they could not possibly have met to begin a discussion of the topic until the morning of the day their report was made and adopted. Without even looking at the text of the rules, it would be suspected that the committee would closely follow the rules of the House of Commons which were referred to them. A close comparison of the two sets of rules justifies the suspicion. Furthermore, the rules of the federal lower House were far from original themselves, having been copied almost verbatim from those of the Legislative Assembly of Canada.[17]

Thus, the rules used in Canada prior to 1867 and those adopted by the province and the federal government are, in all important respects, virtually identical.[18] From the rule that requires the speaker to base his

[14]*Journals*, 1867–68, p. 4.
[15]*Ibid.*, p. 18.
[16]*Ibid.*, p. 20.
[17]Dawson, *Procedure in the Canadian House of Commons*, p. 21.
[18]The three sets of rules compared here were all bound in individual volumes: *Rules, orders and forms of Proceeding in the Legislative Assembly of Canada,*

decisions – in all contingencies unprovided for in the rules or the usages of his own legislature – on the "Rules, Usages, and Forms of the House of Commons of the United Kingdom of Great Britain, as in force at the time," to such detailed provisions as those governing quorums, the business of the Houses (including the setting of the dinner hour), and the regulations governing the libraries, the rules of the three legislatures agree almost to a word. Most of the differences that do occur are simply adjustments to fit the requirements of the unicameral parliament in Ontario. For example, the Ontario rules had to omit the references in the 1860 rules to Black Rod (rule 7), amendments by the upper House (rule 23), bills originating in the upper House (rules 54 and 69), and the rights of the lower House in connection with supply. The other differences have to do with details of limited significance.

The changes that have been made in the written rules since they were formulated first in 1868 have not been very far-reaching and may be noted in some detail. On March 4, 1868, the report of a select committee appointed on February 24 "to revise the Standing Orders of this House affecting Bills relating to Railways, Canals and Telegraphs" was adopted.[19] In the following year an amendment was made reducing from eight to four the number of days required before any private bill could be considered in a committee.[20]

The first complete reappraisal of the rules took place in 1875, when a select committee which had failed to report in the preceding two sessions was reappointed. The committee reported on December 10, and one week later the report was debated and passed without amendment.[21] Most of the changes were of minor importance, dealing for the most part with the procedures relating to private bills, but one innovation had significant implications, for it imposed a limitation on the length of time a member could speak on a motion to adjourn the House or the debate. Rule 30 stipulated that while such a motion was always in order "no member shall speak to such Motion for more than ten minutes; and no second Motion to the same effect shall be made until after some intermediate proceeding shall have been had." Mr. Abram W. Lauder, seeing this limitation on

adopted by the House May 15, 1860 (Quebec: Hunter, Rose 1860); *Rules, Orders and Forms of Proceeding of the House of Commons of Canada*, adopted by the House in the 1st Session of the 1st Parliament, and subsequently amended (Ottawa, 1873); *Rules, Orders and Forms of Proceeding of the Legislative Assembly of Ontario*, adopted by the House, in the 1st Session of the 1st Parliament (Ottawa, 1868).

[19]*Journals*, 1867–68, pp. 71, 79, 84.
[20]*Ibid.*, 1869, pp. 24, 70, 71.
[21]*Ibid.*, 1875, pp. 56, 100–1.

freedom of speech (quantitatively conceived) as the head of the camel in the parliamentary tent, moved that the ten-minute limit be struck out. The amendment lost on division, 25 to 42, and the clause remains in the current rules. In Ottawa in 1913 more drastic action was taken, and adjournment motions, along with a number of other motions, were declared non-debatable.[22]

From 1876, when rule 53 concerning private bills was amended by way of certain additions,[23] until 1885, there were no changes in the rules. On March 11 of that year four rules were added, one to do with committees of the House and three dealing with private bills, but these rules were never incorporated into any complete listing of the rules and apparently lapsed purely by oversight. In 1897 "pairs" were recognized officially by an amendment to the rules instructing the clerk to enter pairs upon the votes and proceedings and in the *Journals*.[24] In 1901 provision was made for recording the questions of members and the answers thereto, except that a minister could require that a motion be made for a return if the answer was of a lengthy or voluminous nature.[25] The next change, in 1904, was merely to spell out the duties of the law clerk in more detail.[26] Further changes were made in regard to private bill procedures in 1907, none of which was of great significance.[27] The functions of the law clerk were again expanded and clarified by an amendment to rule 50 in 1910.[28] Private bill regulations were substantially revised again in 1914.[29]

The second complete revision of the rules took place in 1929,[30] and although the changes introduced in 1929 were more extensive than those

22Dawson, *Procedure in the Canadian House of Commons*, pp. 167–8.

23*Journals*, 1876, p. 163. See also the *Rules, Orders and Forms of Proceeding of the Legislative Assembly of Ontario*, published in a separate volume in 1876. A word of caution needs to be spoken about these editions of the rules in individual volumes for very few of them are accurate when compared to the official versions contained in the *Journals*. For instance, the 1876 edition contains changes in rules 53 and 60 of which there is no record in the *Journals*. On the other hand, the four rules added in 1885 were left out of the 1891 edition, although there is no record in the *Journals* to suggest that the House ever rejected them.

24*Journals*, 1897, p. 122. Pairing was practised before this time but no official record was kept. After a division the Whips would call attention to pairs by asking that the division list be read and stating that certain gentlemen had not voted because they had paired with others. Charles Clarke, *The Member's Manual of Practice and Procedure in the Legislative Assembly of the Province of Ontario, with Decisions of Mr. Speaker, From 1867 to 1893: Rules of the House and Miscellaneous Information* (Toronto, 1893), p. 51.

25*Journals*, 1901, pp. 175, 182. 26*Ibid.*, 1904, p. 296.
27*Ibid.*, 1907, p. 253. 28*Ibid.*, 1910, pp. 202–5.
29*Ibid.*, 1914, p. 313.

30The committee was appointed on March 14 and reported twelve days later. The report was adopted, and the new rules were printed as Appendix 3 of the *Journals*, 1929, pp. 121, 163, 277–94.

made in either 1875 or 1939 (the only other major revisions), they did not alter any of the fundamental procedures of the House. Most innovations were either minor amendments to detailed provisions (for example, the procedures relating to private bills) or additions to existing rules to clarify or expand them. Only a few of the changes merit attention here.

The first innovation in the 1929 edition of the rules was indicative of a new sense of maturity in the Ontario House. Until this time the rules had merely stated that in all unprovided cases the Rules, Usages and Forms of the House of Commons of the United Kingdom of Great Britain and Ireland were to be followed.[31] But rule 1 of the 1929 edition provided that "in all contingencies unprovided for the Question shall be decided by the Speaker and in making such a Ruling the Speaker shall base his decision on: 1st, the Usages and Precedents of this Legislature. 2nd, The Rules, Usages and Forms of the House of Commons of the United Kingdom of Great Britain and Northern Ireland as in force at the time." Clearly, the apron strings were being cut when the ancient practice of the British House was made inferior to the sixty-one-year-old practice of the provincial legislature.[32]

A significant addition to the rules was the instruction to the speaker to "name" any member who persisted in speaking after being requested to discontinue.[33] This provision had already been incorporated into the standing orders of the Canadian House of Commons[34] and had been applied in that House on one occasion in 1913.[35] No doubt the speaker of the Ontario House could have exercised this power without having it written into the rules – since it was a traditional right of the speaker according to British usage – but incorporating it into the written rules removed any possible doubts as to his powers and perhaps this did have a salutary effect on certain members.

Rule 39, added in 1929, had real significance – at least potentially: "Only one amendment may be made to a motion for the Speaker to leave the Chair for the House to go into Committee of Supply or Ways and Means." Before this rule was copied from the standing orders of the Canadian House of Commons, it was "legally" possible for each party group in

[31]*Rules of the Legislative Assembly of Ontario* (Toronto: King's Printer, 1926), rule 113.

[32]Although Nova Scotia was also one of the original provinces in the Canadian federation it did not authorize its speaker to be guided by the usages of its own Assembly until 1955. J. Murray Beck, *The Government of Nova Scotia* (Toronto: University of Toronto Press, 1957), p. 274.

[33]Rule 14, now rule 17 (*a*).

[34]Arthur Beauchesne, *Rules and Forms of the House of Commons of Canada* (4th ed.; Toronto: Carswell, 1958), p. 107.

[35]Dawson, *Procedure in the Canadian House of Commons*, p. 116.

the House to move an amendment to the motion "that Mr. Speaker do now leave the Chair. . . ." With the new rule in operation, only the Official Opposition would have the right to move such an amendment. When the two-party system collapsed in Canada in the twenties, the third party chafed under this rule and had it amended to allow for one subamendment as well;[36] but to this time no such change has been made in the written rules in Ontario, in spite of the fact that the three-party system has become the norm. However, until 1966 this did not affect supply procedure in the province – for the simple reason that there were no motions to go into Committee of Supply – and since that time a special arrangement has permitted the third party to move one amendment to the motion to go into Committee of Supply in each session.[37]

One other change made in the written rules in 1929 that should be noted is the omission of any reference to the "chief clerk of committees." By rule 114 of the 1929 edition, the functions formerly performed by that officer of the House were transferred to "a clerk" in the office of the clerk of the House. Apparently the feeling was that it would be better to leave it up to the clerk of the House to choose from his own staff the person who would function as clerk of committees during sessions, instead of having someone specially appointed to carry out these duties. The clerk of committees did not function as clerk assistant. In fact, there has not been a permanent clerk assistant appointed since 1906.[38]

From 1929 until the next major revision in 1939 there were no changes made in the rules, and the revision of 1939 was notable more for the manner in which the select committee charged with performing the task was appointed than it was for the actual changes that were made. An unusually small select committee, composed of only three members, was appointed on March 29, 1938, to consider the revision of the rules that had been prepared by the Clerk.[39] However, on April 7, the committee reported that it had not been able to complete its labours and recommended that it be given authority to meet during the early part of the recess to complete its work, and that "when completed the Revised Rules be submitted to the *Executive Council* for their approval and if so approved they be brought into force on a day to be named by the Lieutenant-Governor by His proclamation."[40] To have the executive council

[36]Standing order 45 of the House of Commons of Canada, cited in Beauchesne, *Rules and Forms*, p. 161.

[37]For a discussion of this distinctive feature of parliamentary practice in Ontario. See pp. 147–50.

[38]From an interview with Mr. Roderick Lewis, clerk of the Legislative Assembly, June 7, 1965.

[39]*Journals*, 1938, p. 92.   [40]*Ibid.*, p. 138. Italics added.

approve the rules of procedure to be followed by the Legislative Assembly would have been unusual, to say the least, but the recommendation was approved. Nevertheless, the committee did not follow this procedure – probably because it did not complete its work during the recess, but perhaps because it saw the implications of such a course of action – and instead made its report to the House,[41] where it was debated and amended on April 3, 1939.[42] In spite of the time invested in the project, the new rules were not very different from those adopted a decade before.

But, some interesting changes were made in the rules defining the functions of the speaker. For instance, rule 11 now gives him the power to adjourn the House without putting the question or to suspend any sitting for a time to be named by him in the case of a grave disorder arising in the House. Rule 17(b) is quite unique in Canada in that it attempts to define the grounds on which a member may be named[43] and also the procedure to be followed in such an event.[44] Rule 17 (c) provides that if a member who has been suspended under rule 17(b) refuses to obey the direction of the speaker, the speaker shall call the attention of the House to the fact that force is necessary in order to compel obedience to his direction, and the member named will thereupon be suspended from the service of the House during the remainder of the session.[45] Another innovation suggested by the committee, but eventually rejected by the House, would have given the speaker the power to decide whether or not certain dilatory motions were an abuse of the rules and, if so, to forthwith put the question thereupon from the chair or to decline to propose the question to the House.[46] It was indicative of the less hurried pace of proceedings in Ontario that the executive was unable to convince the House of the need for this particular rule.

[41]*Ibid.*, 1939, p. 33.

[42]*Ibid.*, pp. 87–8. The new rules were printed in the *Journals* as Appendix 4, pp. 429–51.

[43]These are: "disregarding the authority of the Chair, or . . . abusing the rules of the House by persistently and wilfully obstructing the business of the House. . . ." No such statement occurs in the standing orders of the House of Commons of Canada, but almost the exact words may be found in standing order 24 of the British House of Commons. The British standing orders referred to in this discussion are those to be found in May, *Parliamentary Practice*, pp. 1065–88).

[44]The speaker forthwith puts the question, on a motion being made, "that such member be suspended from the service of the House," such suspension to be for any time stated in the motion but not to exceed two weeks. Again, this rule is an adaptation of the British standing order 24(2), but no such provision occurs in the Canadian standing orders.

[45]Standing order 22 (4) in the British House of Commons is almost identical to this rule.

[46]This was rule 38 (d) in the original report of the select committee. *Journals*, 1939, p. 428. A similar rule does exist in the United Kingdom as standing order 28.

A noteworthy change in the rules was the recognition of the right of any member to move the adjournment of the House "for the purpose of discussing a definite matter of urgent public importance."[47] As in many other cases where the written rules in Ontario did not keep pace with developments in the procedures followed in the United Kingdom, it probably would have been possible for an MPP to use the adjournment motion for this purpose prior to 1939, in spite of the fact that there was no provision for it in the rules. Since the British standing orders did make room for such an adjournment motion,[48] the speaker could have allowed it to be used in Ontario under the rule governing unprovided cases. But writing the procedure into the rules brings it to the attention of the members and perhaps encourages them to take advantage of the opportunities it presents.

Two things about the Ontario rule distinguish it from its British and Canadian equivalents. First, no mention is made of the grounds upon which the speaker may refuse to accept the motion (as in Ottawa) or of the need for the support of twenty or forty members (as in Ottawa and Westminster, respectively) if the unanimous consent of the House is not given. Motions for the adjournment under standing order 26 of the Canadian House of Commons were quite frequent for about thirty years after the rule was created, but they have since become a negligible factor in the procedure of that House.[49] In Britain, the number of motions for adjournment under standing order 9 accepted by the speaker in any session has declined considerably in recent years. In the first nineteen years of its operation, from 1882 to 1901, an average of 6.9 such motions were allowed; from 1902 to 1920, the average was 6.1; from 1921 to 1939, an average of 1.5 was allowed each year;[50] and at present the standing order is allowed to operate rather less than once a year.[51] In Ontario, motions to adjourn the House to discuss a definite matter of urgent public importance under rule 38 (*a*) meet with success only about once in every five years.[52] The second thing that is different about this Ontario rule is that it specifies

---

[47]Rule 38 (*a*).

[48]"Standing Order 9" was first adopted by the British House of Commons in 1882. *Report From the Select Committee on Procedure* (London: Her Majesty's Stationery Office, 1959), p. xix. In Canada the procedure is provided for by standing order 26, which was first adopted in 1906. Dawson, *Procedure in the Canadian House of Commons*, p. 173.

[49]Dawson, *Procedure in the Canadian House of Commons*, pp. 173–5.

[50]Sir William Ivor Jennings, *Parliament* (2nd ed.; Cambridge: Cambridge University Press, 1957), p. 113.

[51]Peter G. Richards, *Honourable Members: A Study of the British Backbencher* (2nd ed.; London: Faber & Faber, 1963), p. 123.

[52]From an interview with Mr. Roderick Lewis, August 19, 1964.

that no member may speak to the motion for more than ten minutes; no such restriction on the length of speeches is imposed in either Westminster or Ottawa.

The section of the rules dealing with proceedings on public bills was modified significantly in 1939 by the addition of rule 56: "If on an amendment to the question that a bill be now read a second time or the third time, it is decided that the word 'now' or any words proposed to be left out stand as part of the question, Mr. Speaker shall forthwith declare the bill to be read a second or the third time, as the case may be." When this stipulation is followed closely, in most cases only one amendment to a motion for second reading can be made, and the House can divide only once at this stage of proceedings. However, for many years the House did divide on both the amendment and the main motion for second reading, and it was only in the 1965 session that the Speaker decided to begin following the literal meaning of the rule.[53]

The only other changes made in the rules in 1939 that have any general significance were those improving the method of choosing members of select committees and requiring committees to record divisions. Before rule 101 was adopted, if five or more members objected to the names submitted in the motion to establish a select committee, the House was to elect the members of the committee according to a very involved procedure.[54] Under the new rule the member moving the appointment of a select committee may submit in his motion the names of the members proposed to form the committee, and this motion is then open to amendment in the same manner as any other motion. Rule 102(b) provides that the names of the members attending each committee shall be entered by the committee clerk in the minutes and that a record shall be kept of how each member votes on every division in the committee.[55]

An addition was made to rule 63 in the section on private bills on April 24, 1939,[56] but this is included in the rules which are printed as an appendix to the 1939 volume of the *Journals* and in the edition of the rules currently in use,[57] both of which are listed as having been adopted

[53]Ontario, Legislative Assembly, *Debates*, June 21, 1965, p. 4424. (Hereinafter, the short title, *Debates*, will be used to refer to the debates of the Legislative Assembly of Ontario).

[54]See rule 95 in the 1929 version of the rules.

[55]Rule 102 (*b*) notwithstanding, the details concerning divisions are not recorded in committee minutes.

[56]*Journals*, 1939, p. 136.

[57]The rules are printed in Alex C. Lewis, *Parliamentary Procedure in Ontario* (Toronto: King's Printer, 1940), pp. 103–34.

on April 3, 1939. In any case, no amendments have been made to the rules since April 1939.

While not every change that has been made in the rules since 1867 has been noted in the preceding pages, all the innovations that are significant, so far as the balance between the legislative and executive branches is concerned, have been discussed; with the possible exception of the procedures regarding private bills, all changes which have had the effect of streamlining the conduct of parliamentary business have been noted. The important point to notice is that when all of these modifications are added up, they still do not amount to very much. None of the major changes that have taken place in Westminster and Ottawa – such as the time limits placed on certain debates, speeches, or private members' business – has been incorporated into the Ontario rules. In short, the Legislative Assembly is still governed by the mid-nineteenth-century rules it adopted in 1867.[58]

However, a study of the written rules by themselves produces a highly erroneous conception of the true state of parliamentary procedure in Ontario. In practice there have been some extremely significant changes made in the rules of procedure, some of which are in direct contradiction to the written rules. One of the most blatant examples of the violation of the written rules, and one that has a great deal of significance for legislative-executive relations, has been the practice governing the calling of items of business. The rules are quite unequivocal. Rule 31 reads: "All items standing on the Orders-of-the-Day shall be taken up according to the precedence assigned to each on the Order Book, the right being reserved to the administration of taking up Government Orders, in such rotation as they see fit, on the days on which Government Bills have precedence," and rule 28(a) stipulates that Government orders have precedence on Tuesdays and Thursdays of each week. The rules notwithstanding, for at least seventy-five years the premier, as leader of the House, called *all* orders without regard to the precedence assigned to them on the order paper.[59] Perhaps the best statement of the practice of the House until 1966 was given by the Honourable James de Congalton Hepburn, speaker of the House. On March 15, 1948, the order of the day for second reading of Bill 57, An Act to Amend the Election Act, having been read, the member who was responsible for the bill called the

---

[58]In this respect, the Ontario legislature is similar to the New Zealand parliament which has likewise neglected to revise its procedures substantially. Robert N. Kelson, *The Private Member of Parliament and the Formation of Public Policy: A New Zealand Case Study* (Toronto: University of Toronto Press, 1964), p. 12.

[59]From an interview with Mr. Roderick Lewis, August 19, 1964.

attention of Mr. Speaker to rule 31 and claimed that he could not be called on to discuss his bill until those preceding it on the orders had been considered. In reply Mr. Speaker addressed the House as follows:

> While it is true that Rule 31 as at present in the rule book provides that Orders of the Day shall be taken up according to precedence on the Order Paper, it has been a custom which has obtained in the Legislature of Ontario for very many years to allow the Leader of the House the privilege of indicating what Orders shall be considered at any particular stage of proceedings. This custom has met with the consent of the House for so many years past that it has become an acknowledged method of dealing with the Orders. The object of this custom has been to facilitate the business of the House.
>
> In my opinion the custom which has been approved by the House during the lifetime of several Governments in the past obtains the authority of a rule of the Assembly.[60]

Naturally such a rule, if exercised by a fair-minded prime minister who had due regard for the historic rights of all elected representatives, would not necessarily restrict the scope of the activities of private members. Prior to the new arrangements introduced in 1966, Prime Minister Robarts called approximately a third of all private members' orders and allowed them to be debated until at least one representative from each party had spoken. Normally he notified the private member concerned, and sometimes the whole House, when he was going to call a particular private member's order so that preparation could be made for a debate. When he felt that the matter had been sufficiently well aired, he had someone – usually the Government whip – move the adjournment of the debate. This was the equivalent of the "talking out" procedure followed in Ottawa, and now in Ontario. When the motion to adjourn the debate had been carried, the subject was removed from the section entitled "notices" on the order and notice paper and put under the heading, "other public bills and orders" as an order for resuming the adjourned debate. In the case of private members' bills, once they had been called for second reading the wording of the order was changed from "Second Reading Bill . . ." to "resuming the Adjourned Debate on the motion for Second Reading Bill. . . ." Unless the Government was willing to "adopt" the bill or resolution and let it pass, or else was so opposed to the principle of the bill or resolution that it was willing to let the matter come to a vote so that it could display its displeasure, the order was simply never called again, and the matter lapsed at the end of the session. When a private member's order

---

[60]*Journals*, 1948, pp. 47–8. See also the decision of Mr. Speaker on March 22, 1912, as given in Lewis, *Parliamentary Procedure in Ontario*, pp. 207–8.

had once been called, the member was at liberty to put together notice of motion on the order paper.[61]

While the recent practice appeared to be quite fair to the private members, this had not always been the case, and the privilege conferred on the House leader was potentially open to abuse. On some occasions under previous administrations, private members' orders had been ignored completely. More common was the practice of postponing these orders until very late in the session when the House was overburdened with Government orders, and then usually calling them late in the evening or at other times when attendance and interest were at a low ebb. Regardless of whether or not the bulk of private members' resolutions and bills was actually called, the very fact that it was solely up to the premier to decide whether or not they would be called and, if so, when and how long they would be debated, put the backbencher in a very inferior position vis-à-vis the cabinet.

During the 1966 session, a meeting chaired by the speaker and attended by the party leaders and whips resulted in a significant reform.[62] It was agreed that the hour from 5 to 6 PM on Tuesdays and Thursdays would be reserved for the debate of private members' bills and resolutions. The order in which the items were to be called was to be determined by the whips. A maximum of one hour was to be spent on each bill or resolution, and, although no limits were set on speeches, the whips were to encourage the mover to speak for no longer than thirty minutes; other debaters were to limit themselves to fifteen minutes. In return for this concession, the members of the Opposition had to agree that their proposals would not be voted upon and that half of the available hours would be reserved for members of the majority party.

British backbenchers do not have a very high proportion of their proposals debated, but, on the other hand, the times of the debates are established, and the decision as to which motions shall be called is determined by *blind* chance through the ballot box, instead of by an adversary with his eyes open for political advantage, as was the case in Ontario up to 1966. And in Ottawa, although the Opposition has had little more chance to force the Government to a vote on private members' orders, for many years now at least the time of the debates has been set and the Government has been compelled to register its disapproval of the measures to the extent of talking them out. In Ontario under pre-1966 practice the Government

[61]According to rules 44 (*c*) and 44 (*d*), no member may have more than one notice of motion standing on the order paper at one time, not counting notices of motion for the production of papers. This rule does not apply to private members' bills, and any number of these may be listed on the order paper by one member.

[62]*Debates*, June 29, 1966, pp. 5434 ff.

could very magnanimously permit a private member to introduce a subject and then simply adjourn the debate on the matter. Ostensibly, the discussion had simply been postponed, and the topic was still receiving the consideration of the House; in fact, the bill or resolution had been killed without the Government having to so much as record its opposition to it, let alone justify that opposition on the floor of the House. Even in recent years there were occasions when the prime minister would refuse outright to call certain orders. Most frequently these were motions for the production of papers, and therefore such motions were becoming less common on the order paper.[63]

The change that was made in the rules of procedure for the calling of orders was accompanied by another change which had been given added authority by being incorporated into the order and notice paper. The schedules laying out the order of business to be followed by the House on each day in the week had been ignored for decades but in recent years the Clerk of the House formalized this departure from the rules by setting up the order and notice paper according to actual practice, instead of as specified in rule 28. Another minor changer which, because of its nature, has received recognition in the published record of the proceedings in the House is the change affecting answers to questions. Rule 37(b) stipulates that questions put by members, and the replies thereto, shall be entered in the *Journals*. However, since the first session in 1960 these have been included in the *Debates* instead of in the *Journals*, so that all questions and answers, both written and oral, appear in the same place.

A second major change in procedure was not only contrary to the implied meaning of the written rules of the legislature, but also to the whole weight of parliamentary tradition. The Committee of Supply is the vehicle chosen by parliament for considering the supply to be offered to Her Majesty's Government towards defraying the expenses of the public services. For centuries it has been the tradition in England to use the motion "that the Speaker do now leave the Chair and that the House resolve itself into the Committee of Supply," as the occasion on which

[63]If a private bill is distasteful to the Government—but not so unpopular that the Government is willing to allow the bill to come to a vote—the prime minister may make use of his prerogative here as well and refuse to call the order for its second reading. A good case in point was Bill Pr 11, an Act respecting Westminster College, introduced in the 1964 session. The bill was requested in order to gain tax exemption for a residential college at the University of Western Ontario. While the Government was not prepared to grant this concession, it could hardly vote down such an apparently worthy cause, and so the Prime Minister took the way out provided by the practice of the House and bluntly refused to call the order for the second reading of Bill Pr 11.

grievances might be aired. At Westminster and Ottawa such advantage was taken of these opportunities that their number had to be reduced. In the United Kingdom, standing order 17 provides that whenever an order of the day for the House to resolve itself into a committee other than a committee on a bill is read, the speaker shall leave the chair without putting any questions, unless, on a day on which the Committee of Supply stands as the first order, a minister of the crown moves "that Mr. Speaker do now leave the Chair." Although not required to by the standing order adopted in 1947, the Government makes such a motion and so makes way for debate when each of the main branches of the estimates is introduced. This, in effect, provides the Opposition with five occasions when they can air their complaints and criticize the Government in general.[64] In Ottawa, under rules adopted in 1955, only six motions are made each session for the House to go into Committee of Supply. These motions are usually spaced throughout the session so that members will have periodic opportunities to raise questions of a general nature,[65] but on all other occasions the House goes into Committee of Supply without the question being put and hence without any debate. In spite of this great tradition, which even the overworked national parliaments of the United Kingdom and Canada have been able to maintain to some degree, the Ontario Legislative Assembly abandoned the practice of allowing grievances to be aired before going into Committee of Supply.

Up to and including the session of 1960, the Ontario budget was delivered on the motion "that Mr. Speaker do now leave the Chair and that the House resolve itself into the Committee of Supply." This meant that the budget debate and the general supply debate were one and the same. At one time the practice was not to begin a detailed examination of the estimates until after this motion was carried at the end of the budget debate, since the estimates were traditionally considered in Committee of Supply and the House could not get into committee until the motion to that effect was carried.[66] This proved inconvenient for a number of reasons, but mainly because it was difficult to find time in a short session to perform the two functions in sequence. There was a tendency to prolong the budget debate until so late in the session that very little time was left over for the

---

[64]May, *Parliamentary Practice*, pp. 754–6; Harvey and Bather, *The British Constitution*, p. 178.

[65]R. M. Dawson, *The Government of Canada* (4th ed. revised by Norman Ward; Toronto: University of Toronto Press, 1963), pp. 406–7.

[66]For example, in 1929 the motion to go into Committee of Supply was debated on seven days before it was carried, and only then did the House begin to examine the detailed estimates.

Committee of Supply to go over the estimates.[67] In the special four-day session in the summer of 1945, the new Conservative administration took steps to rectify this situation. On July 16 the Committee of Supply and the Committee of Ways and Means were constituted in the usual fashion. The next day, the order of the day for the House to resolve itself into Committee of Supply having been read, Mr. Drew moved "that Mr. Speaker do now leave the Chair and that the House resolve itself into the Committee of Supply," and delivered his budget address. However, when the Opposition attempted to move an amendment to the motion, the Speaker ruled that "at the present stage of proceedings on the consideration of Supply, the amendment offered was out of order and could not be accepted."[68] The Speaker's ruling was appealed but was sustained without a division. The debate continued, and after some time "the House according to Order, resolved itself into the Committee of Supply." The motion that the speaker leave the chair and the House resolve itself into the Committee of Supply was *never* carried, and yet the Committee of Supply was constituted and performed its usual functions.

The summer session in 1945 was unusual in many ways, and the exact procedures followed in those four days, so far as supply was concerned, were never repeated. However, a beginning was made, and the new procedures were established in the next session. These procedures, observed from 1946 to 1960, inclusive, were as follows: Usually on the day before the budget was to be presented the Committee of Supply and the Committee of Ways and Means would be authorized by motions without any opposition.[69] The next day, or shortly thereafter, the provincial treasurer

[67]In the Hepburn era it was not unknown for the Committee of Supply to go through all of the estimates in one sitting. See, for example, *Journals*, 1940, pp. 106–12.

[68]*Ibid.*, 1945, p. 12.

[69]Constituting these committees before the completion of the debate on the address in reply to the speech from the throne is itself a violation of rule 114 which provides that they are to be appointed on motion "at the commencement of each Session, as soon as an address has been agreed to in answer to the Speech of the Lieutenant Governor." On March 7, 1945, Mr. Hepburn demanded a recorded vote on the motion "That this House will on Friday next, resolve itself into the Committee on Ways and Means," and, when the motion was carried, he objected that this was contrary to rule 114. The Speaker attempted to justify this obvious violation of the rule by claiming that "it was optional to present the motion in question either 'early in the Session' or 'as soon as an address had been agreed to in answer to the Speech of the Lieutenant Governor.'" He also pointed out that the previous administration had also adopted a motion to go into Committee of Supply before the throne debate had been concluded (*Journals*, 1945, pp. 43–4). In the United Kingdom the Committees of Supply and Ways and Means are set up in the same manner as in Ontario but only after the conclusion of the debate on the address. Lord Campion, *An Introduction to the Procedure of the House of Commons* (3rd ed.; London: Macmillan, 1958), p. 226.

would present his budget – using the motion to go into Committee of Supply as the occasion for this event. Late in the session, generally on the very last day, this motion would be carried. However, during the intervening days the House on several occasions would have gone into Committee of Supply for the purpose of giving detailed attention to the estimates of the various departments. This was done, not by motion, but simply by calling the order for the House to go into Committee of Supply.[70] On other occasions the order for resuming the adjourned debate on the motion that the speaker leave the chair would be called and the budget debate would be continued. The aspect of this procedure which required the most ingenuity was keeping at least one estimate to carry when the main motion to go into Committee of Supply was carried, thus ending the budget debate.

This whole procedure was confusing, to say the least, and two further changes were made. In 1961 the motion to go into the Committee of Ways and Means was made the budget motion. This allowed the budget debate to proceed sporadically throughout the session without any confusion with the estimates which were still dealt with by the Committee of Supply. The second and finishing touch on the new supply procedure was to avoid all motions to go into Committee of Supply. After the changes made in 1961 the practice was to appoint or authorize the Committee of Supply early in the session at the same time that the Committee of Ways and Means was authorized, rule 114 notwithstanding, in order to get the item down on the order paper. Then, whenever the House needed to go into the Committee of Supply, the prime minister merely called the appropriate order. There was never any motion made that the speaker leave the chair and the House resolve itself into Committee of Supply; the question was never put; no debate was permitted; no amendment could be made. The time-honoured tradition of voicing grievances before granting supply was discarded.

While it must be admitted that this was a remarkable deviation from British parliamentary practice, it was really of very limited significance in the Legislative Assembly of Ontario. The fact was that little, if anything, could be said in a debate on a motion to go into Committee of Supply that could not be said just as well in the Committee itself. The bulk of the time of the House was taken up in Committee of Supply, and there was ample opportunity for members to discuss virtually any subject they chose.

[70]Sometimes a routine motion "that the Speaker do now leave the Chair and the House resolve itself into Committee of Supply" was used, and when this was done it was of course possible for the Opposition to move an amendment. See, for example, *Journals*, 1960, pp. 99–100.

If there was any disadvantage in not having a motion to go into Committee of Supply it was that it limited the number of opportunities for votes of censure. In Ontario, under the 1961 procedures, there were only two definite opportunities for the Opposition to force the Government to defend itself on a vote of confidence, and minor parties in the House had only one such opportunity. The Opposition could challenge the Government on both the throne and budget debates, but a third party was left with only one possibility, namely, a subamendment to the address in reply to the speech from the throne. But even this was not a very grave disadvantage because it was always possible for any member to give notice of his intention to move a motion of censure, and, even though it was the prime minister who decided if and when such a motion would be debated, it was unlikely that such a motion would go uncalled. Perhaps, in view of the shortness of the sessions in Ontario, two motions of no confidence would be sufficient. This hypothesis is supported by the fact that the Opposition has not seen fit to use very many special motions of censure to make up for the ones lost by Ontario's unique supply procedures. Indeed, before the 1961 procedures were introduced members only rarely used the motion that the speaker leave the chair as an occasion to move an amendment censuring the Government.

Nevertheless, in 1966 an agreement was reached whereby three motions to go into Committee of Supply are moved in each session, thus allowing three amendments, two moved by the Official Opposition and one by the third party. The three debates can last a full day each, and the amendments are voted upon at the end of the debates. While this change puts Ontario back in line with the practice of other parliaments, it is still too early to judge whether it will have any significant effect on the operations of the Assembly.

Having discussed the history of the written rules and having indicated some of the more significant modifications that have been made in rules in practice, we may now look more closely at parliamentary procedure in Ontario. In the following pages various aspects of procedure will be analysed with a view to discovering how the rules govern legislative-executive relations in the province. Those procedures which have been designed specifically for the purpose of enabling the Opposition to carry out its functions will naturally be noted, but the operations of many ordinary procedures in the legislative process are just as significant in this regard and therefore merit close attention.

To begin with, it should also be stressed that in Ontario there is no set limit to the length of particular speeches or debates and no set time for adjourning. Potentially, the lack of any regulations in these matters leaves the Opposition with some powerful weapons which have been used with deadly effect on some occasions.[71] Perhaps the best illustration of how such privilege can be used occurred in 1923 when the Opposition wore down the resistance of the Government and finally provoked the Premier, Mr. Drury, into calling the election which he subsequently lost. For a number of successive days the House sat until the not-so-early hours of the morning, and members used every conceivable variety of the filibuster technique, including long excerpts from *Alice in Wonderland*.[72] The Government was helpless: if it allowed the adjournment of the debate before the member speaking had completed his remarks, the same member could speak again when the debate was resumed and the only way in which the debate could be concluded was to wait until all of the Opposition members had had their say on the matter.[73] A yet unchallenged record for the length of any one speech was set on the final night of the sitting. Mr. Alex Lewis, member for Toronto Northeast, Seat "A", who later became clerk of the Legislative Assembly, was asked to hold the floor for the Opposition until Mr. Ferguson, the leader of the Conservative party, was ready to speak. Mr. Lewis performed the task with distinction, speaking for six-and-a-half hours without interruption![74]

[71]Of course, if the Government has a large majority, these same weapons can be used to wear down the Opposition and force through Government legislation.

[72]From an interview with Mr. E. C. Drury, March 19, 1965.

[73]Technically, Mr. Drury did have at least one other alternative. Although he could not interrupt a member who was speaking, at any other time in the course of the debate anyone on the Government side could have moved the "Previous Question." The form of the motion is "that this question be now put." The speaker then presents the question to the House, and, if the decision is in the affirmative, the debate is closed and the original question is put forthwith. Lewis, *Parliamentary Procedure in Ontario*, pp. 37–8. Either Mr. Drury was not aware of this "closure" provision or else he chose not to use it for fear of offending the democratic principles so dear to his own party.

[74]From an interview with Mr. Roderick Lewis (son of the gentleman who was the Member for Toronto Northeast, Seat "A", in 1923), August 19, 1964. On occasion some rather unparliamentary tactics have been used to cut speeches short. For instance, once when the whips had arranged for Sir William Meredith and Sir Oliver Mowat to wind up the debate on the address, a backbencher rose to continue the debate when Sir William sat down. The House then adjourned for dinner, and at 8 P.M. the member, Mr. Tate, rose to continue his speech and was immediately handed a message by a page boy. After a glance at the note Mr. Tate said: "I must apologize to Mr. Speaker for bringing my remarks to an abrupt conclusion. I've just heard that my bakery is on fire." When he found out that he had been tricked into leaving the House, he attempted to resume his speech, only to be informed that he was out of order. Taken from "Notes on the History of Ontario," an unpublished manuscript prepared by Major B. Handley Geary, v.c., sergeant-at-arms, Legislative Assembly of Ontario.

While the members of recent parliaments have not proven equal to the "mighty men of old," they have achieved a degree of notoriety by modern standards. In the budget debate of 1964, the late Member for Bracondale, Joseph Gould, spoke for two hours and forty-two minutes, and in the throne speech debate of that session, Mr. MacDonald, the leader of the New Democratic party, spoke for two hours and fifteen minutes; but both of these were extended beyond one sitting and were not therefore continuous.[75] The average length of speeches in the throne speech debate in the 1964 session was thirty-four minutes, and the average length of speeches in the budget debate was thirty-eight minutes.[76] The record for the longest sitting in the history of the Legislative Assembly was probably achieved on March 24/25, 1926, when the House sat from 3:15 PM until 9:00 AM the next day.[77] A number of recommendations have been made to limit the length of speeches and the number of days devoted to the major debates of the session and to set a definite time for the termination of business, but nothing of a formal nature has been accomplished in these respects.[78] Similarly, although the practice is constantly decried by observers who are not themselves members of the House, no action has been taken to stop members from reading their speeches.

If the rules leave the tongues of the members unbridled, the next questions to be asked are: On what occasions may they exercise their right of free speech, and how have these opportunities been circumscribed in practice? In answering these questions, it is useful to proceed from the general to the particular, and the remainder of this chapter will be given over to a discussion of the general debates and the legislative process common to practically all bills which eventually become statutes. Chapters 6 and 7 will include discussions of the procedures regulating specific opportunities available to the members to restrain and criticize the use of executive powers.

[75]*Debates*, 1964, pp. 170 ff. and 192 ff. (MacDonald); and pp. 1085 ff., 1265, and 1392 ff. (Gould).

[76]While it is impossible to obtain exact measurements of speeches by any method other than timing them during their delivery, these figures may be accepted as fairly accurate. In general, they were calculated in the following manner: the number of columns of Hansard reporting an individual speech was multiplied by 3.04 minutes, the estimated average time required to deliver one column of a speech.

[77]Geary, "Notes on the History of Ontario."

[78]See, for example, the recommendations of the two most recent select committees established to study and make recommendations concerning parliamentary procedure in Ontario: "Report of the Select Committee Appointed to Inquire into the Revision of the Rules of the Legislative Assembly," *Journals*, 1947, pp. 25–46; and Select Committee Appointed April 11, 1960, to Study and Inquire into Matters pertaining to the Transaction of Business in the Legislature, Sessional Paper 55 (printed), *Report*, 1960–61 session.

The General Debates

There are, first of all, the two general debates in most sessions: the debate on the address in reply to the speech from the throne, and the budget debate.[79] The speech from the throne is one of the traditional elements in the formal opening of parliament at the beginning of each session. Until 1895 the formalities used to take two days in Ontario, but since then everything has been compressed into one afternoon. Because Ontario has only one House it was necessary to make a few changes in the traditional opening ceremonies, the main features of which may be briefly summarized: The lieutenant governor enters the House and informs the members, through the provincial secretary, that he does not see fit to declare the causes of the summoning of the legislature until a speaker has been chosen. He then retires and a speaker is elected and escorted to the dais, where, standing on the upper step, he returns his humble acknowledgment to the House for the great honour it has conferred upon him. The House then adjourns during pleasure. Shortly thereafter the lieutenant governor re-enters the House and takes his seat on the throne. The speaker then announces that he has been elected and claims the rights and privileges of the Assembly. Through his provincial secretary, the lieutenant governor grants these requests; he then opens the session with his speech from the throne. Upon the completion of this task, he retires from the chamber and the speaker resumes the chair. As is done at the beginning of each day's sitting, he first reads prayers,[80] and then Bill 1 is introduced and read the first time. Originally this was a dummy bill – as it still is in most other parliaments that are patterned after the Westminster model – but some premiers considered this tradition a waste of time and began using a regular bill for the same purpose, i.e., the immemorial right of the House to attend to its own business before considering the affairs of the crown. Since the Hepburn era this has been the established practice in Ontario, the particular bill usually being quite innocuous and occasionally

[79]Both the throne and the budget debates have been dispensed with for some of the special sessions that have only lasted a few days. Note, for example, the short sessions in the following years: 1937, 1939, 1945, 1951, 1952, 1955, and 1963.

[80]There were no prayers offered as part of the daily opening exercises until a select committee reported in favour of such a practice in 1877. For one session the ceremony was performed by clergymen of the city, but this practice was discontinued because of the difficulty of finding appropriate gentlemen for each day. When Charles Clarke was elected speaker on January 7, 1880, he became the first lay reader, and those who have followed him in the office have carried on the tradition. Charles Clarke, *Sixty Years in Upper Canada, with Autobiographical Recollections* (Toronto: William Briggs, 1908), pp. 220–1.

rather humorous in its title. During Mr. Drew's administration, a number of bills would be introduced on the first day,[81] and, until Mr. Frost's time, motions to authorize the appointment of certain committees, to establish the striking committee and to authorize the recording of debates, the notification of vacancies that had occurred during the time that the House was prorogued, and the introduction of new members who had been elected were all given time on the first day. Now the only such item that occurs is the announcement of vacancies; all others have been relegated to the second day.[82] The final act of the House at its first sitting is to order that the speech of the lieutenant governor be taken into consideration the next day.

In the early years, the address in reply to the speech from the throne merely repeated the original speech verbatim. The paragraphs of the address were duly numbered and separately put from the chair, at which time they were subjected to a nominal second reading and submitted to a committee which invariably reported the address intact. When these formalities were over, the address was ordered to be presented to His Excellency, as the lieutenant governor was then called, by the executive council.[83] Today, the address consists of only one paragraph and simply thanks "His Honour" for his gracious speech. As is the case in other jurisdictions, the honour of moving and seconding the motion to present the address to the lieutenant governor is usually bestowed upon two backbenchers.

In the United Kingdom, the address in reply to the Queen's speech is moved on the first day and generally takes precedence over other business until it is agreed to, the debate usually lasting about six days.[84] At Ottawa the amount of time devoted to this debate has been limited by the standing orders to eight days, in addition to the day on which the address is moved.[85] At Queen's Park, only rule 114, which stipulates that the Committees of Supply and of Ways and Means are to be appointed "at the commencement of each Session, as soon as an address has been agreed to in answer to the speech of the Lieutenant-Governor," applies, but, as is

[81]For example, on the first day of the 23rd Legislature (1947), 22 bills were given first reading. This practice had been followed on rare occasions previously as well: in 1910 when 33 Government bills were introduced on the first day of the session.

[82]In recent years the opening ceremonies have been televised, but even with the elimination of many items of business the programme has not been well received; primarily because of the length of the ceremony and the poor reading of the speech.

[83]Clarke, *Sixty Years in Upper Canada*, pp. 144–5.

[84]May, *Parliamentary Practice*, p. 305; Taylor, *The House of Commons at Work*, p. 56.

[85]Dawson, *Procedure in the Canadian House of Commons*, pp. 138–9.

true with so many other written rules, this provision is ignored in practice. Although in some sessions the address is agreed to before the budget is presented – which is not done before the Committees of Supply and Ways and Means have been authorized – in most cases the throne speech debate continues sporadically for some time after the budget has been brought down.[86] Since the rules are not specific on the point, the decision as to how much time will be given over to the debate rests with the prime minister in his capacity as leader of the House; who shall speak and the order of speaking are arranged by the whips. Minor parties in the House have the opportunity to move amendments to the amendment moved by the Official Opposition.

The throne debate is very significant in the Ontario legislative session so far as length and participation are concerned. A total of approximately twenty-six hours was taken up by speeches in this debate in the 1964 session.[87] The whole debate, including points of order, etc., accounted for 10.2 per cent of the total session. (How this compares with the amount of time spent on other proceedings in the session is shown in Figure 12.) During the throne debate the members of the Government – who constituted 71 per cent of the House in 1964 – used approximately eleven-and-a-half hours for speeches, including the throne speech itself, or 40 per cent of the time; the members of the Liberal party – who made up 22 per cent of the House – accounted for 34.5 per cent of the time; and the New Democratic party – whose seven members made up only 6.5 per cent of the House – spoke for nearly 20 per cent of the total time used for delivering speeches in the throne debate. These figures are depicted in Figure 13, which shows what proportion of the membership of the House is taken up by each party and what proportion of the throne debate each party delivered. Forty-seven members participated in the debate, their speeches averaging thirty-four minutes in length. However, the participation was not quite as evenly distributed as this figure might suggest. For example, Mr. MacDonald's marathon speech took up more than one-third of his party's total contribution. Mr. Sopha spoke for approximately three times as long as most of his colleagues in the Liberal party and Messrs. Robarts and Randall spoke twice as long as the average Government backbencher.

Two conclusions may be suggested on the basis of this evidence. First,

[86]In the 25th and 26th Parliaments the rule – that the address be agreed to before appointing the Committees of Supply and Ways and Means – was followed in half of the eight full sessions, but in both of the first two sessions of the 27th Parliament (i.e., 1964 and 1965) the rule was violated.

[87]This total only includes the formal speeches of more than three minutes and does not take account of such things as points of order or interjections.

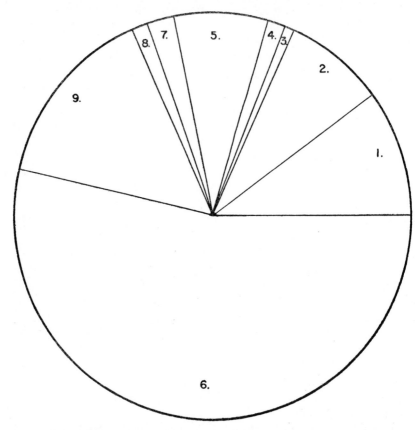

Fig. 12. Distribution of time in the 1964 session of the Legislative Assembly of Ontario: 1. throne debate, 10.2 per cent; 2. formal legislative process, 8.2 per cent (1st reading, 1.8 per cent; 2nd reading, 4.8 per cent; committee, 1.4 per cent; 3rd reading, 0.2 per cent); 3. statements at 1st reading, 0.9 per cent; 4. statements before the orders of the day, 1.3 per cent; 5. budget debate, 7.6 per cent; 6. Committee of Supply, 53.6 per cent; 7. private members' business, 2.1 per cent; 8. private bills, 1.3 per cent; 9. other, 14.8 per cent – The major items included in this category are speakers' rulings, questions, and divisions.

as at Ottawa and Westminster the debate on the address in reply to the speech from the throne in Ontario has become the preserve of the backbenchers. A higher proportion of the private members of the House participated in this debate than in any other debate that came before the House in the session of 1964. Only two cabinet ministers and six prominent Opposition members spoke, leaving thirty-nine other contributors.

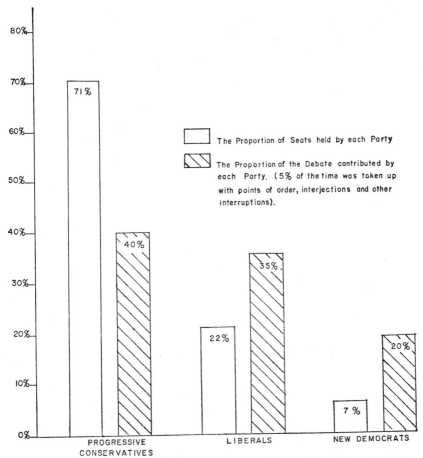

FIG. 13. Proportion of the time spent on the throne debate by each party in the 1964 session.

Although the big guns in the three parties used their time for party purposes, the new members of the House used the throne debate to deliver their traditional maiden speeches extolling the good people who had been kind and intelligent enough to elect them to parliament.

The second conclusion the above analysis suggests is that most of the time of the throne debate is taken up by the Opposition.[88] Although the Government is able to structure the debate to some extent by means of the

[88]While this is true, perhaps it should be pointed out here that the throne debate is not unique in this respect. In fact, the Government accounts for a larger percentage of the time spent on this debate than it does on any other major debate in the session.

terms of the speech from the throne and by ministerial statements in the course of the debate, the Opposition looks upon it as one of its best opportunities to criticize the Government on general issues of its own choosing. Members also attempt to use the debate to raise particular instances of the alleged abuse of powers that have been delegated to ministers or to extra-departmental agencies.[89] Grievances received from constituents are often aired during a member's speech on the address in reply, perhaps because the traditional opportunity for raising such matters – the debate on the motion to go into Committee of Supply – was for years non-existent in Ontario.

The second major debate in each session is on the budget. In their study of twelve parliaments associated in the Inter-Parliamentary Union, Campion and Lidderdale found that in every country except Sweden use was made of debates on financial matters in order to bring forward criticism of non-financial aspects of administration.[90] Ontario conforms to the general pattern, and the budget debate embraces virtually everything the members care to dicuss. At Ottawa and Westminster, where broad debates were allowed on the supply motions, the subject matter of the budget debates is usually more limited. At Ottawa the standing orders have further limited the debate by restricting it to six days.[91] However, while the standing orders of the Canadian House of Commons impose a time limit on the whole debate such as does not exist in Ontario, since 1927, they have also provided at least the third largest party in the House with the right to move a subamendment to the main amendment. No minor party in the Ontario House enjoys this privilege because rule 42 stipulates that only one amendment may be made to a motion for the speaker to leave the chair for the House to go into Committee of Supply or Ways and Means. The budget debate is arranged by the whips and continues off and on until the last day of the session when the House finally passes the motion that the speaker leave the chair and the House resolves itself into the Committee on Ways and Means.

The budget debate of 1964 was neither as long nor as popular a forum as was the throne debate of that session. It took up only 7.6 per cent of the session, and only thirty-one members, or 28 per cent, of the House participated in it. Although the subject matter of the budget debate is slightly more narrowly circumscribed than that of the throne debate, in

[89]Most of the leading private members interviewed by the author gave the throne debate as one of the most useful occasions available to them to check the exercise of delegated powers.
[90]Campion and Lidderdale, *European Parliamentary Procedure*, p. 34.
[91]Dawson, *Procedure in the Canadian House of Commons*, p. 140.

many respects the two debates are quite similar. For example, private members without prominence in their respective parties tended to occupy the bulk of the time: of the eleven Conservatives who took part, only three were cabinet ministers, and one of those was the Provincial Treasurer who had read the budget statement; approximately half of the twelve Liberals who participated were party luminaries; and probably only two of the six New Democrats who contributed to the debate would have been considered frontbench material. The average length of the speeches was thirty-nine minutes, but when the budget address and the protracted speech by Mr. Gould are eliminated from the calculation, the speeches in this debate were about the same length as those in the throne debate.

The proportion of the total time of the debate which each party spent as compared to the relative size of each party in the House is shown in Figure 14. From this it may readily be seen that the Opposition dominated this debate even more than it did the throne debate. Including the budget address itself, the governing party took up only slightly more than 28 per cent of the total time spent delivering speeches.[92] Thanks largely to the Herculean efforts of Mr. Gould, who spoke for one-quarter of the time spent in the debate by his party, the Liberals took up over 44 per cent of the time. The six members of the New Democratic party who participated in the debate used up nearly 23 per cent of the total time.

The fact that the budget debate usually begins within about one month of the opening of the session – unless the session happens to begin in the fall – and often before the debate on the address has been completed, coupled with the leniency with which the rules of relevancy are applied, has meant that there has been a great deal of duplication in the two debates. Government and Opposition leaders usually confine their speeches to the Government programme for the session and to the fiscal policy of the Government in the throne and budget debates, respectively, but some backbenchers on both sides of the House range over much the same material in both debates and, not infrequently, repeat themselves while doing so. On top of this, it is sometimes the case that the same ground is gone over again during the consideration of the estimates by the Committee of Supply, and the Clerk of the Legislative Assembly has remarked that proceedings in the Committee of Supply amount to something approaching a whole series of throne and budget debates.[93] Suggestions have

[92]Some 5 per cent of the time was taken up with other things such as speaker's rulings, interjections, etc.

[93]Roderick Lewis, "Memorandum to the Select Committee on Administrative and Executive Problems of Government," p. 19.

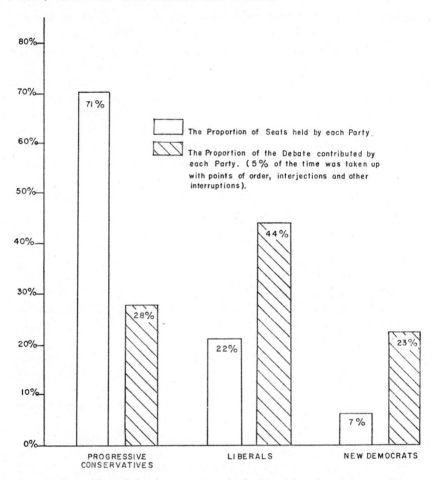

FIG. 14. Proportion of the time spent on the budget debate by each party in the 1964 session.

been made to eliminate some of this duplication either by curtailing the length of time spent in these debates or by getting private members to agree to speak on only one of the general debates.[94] Some have also suggested that if ministers were required to make their departmental reports during one of the general debates instead of waiting until the presentation of their estimates in Committee of Supply, a good deal of overlapping could be

[94]Members are not unanimous in the opinion that this kind of duplication should be eliminated. In particular, some opposition members feel that the more times they can drive home their points the better.

eliminated.[95] So far little progress has been made in any of these directions. In the session of 1964 the address in reply to the speech from the throne was debated on fifteen different days and the budget debate extended over twelve separate sittings. Seventeen members spoke on both debates and so delivered over half of the speeches that were made. The same points were often not only reiterated by the same speaker in both debates but by other MPPS as well. During Committee of Supply, long ministerial statements were the rule rather than the exception, and such speeches naturally tended to encourage an answer in kind from the Opposition.

So far as legislative-executive relations are concerned it may be stated quite emphatically that the Opposition has every conceivable opportunity to perform its legitimate functions in both the throne and budget debates, with the relatively insignificant exception that minor parties do not have the right to move amendments to the main Opposition amendment to the motion for the House to go into Committee of Ways and Means. The practice of the House allows members to speak as long as they like on any subject of their choice – and there is little evidence that they have seen fit to impose any restrictions on themselves in respect to either length or subject matter. If members do not speak it is of their own choice. If what they say is insignificant, picayune, or redundant, the responsibility is also theirs. However, the effectiveness of private members is dependent upon many factors other than freedom of speech on the floor of the House during the great debates and these too must be assessed before arriving at any final judgment about their ability to criticize and check the use of executive powers.

The Formal Legislative Process

It may be that the great traditional debates are an essential feature of the parliamentary session, but to the ordinary citizen the real function of a legislature is to enact laws and, from the moment the first motion is moved to the time the last question is put, the rules which govern how legislative proposals are to be dealt with also determine the respective roles of the legislative and executive branches.

Since all of the business of the House is conducted by motions, the first

[95]In this case as well there is something to be said for the existing situation. If ministers made their reports in one of the general debates, these could not be debated in the same way as they are during Committee of Supply. When the House is in committee, members can question ministers about their reports and pursue topics to some sort of conclusion. This kind of procedure is not possible in the throne and budget debates.

step in the legislative process is the moving of a motion, which may be thought of as the opinion or wish of one member. The House will then express its opinion on the subject by either agreeing to the motion, negativing it, or amending it. However, according to the written rules, there is at least one and possibly three steps which must precede the introduction of a bill. Rule 39 stipulates that two days notice shall be given of a motion for leave to present a public bill, except for the one bill introduced on the opening day of each session. The notice includes the name of the member and the long title of the bill and is handed to the clerk of the Legislative Assembly before 5 PM on any day of sitting. The clerk then puts this information on the votes and proceedings for the same day under the heading "notices of motion" which appears after the speaker's signature. Two days later the bill appears on the order and notice paper in the section entitled "notices" under the subheading, "intention to introduce bills."

Rule 112 quotes the British North America Act to the effect that the House may not adopt or pass "any vote, resolution, address or bill for the appropriation of any part of the public revenue, or of any tax or impost, to any purpose that has not been first recommended by a message of the Lieutenant-Governor." And rule 113 specifies: "If any motion be made in the House for any public aid or charge upon the people, the consideration and debate thereof may not be presently entered upon, but shall be adjourned till such further day as the House shall think fit to appoint; and then it shall be referred to a Committee of the Whole House, before any resolution or vote of the House do pass thereupon." In other words, at least two days notice must be given before a bill is introduced and, if it is a "money bill," it probably should be preceded by a recommendation from the lieutenant governor and a financial resolution passed by the Committee of the Whole House – although the wording of rules governing these latter stipulations is somewhat vague as to whether they must actually precede the *introduction* of the bill.

The exact meaning of these rules is of little significance, however, because they have been substantially modified by practice. For example, rule 39(*b*) notwithstanding, quite frequently bills are introduced without any previous notice whatsoever.[96] So far as the recommendation of the lieutenant governor is concerned, Mr. Speaker Hipel in 1936 interpreted the quotation from the British North America Act to mean that the

[96]From a lecture by Mr. L. R. MacTavish, QC, senior legislative counsel of Ontario, at a seminar in the Junior Executive Officer Training Programme in the summer of 1963. The introduction of a number of bills on the first day of the session, in violation of Rule 39 (*b*), has already been noted.

message from the lieutenant governor had to be received before *third reading* of the bill but not prior to its *introduction,* and he applied the same reasoning to the rule requiring a resolution from the Committee of the Whole.[97] To bolster this interpretation he searched the records and found that of the 254 money bills introduced in the previous thirty years only 12 had been preceded by the supporting resolution. The current practice followed in the case of money bills is as follows. When the bill has been introduced and given a number, the legislative counsel's office prepares the necessary resolution and gives it to the clerk of the Legislative Assembly. When the bill has received second reading, the clerk puts it and the resolution related to it under the order for Committee of the Whole House, which is listed under the heading "government bills and orders" on the order and notice paper. (He also sends a copy to the lieutenant governor for his signature.) The House goes into Committee of the Whole House when the order is called. When the prime minister calls a bill which has a resolution attached to it, the clerk of the House stands and reads the resolution. The chairman asks: "Shall the Resolution be concurred in?" Hearing no objections he says "Carried," and the clerk calls the number of the bill to which the resolution relates. When the Committee of the Whole House rises, the chairman reports the resolutions with the bills that have been passed and upon the adoption of this report the bills are ready for third reading.[98]

How do these rules affect the private member? Of primary importance is the fact that any member may introduce as many public bills as he desires, as long as they do not call for either the appropriation of any public revenue or the imposition of any tax, in which case they would have to be introduced by a minister of the crown. The House could conceivably refuse to grant leave to a member to introduce a certain bill but such action would be considered highly discourteous to the honourable member concerned and is, in fact, never done.[99] It should also be noted that in Ontario the introduction and first reading of a bill are done at the same time. For example, when the speaker puts the question, he uses this form: "Mr. ———— moves, seconded by Mr. ———— That leave be given to introduce a Bill entitled 'An Act to . . .' and that the same be now read the

[97]Lewis, *Parliamentary Procedure in Ontario,* pp. 249–50.

[98]From interviews with Mr. Roderick Lewis on August 19, 1964, and July 7, 1965. Until 1947 the orders for these resolutions were placed on the order paper under the heading "government notices of motion" and remained there until the prime minister brought them forward sometime when the House was in Committee. The bills connected with the resolutions would usually not come before the House until some days later.

[99]More will be said about private members' bills and resolutions in chap. 6.

first time." Since, according to rule 54, a motion for first reading must be decided by the House without amendment or debate, the motion to introduce a bill is likewise exempted from debate. In practice, then, both the motion to introduce a bill and the motion for its first reading are taken together and are non-debatable. Until the 1965 session, only ministers were allowed to make statements on first readings, but now this privilege has been extended to all members whether or not they are specifically asked to explain their bills. It also ought to be mentioned that there is nothing in the rules to prevent the House from debating the resolutions which accompany money bills, but in practice few such debates ever take place.

The position of the MPP in Ontario in these initial stages of the formal legislative process becomes apparent when it is compared to the situations obtaining at Ottawa and Westminster. In the Canadian House of Commons any member may introduce a bill and even private members are permitted to give brief explanations.[100] However, since 1913 the motion for leave to introduce a bill is no longer debatable[101] and once this question has been decided in the affirmative, the separate question, "That this Bill be *now* read a first time," must also be decided without debate or amendment.[102] In practice this is very similar to the procedure in Ontario, although technically the Ontario rules are a little more generous in that they do not specifically forbid debate on the motion to introduce bills. So far as the resolutions for money bills are concerned, standing order 61 of the Canadian House of Commons is identical to rule 113 in Ontario. But, as already indicated, practice in Ontario has so modified the original intent of this rule as to almost do away with the resolution stage, which has become a mere brief formality. At Ottawa, however, the House in Committee on a Resolution is a distinct stage in the passing of a money bill, and, in spite of the obvious duplication and inefficiency involved, there is often fairly lengthy debate before the resolution is passed.

In the United Kingdom the pressure of business has resulted in a number of restrictions on debate in the initial stages of the legislative process. In the first place, private members have little chance even to introduce bills. Although there are other possibilities – for example, the "ten minute rule" – most private members' bills are introduced upon written notice in the same manner as Government bills. However, only twenty bills may be introduced in this manner, and the 250 to 300 members who wish to give their schemes legislative effect must ballot for the

---

[100]Standing order 71 (2).
[101]Dawson, *Procedure in the Canadian House of Commons*, p. 230.
[102]Standing order 73.

privilege of being numbered among this favoured few.[103] Secondly, there is usually no opportunity for members to debate Government bills until second reading. The procedure whereby bills may be introduced on motion has fallen into disuse, and virtually all Government bills are introduced on written notice as prescribed in standing order 35. The procedure in this case is as follows. On the day on which the bill is to be introduced the order paper will have an entry giving the long title and the short title of the bill and the name of the minister introducing it. At the appropriate time the speaker will call upon him; he will then rise and bow, and the clerk will read out the short title of the bill. The speaker then asks the minister to name a day for second reading and repeats this information to the House. These very brief formalities constitute introduction and first reading, and, since there is no motion before the House, there can be no debate.[104] Up until 1938, money bills had to be preceded by a resolution in Committee of the Whole House, and this provided for a general debate on the bill before it even received first reading. Since then all Government bills proposing the expenditure of public money must receive authorization by a financial resolution, but this now takes place after second reading. The object of this change was to reduce the likelihood of debate on the resolution, since the principle of the bill would have been agreed to already, and this has been the result.[105]

From this brief comparison it may be seen that the backbencher in Ontario is in a position somewhere between the Canadian and British members so far as his opportunities to initiate legislation and debate Government bills in their early stages are concerned. The federal MP is in a slightly more advantageous position because he has the same freedom to introduce bills as his provincial counterpart but more specific opportunities to debate the Government's money bills. However, the British member is far worse off, having only about a one-in-twelve chance to introduce his own bill and little or no opportunity to debate Government legislation before it comes up for second reading. When making these comparisons, it should be noted of course that, on the one hand, the opportunity to introduce private members' bills and resolutions is not very significant if there is little time to debate them and no chance of any of them passing, and, on the other hand, the inability to debate Government bills in their early stages is hardly important if there is ample time for

[103]Richards, *Honourable Members*, p. 204.

[104]Taylor, *The House of Commons at Work*, pp. 136–7. Mr. Taylor discusses the procedure for introducing a bill upon a motion for leave to bring in a bill on pp. 151–2 of his book, but this procedure is used so rarely that it does not warrant our attention here.

[105]*Ibid.*, pp. 154–5.

debate on second reading, as there is in Ontario. Final judgment on the position of the Ontario member as compared to those of his counterparts in Britain and Canada must therefore be reserved until the end of the discussion of the procedures governing the formal legislative processes in the three jurisdictions.

Before proceeding to a discussion of the other stages through which bills must pass, something more should be said about one practice which is apparently peculiar to the Ontario legislature, namely, the habit of ministers making explanatory statements on bills immediately after they have received first reading. The nature of the procedures used for introducing bills in the United Kingdom makes such statements quite unlikely. In Ottawa it is quite common for ministers to make brief statements when introducing bills, but this is done *before* they are given first reading.

The procedure at Queen's Park is distinctive in two ways: the statements are made *after* first reading has already been agreed to, and they are sometimes major speeches. The practice is of recent origin and was introduced mainly in response to Opposition demands. In 1960, for example, when the Hon. Mr. Spooner moved first reading of the Wild Rice Harvesting Act, Mr. Wren, the member for Kenora, asked for an explanation, but the Minister replied that he would give a complete explanation on second reading. The following exchange then took place:

> **Mr. Wintermeyer:** Mr. Speaker, is it not customary to make some brief explanation of the significance of the Bill on the occasion of first reading?
> **Hon. Mr. Spooner:** Not usually on first reading.
> **Mr. Wintermeyer:** I believe the hon. member for Kenora has asked exactly for that. . . .
> **Hon. Mr. Spooner:** It is departing from the usual practice.[106]

Since 1960 it has become customary for ministers to make explanations of bills following first reading, even if members do not request such information. The Opposition has become very critical of the practice, primarily on the grounds that such statements are not subject to debate because there is no motion before the House when they are made. Ministers will sometimes use these opportunities to set out Government policy and attack their critics but the Opposition members have no right to reply. Thus the Government is able to capture all the publicity attendant upon the introduction of new legislation while avoiding any possible criticism from the Opposition. In the session of 1964, 136 ministerial statements were made at this stage of proceedings. Together they took up some two-and-one-half hours of the time of the House.

[106]*Debates*, January 28, 1960, p. 35.

It may well be argued that statements by ministers upon the introduction of their bills is a service to the Opposition. It takes at least one day for bills to be printed, and unless some statement of their content is made most Opposition members would not know what they were about until copies were placed in their binders, since only one copy is made available to each party in the Opposition at the time of first reading.[107] Until something is done to prevent bills being called for second reading before members have had ample time to study them, it probably *is* necessary for ministers to offer brief explanations when they are introduced, and surely no Opposition member would complain if all of these statements were kept short and to the point. The problem is, however, that not all of them are short. One such statement in the 1964 session went on for nearly half an hour.[108] In the 1965 session, the statement following first reading of the Medical Services Insurance Bill ran to five pages of Hansard. On the latter occasion, the Leader of the New Democratic party, Mr. MacDonald, complained that the Minister was making a political speech instead of a short statement of explanation. Rising on a point of order he said:

It is one thing to give a short explanatory statement on first reading, which the rules permit when there is going to be no debate. It is another thing for the hon. Minister to get up and to indulge in highly controversial political debate when we on this side of the House are going to have no opportunity to say anything until second reading comes.[109]

A similar tactic used by cabinet ministers is the statement before the orders of the day. Again, since these statements are made at a time when no particular motion is before the House, there is no right of reply available to the Opposition. In the 1964 session forty-four such statements were made, averaging more than five minutes each in length and taking up a total of nearly four hours.[110] As in the case of statements following first reading, there is a useful place for some speeches by ministers, aside from those allowed in the normal proceedings of the House. Sir Erskine May says they may be made by ministers on behalf of the Government regarding policy: "stating the advice they have tendered to the Sovereign regarding their retention of office or the dissolution of Parlia-

[107]This argument was suggested by Mr. Dalton Bales (PC: York Mills) in an interview on May 17, 1965.

[108]This was Premier Robarts' statement following the introduction of the bills to establish a Department of University Affairs and to incorporate the Ontario Universities' Capital Aid Corporation. *Debates*, April 22, 1964, pp. 2332–6.

[109]*Debates*, May 11, 1965, p. 2759.

[110]Only speeches by cabinet ministers are considered here. Statements of a ceremonial nature—such as those honouring the birthdays of famous men, marking certain holidays or acknowledging athletic achievements—are excluded.

ment; announcing the legislative proposals they intend to submit to Parliament; or the course they intend to adopt in the transaction and arrangement of public business."[111] The complaint by the Opposition in Ontario is that ministers too often go far beyond these limits in their statements before the orders of the day. For example, in the 1964 session the Minister of Economics and Development, Mr. Randall, rose before the orders were called in order to reply to certain remarks made at the previous sitting by Mr. Sargent, the Liberal member for Grey North, in his maiden speech delivered during the throne debate.[112] When the Minister had spoken for twenty minutes – answering the charges that had been made and castigating Mr. Sargent for *inter alia* attempting "to make political capital out of a genuine effort of this government to assist the employment situation" – Mr. Bryden (NDP, Woodbine) rose to call the attention of the Speaker to the "persistent abuse by the government of the right of hon. Ministers to make statements before the Orders of the day." Mr. Bryden contended that the Minister's remarks would have made a proper contribution to the Throne debate, and, after some discussion of the point, the Speaker agreed and asked the Minister to desist from "any further remarks regarding the member for Grey North and his intentions." While the Opposition won a technical victory on that occasion, it did not succeed in stopping the abuse of ministerial statements entirely. The Government continues to use them for purposes other than those for which they were intended, much to the annoyance of the Opposition members.

The procedure followed at the second reading stage of the formal legislative process in Ontario is quite similar to that of the British and Canadian lower Houses. Rule 55 stipulates that, except by unanimous consent of the House, no bill may be read the second time until it is printed, distributed, and marked "printed" on the order paper. In recent sessions a further stipulation has been added informally: no bill may be called for second reading until it has been in the members' binders for at least twenty-four hours. Thus, in practice, there are usually two days between first and second readings of a bill, one day for printing and one day for the members to study the proposed legislation. Before the 1965 session this one-day waiting period was even more important because there were usually no copies of bills made available at first reading, except one to the clerk of the House to give to the printer and one for the press gallery. Now, however, one copy of the bill is given to each opposition

[111]May, *Parliamentary Practice*, p. 358.
[112]*Debates*, February 3, 1964, pp. 372 ff.

party immediately after first reading so that the members are at least as well informed as the reporters.

The fate of any bill is usually decided at the second reading which, if granted, constitutes approval of the principle of the proposed act. On occasion this is a mere formality with no debate whatsoever. Sometimes when this happens the Government may want to force the Opposition to record either agreement or disagreement with the bill and will therefore insist on a recorded vote. If there has been debate on the motion for second reading, the Opposition will sometimes force a formal division of the House on the question.[113]

Second reading debates are quite strictly limited. Members are not supposed to discuss anything but the principle of the bill before them, not the details of the bill nor matters outside the subject matter of the bill. Since no member is allowed to speak more than once, it is quite improper to ask questions of the person sponsoring the bill. The detailed provisions of the bill are not subject to amendment at second reading, but only the motion "that the Bill be now read the second time." A direct negative decision on this motion does not actually remove the bill from future consideration by the House but merely decides that it shall not be read the second time "now." It still remains on the order paper, and technically the sponsor may have another opportunity to bring it forward. Hence, the ordinary method used to remove a bill from possible further consideration is to move a "hoist," that is, that the bill "be not now read a second time but be read a second time this day six months." If such an amendment carries, the session will have prorogued before the day set, and the bill will have automatically lapsed.[114] It is also possible to move what is known as a "reasoned amendment" if a member wishes to make known his special reasons for not agreeing to the second reading of a bill. Such an amendment takes the form of a motion to leave out all the words in the main

[113]In the 1964 session the House actually divided on motions for second reading on only four occasions (second reading of Bill 41 was declared carried on the same division as Bill 40, although the House did not actually divide), all at the insistence of the Opposition, and one of these divisions was both unnecessary and contrary to rule 56. A "reasoned amendment" to the motion for second reading had already been defeated, and, according to rule 56, the Speaker should have forthwith declared the bill to be read a second time. However, since the Liberal members had opposed the amendment this would have technically left them voting for second reading of the bill, to which they were also opposed. The way out of this dilemma was provided by the Speaker who ruled that rule 56 only applied to hoist motions. *Debates*, March 4, 1964, pp. 1263–4.

[114]Lewis, *Parliamentary Procedure in Ontario*, p. 57. Even if the House were still in session when the six-month period was over, the bill would probably not be called again, since the intention of the "hoist" is obviously to "kill" the bill.

question after the word "that" and to add other words.[115] However, in Ontario neither type of amendment is very common because few bills are important enough to warrant such attention, and since one tactic is as futile as another, Opposition members are generally content to register their dissatisfaction by simply voting against the main motion. In the 1964 session there was only one occasion when the Opposition moved an amendment to a motion for second reading.[116] When an order for the second reading of a bill has been called there is one other way in which it can be disposed of: the member in charge of the bill may move that the order be discharged.[117] This method is rarely implemented, but it was used by the Government to remove the infamous Bill 99 and four other bills from the order paper in 1964.[118]

The Ontario Legislative Assembly has incorporated into its rules the standing order adopted by the British House of Commons in 1919, which in effect allows only one amendment to the motion for second reading in most cases.[119] Rule 56 reads: "If on an amendment to the question that a Bill be now read a second time or the third time, it is decided that the word 'now' or any other words proposed to be left out stand part of the question, Mr. Speaker shall forthwith declare the Bill to be read a second or the third time, as the case may be." Although the Canadian House of Com-

[115]May, *Parliamentary Practice*, p. 527.

[116]This was a reasoned amendment to the effect that the motion for second reading of the bill to amend the Gasoline Tax Act should be amended by striking out all the words after "that" and substituting the following: "in the opinion of this House the government should give consideration to the imposition of a weight-distance tax in preference to an increase in the gasoline tax." *Journals*, 1963–64, p. 78.

[117]May, *Parliamentary Practice*, p. 387.

[118]*Journals*, 1963–64, pp. 107, 138. In the first case, the motion "that the Order of the Day for second reading of Bill 99 be discharged and that the Bill be referred forthwith to the Standing Committee on Labour, Legal and Municipal Bills for consideration, examination and report" was actually moved by Mr. Robarts and not by Mr. Cass, who was originally responsible for the Act. Although this appears to have contravened the practice of the British House of Commons, which should normally be followed in Ontario, it may have been that Mr. Cass had already tendered his resignation by that time. In any case he was not in the House. The other four bills were discharged on the motion of the new Attorney General, Mr. Wishart. There was a great deal of opposition to the motions to discharge these bills and refer them to a standing committee, but the Opposition was not directed towards that aspect of the motions dealing with the discharging of the orders but towards the aspect referring them to a standing committee. To refer them to a committee at that stage appeared to the Opposition members as a clear violation of rule 60 which states: "Every Public Bill should be read twice in the House before commital or amendment." It looked as if the Government was trying to avoid an embarrassing division in their party, since some Conservative members had publicly denounced the bills.

[119]Jennings, *Parliament*, p. 253.

mons has not adopted a similar standing order, the same rule nevertheless holds.[120] However, until the 1965 session, speakers of the Ontario House interpreted this rule to apply only to hoist motions so that a negation of other types of amendments did not rule out a division on the original motion for second reading as well.[121] This was confusing to members, and towards the end of the 1965 session the Speaker announced that the literal meaning of rule 56 would be followed in the future.[122]

When one considers the popular image of the legislature as an institution for making laws, it is interesting to note the proportion of the time of the House that is actually devoted to the discussion of specific items of legislation (*see* Fig. 12). The second reading of Government bills, generally considered the most important stage in the formal legislative process, occupied the House for only 4.8 per cent of its time in the 1964 session. Of the 135 Government bills which received second reading in that session, only 24, or 17 per cent, were debated, and the debates on these bills averaged only thirty-three minutes each. The other 111 bills, or 83 per cent of the total, were given second reading without debate or division. Obviously, the members of the Opposition do not look upon this stage of proceedings in the House as particularly useful for their purposes, probably because so few of the bills are really very significant.

Omitting the role of the standing committees – which was dealt with in the last chapter – the third stage through which all bills must pass on their way to becoming statutes is consideration by the Committee of the Whole House. This is one of the distinguishing features of the British parliamentary system that has been adopted by the province of Ontario, as it has in most places where British institutions have been copied.[123] Until quite recently the Committee was "appointed" anew for each bill, the order paper showing a separate order of the day for House in committee on each, and theoretically debate would have been permissible on the motion to go into Committee of the Whole for every bill that reached that stage. To streamline procedures and bring the form of the order paper into conformity with the practice of the House, the Clerk of the Legislative Assembly, Mr. Lewis, suggested to the Select Committee on Administrative and Executive Problems, appointed in 1960, that there should be only one order of the day for the House to resolve itself into Committee of Bills. All bills standing referred to the Committee of the Whole could then be listed under this order. The clerk would read the order and the speaker

---

[120]Beauchesne, *Rules and Forms*, pp. 169–70.

[121]For example, see n. 113.

[122]*Debates*, June 21, 1965, p. 4424.

[123]The Committee of the Whole House is not used in continental European parliaments. Campion and Lidderdale, *European Parliamentary Procedure*, p. 35.

would leave the chair without putting any question.[124] Another select committee appointed in 1960, on the Transaction of Business in the Legislature, accepted this suggestion and incorporated it into its report as recommendation number seven.[125] No formal action was ever taken on this committee report, but this particular recommendation has been given effect in practice so that the House now goes into Committee of the Whole automatically when the House Leader calls the order.

At Queen's Park the Committee of the Whole House serves two primary functions: it passes the resolutions which accompany money bills,[126] and it considers the detailed provisions of all bills. All public bills, except the supply bill, and all private bills are referred to the Committee of the Whole, either immediately after second reading or on being reported back by a standing committee.[127] If a bill is referred to a standing committee, it is technically possible for the House to debate its report, in which case another stage would be added to the legislative process. However, in practice such debates seldom occur.

When bills are before the Committee of the Whole House, they are supposed to be considered section by section. The principle of each bill has already been accepted by the House and usually there is no general debate such as takes place at Ottawa.[128] Rule 96(*b*) requires that "speeches in Committee of the Whole House must be strictly relevant to the item or clause under consideration," and there are few violations of this. It is at this stage that bills may be amended. Most of the amendments made at this point come from the departments concerned with the bills. Amendments which have not been introduced by the Government, or at least adopted by the Government, have very little hope of success.[129] If an

[124]Lewis, Memorandum to the Select Committee on Administrative and Executive Problems of Government, p. 3.

[125]Ontario, Legislative Assembly, Select Committee Appointed April 11th, 1960, to Study and Inquire into Matters Pertaining to the Transaction of Business in the Legislature, *Report*, p. 6.

[126]This function has already been discussed in some detail on pp. 162–63.

[127]If there is no indication to the contrary from the responsible minister, each bill is automatically referred to the Committee of the Whole. If the minister wants a particular bill to go before one of the standing committees, he is expected to state this during second reading proceedings. Not infrequently, the clerk of the House has to go to the minister after a bill has been read the second time in order to find out where he would like it to go.

[128]Although the rules strictly forbid it, the Committee of the Whole in the House of Commons of Canada holds a general debate, similar to that on second reading, when clause one is called. Dawson, *Procedure in the Canadian House of Commons*, p. 234.

[129]Kenneth Bryden, "Committees of the Ontario Legislature," an unpublished paper prepared for a graduate seminar in public administration conducted by Professors W. E. Grasham and M. Brownstone, April 15, 1965, p. 3.

amendment moved by a member of the Opposition seems to the minister to have some merit, he will usually wait a day or so – until the department has had a chance to study it – before deciding to accept it or have it rejected.

It will be seen readily from Figure 12 that proceedings on public bills and resolutions in Committee of the Whole do not occupy much of the time of the House. If the amount of time taken up by the purely formal proceedings is subtracted, the House actually spent half an hour less on this function than it did on ministerial statements before the orders of the day in the 1964 session. In other words, the House spent less time on what is popularly considered to be a major function of legislative bodies than it did on proceedings which the Opposition considered to be frequently out of order. In that session, 134 Government bills were called in Committee of the Whole, but only 17 were debated. The 17 which were discussed occupied approximately three hours of the time of the House, an average of eleven minutes each. If one hour is added to this total to cover mere formalities, the total time of the House expended in the consideration of Government bills and financial resolutions in Committee of the Whole amounted to only 1.4 per cent of the total time of the session.

It must be made clear that the small amount of time used for this purpose is not the consequence of any particular strategem devised by the Government – except, perhaps, the late introduction of legislative proposals – because there is nothing at all to stop members from proposing and debating amendments to Bills, except their own taciturnity during these proceedings. Why is it, then, that members do not utilize these opportunities more fully? A number of reasons may be suggested.

First, if a member is opposed to a bill in its entirety, the place to voice this opposition is during second reading and not during committee proceedings. However, it has already been noted that second readings are not very frequently debated either, so this is not a complete answer to the question of why so little is said at committee stage. A second possible reason is that the throne and budget debates provide far better occasions for criticizing the Government in a general way, and members find greater rewards for their efforts there – in the coinage of publicity – than in the proceedings on bills. Thirdly, debates on second reading and on amendments in Committee of the Whole House tend by their very nature to be somewhat hypothetical. Since the legislation is new, it is not always easy to foresee exactly what results it will have nor how any specific amendment will modify its effects. A fourth conceivable reason why members do not make much effort to improve upon bills when they come before the committee, is the crass political one: either they do not want to embarrass the Government, or they do not want to assist the Government – depending upon which side of the speaker they happen to sit. If a member belongs to the governing party he will make his suggestions to the minister privately; and if he belongs to another party he will keep his ideas to himself in the hope that he will be able to use the points either in a forthcoming election campaign or, more optimistically, as a piece of legislation when his side "gets in." But, fifthly, probably the chief reason why members do not bother to debate Government legislative proposals is because they are simply routine in nature and do not merit the attention of the House. Besides, if a bill has already been to a standing committee it may have received sufficient consideration there.

The House in Committee stage ends for each bill when, after all of the sections have been called, the chairman says, "Shall the Bill be Reported?" and, if he hears no objections, "Carried." There is seldom any debate or division at this point because all the bill's sections have been agreed to already. Likewise, there is no debate or division when the prime minister decides to move "that the Committee rise and report certain Bills without amendment and certain Bills with amendments and certain Resolutions and ask for leave to sit again." The House must receive the report forthwith. Rule 62 allows debate and amendment after report if the bill was amended in committee, but any debate at this point would be clearly redundant and in fact rarely occurs. If a bill is reported without amendment, it is "forthwith ordered to be read a third time, at such time as may be appointed by the House." If a bill is amended in committee, it must be reprinted before it can receive third reading.

Like most parliaments, the Ontario House generally considers third reading a mere formality. In the 1964 session only three bills were debated at all, and these for an average of less than five minutes each.[130] One amendment was declared to be out of order because it was neither a hoist motion nor a reasoned amendment but a hybrid motion designed to delay the bill.[131] However, the House did divide on a simple hoist motion to another bill.[132] Except for the Supply Bill, which was given third reading on the last day of the session, all bills received third reading on one of two days; either on March 25, just before royal assent, or on May 7, the day before prorogation. Including the Speaker's rulings and all formalities

---

[130]Debate on third reading is such an unusual occurrence that when the Leader of the New Democratic party began to speak on third reading of Bill 99, a leading parliamentarian in the House, Mr. Vernon Singer, objected, claiming there could be no debate at this stage. *Debates*, May 7, 1964, p. 3032.

[131]*Ibid.*, p. 2004.

[132]*Ibid.*, p. 2005.

except the formal division,[133] third reading in the 1964 session only took up approximately half an hour, or 0.2 per cent of the total time of the session.

With only 8.2 per cent of the time of the session devoted to processing Government legislation, it may be justifiable to conclude that members do not look upon the formal legislative process as a particularly useful occasion for the exercise of their talents. Possible explanations for this reticence have already been suggested, but the basic reason must be that other opportunities provide more scope for criticism with less risk. Whereas in the legislative process the Government takes the initiative, captures the publicity and usually holds its own in debate, at other times the members of the Opposition have opportunity to choose the focal point of debate and thus to win some attention and put the Government on the defensive. Similarly, if the Opposition delays passage of Government legislation – which invariably includes some popular measures – it lays itself open to the charge of obstruction; but if it raises general criticisms in the throne debate, objects to certain taxes in the budget debate, investigates Government expenditures in the Committee of Supply, introduces its own legislative proposals in the form of private members' bills, or utilizes any of the other special procedures specifically designed for its use, it is thought to be exercising its legitimate prerogatives.

[133]Mr. J. J. Young, clerk of the executive council, estimates that the average division takes approximately ten minutes to complete. Divisions are not included in any of the calculations in this chapter and therefore fall into the "other" category in Figure 12.

PARLIAMENTARY
PROCEDURE:
PRIVATE MEMBERS'
BUSINESS,
QUESTIONS, AND
SPECIAL
PROCEDURES

6

Private Members' Business

RULE 28 GIVES private members' business precedence on Mondays, Wednesdays, and Fridays throughout the session but, as was pointed out in the previous chapter, the order of business set out in the rules was completely ignored in practice and until 1966 it was left to the prime minister to decide if and when private members' orders were to be called. The inappropriateness of such a practice was readily apparent, and nearly all of those who suggested amending the rules recommended that definite times throughout the session be set aside for the consideration of private members' legislative proposals.[1] At Ottawa for many years six Mondays and two Thursdays were set aside early in the session for this purpose, but in the 1960–61 session these eight days were replaced by forty one-hour periods, one hour on each of the first three days of each week.[2] At

[1]For example, the select committee appointed to inquire into the revision of the rules of the Legislative Assembly in 1946 recommended that private members' business have precedence on Wednesdays (Ontario, Legislative Assembly, *Journals*, 1947, p. 26. Hereinafter, the short title, *Journals*, will be used to refer to the Journals of the Legislative Assembly of Ontario), and the select committee appointed in 1960 to study matters pertaining to the transaction of business in the legislature recommended that private members' business "have precedence on Mondays and Fridays immediately after Third Readings, in the first hour and a half after the commencement of the day's sittings" (Ontario, Legislative Assembly, Select Committee Appointed on April 11th, 1960, to Study and Inquire into Matters Pertaining to the Transaction of Business in the Legislature, *Report*, p. 2. Hereinafter this Committee will be called the Committee on the Transaction of Business).

[2]R. M. Dawson, *The Government of Canada* (4th ed. revised by Norman Ward; Toronto: University of Toronto Press, 1963), p. 384.

Westminster the dominance of the Government over the parliamentary timetable steadily increased from the beginning of the nineteenth century, when only one day a week was reserved for the Government, to the period of the second world war, when no time whatsoever was left for private members. During the reconstruction period following the war the opportunities of private members were again sacrificed for the sake of Government legislation. However, since the 1950 session backbenchers have usually had the use of twenty Fridays, ten for bills and ten for motions.[3]

Private members' business in Ontario takes the form of either *private members' bills*, which in official publications go under the title "public bills" to distinguish them from "Government bills," or *Resolutions*, which are sometimes referred to as "notices of motion." In other parliaments the opportunities for ordinary members to make their legislative wishes known are considered a very important means for influencing or attacking the Government and something should be said about the effectiveness of both private members' bills and resolutions in Ontario.[4]

The reduction in the amount of time allotted to private members in the Ontario Assembly has been at least as marked as in other parliaments, and the number of private members' bills and resolutions that is finally passed has been reduced to nil. In the first session of the provincial parliament in 1867–68, the backbenchers were more active than the members of the executive council in initiating legislation, and although most of their bills were listed as "private" there was no doubt that many of them were of a "public" nature. When, following the New Year's recess, the Government had only two bills to introduce while a private member, Sir Henry Smith, had no less than five, the *Globe* remarked: "If the Attorney General is not careful it will soon become a doubtful point whether he or Sir Henry Smith is to lead the House, and direct its legislation."[5] Eventually Premier Macdonald resumed some control over the legislative programme, but by the end of the session private members had introduced fifty bills, twenty-four of which had passed as separate statutes and two of which had been incorporated into other acts.[6] Even after the Opposition

[3]Peter G. Richards, *Honourable Members: a Study of the British Backbencher* (2nd ed.; London, Faber & Faber, 1964), pp. 201–2.

[4]The opportunities and procedures for *introducing* private members' Bills and Resolutions have been described on pp. 163–66.

[5]Quoted in Adam Shortt and Arthur G. Doughty, eds., *Canada and its Provinces: A History of the Canadian People and their Institutions by One Hundred Associates*, vol. 17, *The Province of Ontario* (Toronto and Glasgow: Brook & Company, 1914), p. 112.

[6]The 24 private members' bills passed constituted 30 per cent of the 79 statutes enacted that session.

TABLE 13

PRIVATE MEMBERS' BILLS INTRODUCED AND PASSED IN
SELECTED YEARS 1900–60

Year	Number introduced	Number passed	Number embodied	Total enacted
1900	110	12	19	31
1905	63	10	2	12
1910	75	16	20	36
1915	57	7	20	27
1920	104	37	18	55
1925	46	16	14	30
1930	42	5	26	31
1935	27	12	6	18
1940	9	—	3	3
1945	27	—	—	—
1950	22	—	—	—
1955	2	—	—	—
1960	12	—	—	—

SOURCE: Data derived from the register of bills compiled
by the legislative counsel's office, the *Bills of Ontario*, and
the *Journals* for the years concerned.

became established and party discipline was applied, private members
continued to be responsible for a large proportion of the bills introduced
in the early years of the province.

The trend in this century is set out in Table 13 and depicted in graph
form in Figure 15. Under the heading "embodied" in Table 13 are included all bills which were introduced by private members but which were
accepted by the Government and incorporated into one or other of the
general acts governing large legislative fields. For example, the bulk of
these bills concerned municipal affairs, and, upon the recommendation of
the Committee on Municipal Law, they were generally embodied in one
bill entitled the Municipal Amendment Act.[7] With the creation of the
Department of Municipal Affairs in 1934 to administer this area of government concern, such bills became unnecessary and/or an embarrassment to the Government and hence lost their place in the legislative
process. The unusually large number of private members' bills passed in
1920 is a reflection of the attempt on the part of the UFO government of
that time to return to the undisciplined pattern of an earlier day. Premier
Drury made his desires in this respect known in his first speech to the
House:

We invite the co-operation of the gentlemen on the other side of the House. We
invite you to come to us with your suggestions, and I think among us we can

[7]In 1930, for instance, of the 22 separate bills introduced to amend the Municipal
Act, 21 were incorporated into Bill 163, The Municipal Amendment Act, 1930.

loosen up a whole lot of these unreasonable parliamentary rules that have grown up more in the last forty years than ever before when the House has resolved itself into two cast-iron sections.[8]

The leader of the UFO government suggested that legislation should be the responsibility of all members of the legislature instead of emerging full-blown from the cabinet and being passed by a submissive majority. Although he eventually had to give up his idea of a co-operative business government in the face of charges from the Opposition that he was neglecting his responsibility, private members probably enjoyed greater freedom under his regime than at any other time in the province's history.

Figure 16 depicts the proportions of the legislative output accounted for by Government, private, and private members' legislation in selected years of this century. As one would expect, the decline and eventual elimination of private members' legislation is more than compensated for by an increase in Government legislation. Since the war, private legislation has also declined as a proportion of total legislative output. Since the end of the second world war there have been only half a dozen private members' bills passed, and none has been placed on the statute book since 1954.[9]

This leaves the private member of the Ontario legislature in a far worse position than his counterparts in Ottawa or Westminster. Even in the United Kingdom, where the burden of Government legislation is much greater than that experienced at Ottawa, let alone Queen's Park, a few private members' bills still become law in most sessions. For example, in 1951–52, twelve became law; in 1955–56, eighteen became law; and in 1959–60, nineteen became law.[10] The fact that no private members' bills have been successful in Ontario in more than a decade helps to explain

[8]Toronto *Globe*, March 17, 1920, as quoted in Jean MacLeod, "The United Farmer Movement in Ontario, 1914 – 1943," an MA thesis submitted to the Department of Political and Economic Science of Queen's University, 1957, p. 86.

[9]The last private members' bill passed in Ontario was an Act to amend the Theatres Act. This Act was sponsored in 1954 by H. C. Nixon, a former premier, and a highly respected senior member of the House (*Statutes of Ontario (SO)*, 1954, c. 96). In the 1965 session there was another public bill introduced by a private member that became law, but it hardly merited the description "private members' bill" because it was really a Government bill introduced by a private member as a matter of courtesy. The Bill had to do with the University of Ottawa and was introduced by Mr. Guindon (PC: Stormont), the only graduate of the University of Ottawa in the House. The motion to introduce the Bill was seconded by a Minister. *SO*, 1965, c. 137 and Ontario, Legislative Assembly, *Debates*, May 27, 1965, p. 3300. Hereinafter the *Debates* of the Legislature of Ontario will be referred to simply as the *Debates*).

[10]Eric Taylor, *The House of Commons at Work* (4th ed.; Middlesex: Penguin, 1961), p. 131, n. 1.

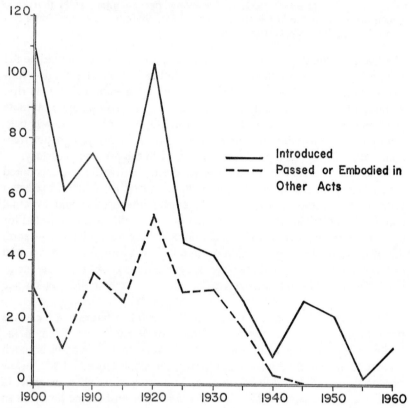

Fig. 15. Private members' bills introduced and passed in the Legislative Assembly of Ontario, 1900–60.

why such a small number are introduced in each session. During the four sessions of the 26th Parliament, 1960–63, an average of only fourteen was introduced each session, approximately half the number usually introduced in the House of Commons of the United Kingdom. However, even this is not the complete picture of private members' legislative proposals in Ontario. The most significant fact is that during the 26th Parliament an average of only 3.25 private members' bills was debated in each session. The exact figures are set out in Table 14.

Even the term "debated" needs some qualification in this context. Only six of the thirteen bills called for second reading were discussed for half an hour or more, and the average length of time spent on each bill was just over twenty-six minutes. The total time spent on private members' bills in the four sessions of the 26th Parliament was just over five-and-a-half hours

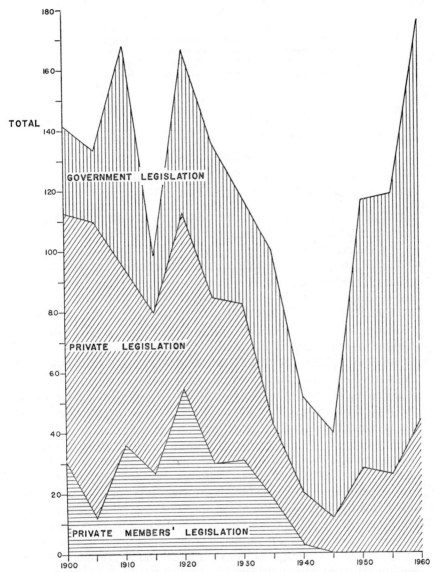

FIG. 16. Government, private, and private members' legislation passed in the Legislative Assembly of Ontario for selected years, 1900–60.

or about the equivalent of one sitting day. In the 1964 session one hour and eighteen minutes were spent discussing the three private members' bills which were called for second reading. This accounted for less than

TABLE 14

PRIVATE MEMBERS' BILLS INTRODUCED AND DEBATED
IN EACH SESSION OF THE 26TH PARLIAMENT, 1960–63

Session	Number introduced	Number debated	Length of debates
			(in minutes)
1960	12	1	24
1960–61	14	5	166
1961–62	17	4	106
1962–63	12	3	43
TOTALS	55	13	339

SOURCE: Data compiled from the *Journals* and the *Debates* for the years concerned.

half of one per cent of the total time spent in the session. It should also be borne in mind that not one of these bills ever came to a vote; debates were simply adjourned and never called again.

The responsibility for the lack of debate on private members' bills prior to the 1966 reforms necessarily rested with the prime minister who organized the business of the House and called all orders. The private members usually introduced their bills early in the session before the order paper filled up and before the Government brought in its own legislative programme. In 1960, ten private members' bills were introduced in the first month of the session. The only bill debated in that year was introduced on the twenty-first day of the session, but it lay on the order paper for more than two months before being called in the dying days of the session. In the 1960–61 session, eight bills were introduced by private members in the first month (excluding the Christmas recess). The third session, 1961–62, saw ten private members' bills on the order paper in the first month, but none was debated until the second to the last day of the session. During the 1962–63 session only three private members' bills were introduced in the first month, but eleven were on the order paper at least one month before the session prorogued. The three bills which were debated were all taken at the same sitting, four days before prorogation. The same pattern continued with the new parliament which had its first session, two days in length, in the fall of 1963. In its second session nine bills were introduced, six of them in the first month, but only three were debated and these all on the same day, about two weeks before the prorogation of the four-month-long session.

One further point should be noted about the use of private members' bills before 1966: they were used almost exclusively by members of the Opposition. From 1959 to 1965 only three public bills were introduced

TABLE 15

PRIVATE MEMBERS' RESOLUTIONS PUT ON THE NOTICE PAPER AND DEBATED
IN EACH SESSION OF THE 26TH PARLIAMENT, 1960–63

Session	Number put on the notice paper	Number debated	Length of debate (in minutes)
1960	20	5	719
1960–61	10	2	395
1961–62	6	—	—
1962–63	4	—	—
	40	7	1114

SOURCE: Data compiled from the *Order and Notice Papers*, the *Journals*, and the *Debates* for the years concerned.

by members of the Government outside the cabinet, two in the 1960 session, and one in 1965. One of those introduced in 1960 was sponsored by Allan Grossman, who later became a cabinet minister, and the other was sponsored by John White, who became chief government whip. The former was debated, the only private members' bill so honoured in the session of that year. The public bill introduced by a backbencher of the majority party in 1965 has already been mentioned.[11] Except for the fact that it was introduced by a private member it was in every respect a Government bill.

The situation with regard to private members' resolutions in the 26th Parliament is set out in Table 15. However, when calculating the proportion of resolutions which is debated, it should be borne in mind that in many sessions the subjects of some resolutions are dealt with in the course of other proceedings, such as in Committee of Supply. To debate such subjects again would be futile, and the resolutions concerned are sometimes either withdrawn or discharged at the request of the members responsible for them. Usually, however, they were just left on the order paper and the prime minister simply did not bother to call them.

Although there are certain advantages to the Opposition in using private members' bills rather than resolutions,[12] members generally agree that resolutions are both easier to use and more effective.[13] In the first place, the drafting of resolutions does not require the same care as does

[11]See n. 9.

[12]Andrew Thompson, the leader of the Ontario Liberal party, suggested that a bill is more impressive than a resolution. It looks as if the member has been more careful in doing his homework. (From an interview, May 13, 1965).

[13]This point of view was expressed by leading figures from all parties in the Ontario House in interviews with the author. For example, Dalton Bales (PC: York Mills), in an interview on May 17, 1965; Kenneth Bryden (NDP: Woodbine) in an

that of bills. However, since private members receive assistance in drafting bills from the Legislative Counsel's office, the relative ease with which a resolution may be drawn up is probably not an important consideration in very many cases.[14] Secondly, resolutions may be broader in scope and more abstract than an ordinary bill, and, if carefully worded, they may even manage to advocate the expenditure of public revenue. The broader a resolution is the less vulnerable a member is to attack on the details of his proposal. Thirdly, resolutions may be used by Government ministers without the same stigma that is usually attached to bills introduced by backbenchers of the governing party. It is one thing for a member to suggest in the House that the leaders of his party should give attention to a certain proposal and quite another thing to lay before the House a specific piece of legislation which the cabinet has apparently ignored or refused to introduce. Even so, few private members on the Government side have made use of the device of the resolution; only one of the forty put on the order paper during the 26th Parliament was from a member of the majority party. However, another one was brought in in the 1964 session and debated for nearly two hours.[15] Fourthly, it is generally thought that resolutions "go farther" than bills. Since neither type of private members' business has any hope of ultimate success, this contention is open to some discussion. The evidence provided by the 26th Parliament is of little help in settling the question. On the one hand, fewer resolutions than bills were introduced, and, while 24 per cent of the bills introduced were debated, only 17.5 per cent of the resolutions proposed were ever called for debate. On the other hand, the seven resolutions were debated for nearly nineteen hours, or for more than two-and-a-half hours apiece, while the thirteen bills were debated for only six hours, an average of only twenty-six minutes each. Also, one of the resolutions was actually brought to a vote,[16] whereas none of the private members' bills was ever so

---

interview on May 12, 1965; Vernon Singer (Lib. Downsview) in an interview on May 14, 1965; Andrew Thompson (Lib. Parkdale) in an interview on May 12, 1965; and John White (PC: London South) in an interview on May 13, 1965.

[14]Obviously, the ease with which resolutions are drafted cannot be the most important factor to be taken into account, since there are still more bills than resolutions introduced by private members.

[15]The significance of this may be somewhat diminished by the fact that it was introduced by A. F. Lawrence (PC: St. George), who had achieved a degree of notoriety through his open criticism of Conservative party leadership, notably during the Police Act episode.

[16]This was the resolution moved by Mr. Manley and seconded by Mr. Wintermeyer and debated on March 24, 1960. It is particularly interesting because it serves as a good illustration of what the Government has done in a number of similar cases. The original motion was "that this House petition the federal government to locate at Elliot Lake the nuclear research station which was scheduled for construction in

well treated. As far as the point in the session at which the orders were called is concerned, resolutions fared neither better nor worse than bills and were usually debated late in the session, in spite of the fact that most of them were also submitted in the first few weeks. In any case, in view of the very limited significance of either bills or resolutions introduced by private members at Queen's Park prior to 1966, the question of which was best is little more than academic.

This is not the case at Ottawa or Westminster, where private members' bills and resolutions are both such popular vehicles for the expression of the legislative ideas of the members that ballots must be held to decide which member's proposal shall have precedence.[17] In the 1961–62 session – when the backbenchers of the Legislative Assembly of Ontario put down six resolutions, none of which was debated – the British House of Commons had seventeen resolutions come before it, fifteen of which were debated and eight of which were passed.[18] In the 1964 session in Ontario, when seven resolutions were debated, the time spent in this way was just over four-and-a-half hours, only 1.6 per cent of the total time of the session. The House of Commons in Britain spends an average of five days on this type of business each year, nearly 3.5 per cent of the total time of the session.[19]

Since in practice there was apparently very little difference between private members' bills and private members' resolutions in Ontario before the changes introduced in 1966, they may be dealt with together in arriving at conclusions about the extent and effectiveness of private members' business in the province at that time. With regard to the extent of private members' business, the situation existing in Ontario up to 1965 was rather dismal when compared to that in other jurisdictions. The Ontario Assembly spent approximately only 2 per cent of its time on this aspect of its

---

Manitoba," but the Premier moved an amendment striking out all the words after "that" and substituting a long paragraph commending the Government for what it was already doing for Elliot Lake. By such a manoeuver the Government was able once more to assume the initiative and so evade some of the force of the original criticism. The 1964 session also witnessed a division on a private members' resolution, this one defeated without amendment. *Journals*, 1964, p. 24.

[17]See W. F. Dawson, *Procedure in the Canadian House of Commons* (Toronto: University of Toronto Press, 1962), pp. 98–101 and Sir Ivor Jennings, *Parliament* (2nd ed.; Cambridge: Cambridge University Press, 1957), pp. 360–4.

[18]These figures on the British session have been calculated from the table given in Peter G. Richards, *Honourable Members*, p. 213.

[19]This figure has been calculated from the data given in Lord Campion, *Introduction to the Procedure of the House of Commons* (3rd ed.; London: Macmillan, 1958), Appendix III, p. 337. The regular sessions from 1945 to 1955 are all included in the calculation even though no time at all was spent on resolutions in the first four of those sessions.

proceedings in the 1964 session. The British House of Commons, on the other hand, spent an average of more than 7 per cent of its time on private members' business in the ten regular sessions from 1945–46 to 1954–55.[20]

Critics of Ontario procedures argued that if private members' business was given more time and if the important decisions about the use of private members' time, such as which item should be debated, when, and for how long, were taken out of the prime minister's hands, private members' bills and resolutions could become very effective means for criticizing and so controlling the executive branch. It was true that backbenchers did have other opportunities to speak, but on most of those occasions the initiative was taken by the Government which was thus able to structure the debate along lines of its own choosing. Members of the Opposition were then limited to criticizing some action that the Government had taken or was about to take. But, it was argued, if a fixed time were set aside for private members and some unbiased means was used for assigning precedence on the order paper, members of the Opposition would have a chance to take the initiative occasionally and so capture the publicity. The Government then would have to assume a defensive position and debate on the terms laid down by the Opposition. This would put the members of the cabinet in a position which would be quite a new experience for them. It would not be possible to have their speeches written for them ahead of time – because it would be impossible to know exactly what line the Opposition was going to take – and it would be inappropriate for them to be assisted by their officials, as they are when their estimates are being considered. They would be left to their own devices, and, while the experience would probably be revealing, there is little doubt that it would also be salutary.

Advocates of reform claimed that, besides enabling the Opposition to perform better its controlling function, extending and improving private members' time would add new life to proceedings at Queen's Park. Greater variety in subject matter would probably make debates more interesting to outsiders, and the chance to put forward their own ideas would probably make the backbenchers' position more attractive to the members themselves. If a certain set time was allowed for private members' business, Government backbenchers would also have to participate or else the whole period would be monopolized by members of the Opposition. Giving these majority party members something constructive to do would lend some dignity to their position and might in the long run raise the general tenor of debate.[21] It was also argued that if a significant

---

[20]*Ibid*. The short session of 1948 was not included in his table.

[21]During other proceedings of the House, Government backbenchers hardly contribute to debates at all. The Progressive Conservative members occupy nearly

number of private members' bills and resolutions were allowed to come to a vote and if the whips were used sparingly, private members' time could become a useful forum for the expression of public opinion on specific issues.

With so many conceivable benefits to accrue to the House from a more liberal approach to private members' business and with the examples of what had been done elsewhere, why, one may ask, did the Government of Ontario give such short shrift to private members' time until 1966? The reason could hardly have been the press of Government business, because the House has since very easily extended its sitting time enough to accommodate private members' business. Furthermore, the time that has been given to the private members more recently could probably have been found without lengthening the session at all if it had been scheduled early in the session before much of the Government's legislative programme was introduced. It seems that the only explanation for the limited amount of time devoted to private members' business was the desire on the part of the Government to keep the initiative in its own hands as much as possible. What the objective observer might justly consider to be improvements in the organization of legislative business, cabinet ministers probably saw as threats to their pre-eminence. It took a cabinet with a more long-term view of the public good to hand over to members of the Opposition the opportunity to capture headlines with their own legislative proposals and to force cabinet ministers to justify their deeds and omissions during debates over which the ministers would have little control.

Questions

Questions put to ministers are another British invention and one which has been meticulously copied in Ontario. It is generally agreed that the first such question was the one concerning the detention in Belgium of an important witness in the South Sea Bubble affair, addressed by Earl Cowper to the Prime Minister, the Earl of Sunderland on February 9, 1721, in the House of Lords.[22] However, questions as we know them today are largely a development of the nineteenth century: in 1847 there

---

three-quarters of the House and, lacking the opportunity to make formal debates, a number of them content themselves with making humorous (and not so humorous) interjections.

[22]See D. N. Chester and Nona Bowring, *Questions in Parliament* (Oxford: Clarendon, 1962), p. 12; Patrick Howarth, *Questions in the House* (London: The Bodley Head, 1956), pp. 11–14; Jennings, *Parliament*, p. 99; Taylor, *The House of Commons at Work*, p. 113.

were only 129 questions asked, compared to 6,448 in 1901. They have become, in the words of the Clerk of the British Estimates Committee, "one of the more effective methods of control of the executive ever invented."[23]

To serve this purpose three types of questions are used.[24] In the first place, they may be used simply to gain specific information which members may then use as political ammunition in future debates or election campaigns.[25] Secondly, questions may be used for the sole purpose of embarrassing the Government. In fact, this is probably the primary reason for asking the oral questions which have been such a prominent feature of parliamentary proceedings at Ottawa and elsewhere. The relatively few oral questions asked in Ontario almost invariably reflect such an intention, as does a considerable portion of the written questions. Thirdly, questions may be used to secure redress of individual grievances suffered by constituents. If individual representations to the department or other agency of government do not get results it is not unusual for members to bring the matter before the court of public opinion by means of a question to a minister. When a case arises which looks as if it could be used for larger political purposes without undue harm to the individuals involved, a member may use the question technique immediately rather than try to rectify the situation privately through representations to the appropriate officials. Whether they are used to obtain information, embarrass the Government, or remove minor oppressions – or serve all three purposes at the same time – parliamentary questions are one of the most direct avenues of confrontation between the executive and legislative branches of government, and the place they hold in the procedures of the Legislative Assembly of Ontario must be investigated.

The rules of procedure adopted by the House in its first session made provision for members to put questions to ministers of the crown relating to public affairs and to other members relating to any bill, motion, or other public matter connected with the business of the House.[26] Although this provision did not specify whether it was referring to oral or written

[23]Taylor, *The House of Commons at Work*, p. 114.

[24]All of the written questions asked in the 1964 session of the Ontario legislature are given in Appendix C.

[25]Sir Ivor Jennings has suggested that some questions are asked to enable a friend to include hitherto unpublished material in a book. (*Parliament*, p. 102). While the present writer takes some pride in the research techniques he has devised he must confess that he has not used this one, although answers to questions asked without his request have been profitably utilized.

[26]It is interesting to note that questions were not recognized in the British standing orders until March 7, 1888, twenty years after the Ontario rules were adopted. Chester and Bowring, *Questions in Parliament*, p. 289.

questions, it was probably understood to cover only the latter. Any possible doubt about this was removed in 1901, when a select committee which had been set up to consider changing the rules in regard to questions recommended that the questions of members and the answers thereto be recorded. The House concurred in the recommendation and added two sections to the rule governing questions.[27] The first stipulated that "questions and replies thereto shall be in writing and shall be entered in the Journal," and the second allowed a minister, with the consent of the House, to require a motion to be made for a return if he was of the opinion that the answer was of a lengthy or voluminous nature. As a result, the only questions recognized by the official rules of the Ontario Legislative Assembly are the formal written ones which were recorded in the *Journals* until 1960 and which are now printed in the *Debates*.[28]

Until the 1930s the procedures for written questions in Ontario were quite similar to those for "starred" questions in the United Kingdom.[29] If the questions were handed to the clerk before 5 PM on any afternoon, they were printed in the votes and proceedings for that day and would then appear on the order and notice paper two days later. When the answer to a question was ready – and when the prime minister was willing to give it – he would read it in the House and then table it. Reading the answer allowed the members to ask supplementary questions. The only significant way in which this procedure differed from the procedure now followed in Britain was that no particular haste was exerted in attempts to provide answers in Ontario, whereas in the United Kingdom the two-day notice period was considered to be the length of time in which answers must be prepared.

Currently, there are two types of questions used in Ontario. First, there are the written questions authorized by the printed rules. The procedure followed in this case is the same as outlined in the preceding paragraph except that answers are no longer read aloud before being tabled. Written questions are the subject of a notice under the same rule that governs notices of motion.[30] They are also subject to the same scrutiny at the table

---

[27]These additions of 1901 appear in the 1939 edition of the rules as rules 37(*b*) and 37(*c*).

[28]It need hardly be pointed out that the current practice of printing questions and answers in Hansard instead of in the *Journals* is in direct violation of rule 37(*b*). But from the researcher's point of view, the real foible in the new system of recording questions and answers is that they are no longer indexed. Hence it is no small task to discover so much as how many questions have been asked in a given session, let alone to locate the questions and answers themselves.

[29]From an interview with Mr. Roderick Lewis, August 19, 1964.

[30]Rule 39(*a*): "Two days' notice shall be given of a motion for leave to present a Bill, Resolution or Address; for the appointment of any Committee; or for the

as is given to notices of motion, and, if they contain unbecoming expressions, infringe the rules, or are otherwise irregular, they may be corrected by the clerk at the table under the authority of the speaker. If a question is manifestly out of order, the speaker refuses to accept it, and if a question is obviously designed to give annoyance, he can direct that it shall not be printed.[31] The rules that the speaker applies to the form and content of questions are those followed in the British House of Commons, the fundamental provision of which is that

The purpose of a question is to obtain information or press for action within the responsibility of the Member to whom it is addressed; it should not be in effect a short speech, or limited to giving information, or framed so as to suggest its own answer or convey a particular point of view.

A question should be addressed to the Minister who is primarily responsible. . . .[32]

On April 11, 1912, the Ontario Legislative Assembly adopted a resolution which incorporated some other basic rules governing questions. It was resolved

That under the Rules and procedure of this House, questions put to members must not put forward any debatable facts, nor any matter that will involve opinion, argument or inference, nor can any fact be stated, nor any opinion or intention as to matters of policy; nor should any question be put upon a matter which is not within the recognition of the House.[33]

When the Hepburn administration assumed office in 1934, the ministers began the current practice of tabling answers to questions without first reading them. This procedure allows no opportunity for oral supplementary questions, and written supplementaries would have to go through the same process as the original question. When members objected to the innovation during the session of 1935, Mr. Speaker Hipel ruled:

There is nothing in the Rule [34(a), now 37(b)] or elsewhere in the Standing Orders which implies that questions must be answered orally, on the contrary

---

putting of a Question. . . ."
[31]Alex C. Lewis, *Parliamentary Procedure in Ontario* (Toronto: King's Printer, 1940), p. 44.
[32]Great Britain, House of Commons, *Manual of Procedure in the Public Business* (9th ed.; London: Her Majesty's Stationery Office, 1959), p. 48. The rules are set out in detail in Sir Erskine May, *Parliamentary Practice* (London: Butterworths, 1964), pp. 351–6 and Lord Campion has summarized them in the form of thirty-eight specific regulations, to be found in his *Introduction to the Procedure of the House of Commons* (3rd ed.; London: Macmillan, 1958), pp. 151–4.
[33]Quoted in the ruling given by Mr. Speaker Thompson, March 10, 1926, as recorded in Lewis, *Parliamentary Procedure in Ontario*, p. 234.

it appears to me that the Rule quoted carries the implication that the questions and replies thereto would properly be handed to the Clerk for inclusion in the Votes and Proceedings of the day and the Journals of the House.

In my opinion it is a matter within the discretion of the Minister to whom a question is addressed as to whether he reads his reply or Tables it for inclusion in the Votes and Proceedings.[34]

In the House today answers to questions are never read aloud. The prime minister waits until he has a number of answers ready and then tables them all at the same time. If an answer is very long the prime minister informs the House that the Government requires that it be made an order of the House for a return. It then becomes a sessional paper instead of an answer printed in Hansard.[35] Once an order has been made for a return it does not lapse with the prorogation of the House,[36] as unanswered questions do, but this is of little significance since the premier never seeks an order for a return until he has the required information ready. It is, of course, possible for a private member to put a motion on the order paper for an order of the House or for an address to the crown[37] asking for a return but this is an exercise in futility unless the House leader sees fit to call the order for the motion, something he is not inclined to do unless and until he has the information requested ready.[38] Hence, there are seldom any orders for returns left on the order paper at the end of any session.

At both Ottawa and Westminster there are what are known as "starred" questions which take their name from the fact that they have asterisks beside them on the order paper, indicating that the questioners desire that they should be answered orally.[39] As has already been indicated, in Ontario the practice of reading the answers to written questions prevailed until 1935, but since that date answers have been read in the House only

[34]*Journals*, 1935, p. 63.

[35]This causes some inconvenience for MPPs and researchers, aggravated by the decision in 1949 to stop printing sessional papers in bound volumes for each session. Members may view current sessional papers in the office of the clerk of the Legislative Assembly and later the public may be able to obtain them from the vault attached to that office.

[36]Rule 48.

[37]The late Clerk of the House, Alex Lewis, made a formal distinction between an address to the crown and an order for a return (*Parliamentary Procedure*, p. 93), but there is no longer any difference in practice.

[38]According to Alex Lewis (*Ibid.*) a member may, after two days notice, ask for consideration of his motion for a return or an address but this is never done. From an interview with Mr. Roderick Lewis, August 19, 1964.

[39]Starred questions were first adopted at Westminster in 1902 and at Ottawa in 1910. (Chester and Bowring, *Questions in Parliament*, pp. 49–84; Dawson, *Procedure in the Canadian House of Commons*, p. 149.

rarely. The 1960 Select Committee on the Transactions of Business in the Legislature recommended the amendment of rule 37 to provide for starred questions to which oral answers would be made, but no action was taken on this aspect of their report.[40]

The second type of question permitted at Queen's Park is the oral question before the orders of the day. There being no provision for this type of question in the printed rules of the House, it may be assumed that the practice is derived from the procedure followed in Britain for "private notice" questions. The distinguishing feature of questions of this type is indicated by the name given to them in Britain: they are termed "private notice" questions because no public notice is given of the intention to ask them, i.e., they are not printed in the order paper. Both the British House of Commons and the Ontario House require notification to be given to the speaker before 12 noon on the day the question is to be asked. The purpose of this type of question is mainly to gain information needed immediately or to elicit a statement from the Government on some matter of urgent public importance. In the United Kingdom the private notice question is also used by the leader of the Opposition who, by custom, does not put questions on the order paper. The practice at both Queen's Park and Westminster is markedly different from that at Ottawa, where oral questions are put to ministers before the orders of the day almost every day without any previous notification whatsoever.[41]

The use of questions before the orders of the day in Ontario is strictly regulated. Before he will allow them to be asked, the speaker must first be convinced that there is some urgency involved.[42] If this hurdle is surmounted and the question is deemed to be in order, its wording may be edited in order to shear it of any unnecessary preamble which the member may have hoped to attach.[43] If an oral question is allowed, the speaker will usually also allow one or two supplementary questions. These supplementary questions are the closest thing Ontario has to the free-wheeling question period that attracts so much attention at Ottawa and, if the

[40]Ontario, Committee on the Transaction of Business, *Report*, p. 3.

[41]For a discussion of the Canadian practice and the problems attendant thereupon see Dawson, *Procedure in the Canadian House of Commons*, pp. 146–60.

[42]See the Speaker's statement on the appropriate use of questions before the orders of the day in *Debates*, February 15, 1960, p. 369.

[43]In a speech to the Parliamentary Association in September, 1963, Donald H. Morrow, speaker of the Ontario House, claimed that his greatest difficulty was "training the Members not only what questions should be asked orally and what questions should be placed with the clerk for the notice paper, but most important, how the question should be asked. Invariably, Members insist upon winding up like a baseball pitcher, with a half page preamble before asking their questions. For some reason or other, they feel cheated if they don't get in a few political licks at the Government in this preamble portion of the Question."

speaker is lenient in his attitude towards these questions, the period before the orders of the day becomes quite similar to the British question period, which includes the reading of answers to starred questions as well as supplementary questions and lasts nearly an hour each day.

As with most aspects of parliamentary procedure, a bare description of current practice is an inadequate basis for evaluation. To assess accurately the utility of questions put by members as a means of gaining information and exercising control over the executive, it must first be discovered how successful members are in their attempts to make use of this device. When this is done one soon discovers that there are other hindrances encountered by the ambitious member besides the purely formal requirements of the rules.

In the first place, even when he does get a question put on the order paper or on the floor of the House before the orders of the day, a member soon discovers that the minister is under no obligation to answer it. The convention in such a case is clear and was summarized by Lewis: "A Minister may refuse to answer a question on the ground of public interest and a question so refused cannot again be placed on the Order Paper. A member cannot plead such a refusal as a matter of privilege, nor can it be used as a ground for moving the adjournment of the House."[44] The British speaker has from the earliest days of questions made it clear that he has no power to insist on a minister answering a question put to him.[45] In Canada there was at least one occasion when the Speaker ordered an answer to be expunged from Hansard as irrelevant to the question and ordered that an answer be given should the question be asked again,[46] but this was quite exceptional and even in that case the minister could possibly have refused an answer for reasons of public policy. If the speaker did take it upon himself to require recalcitrant ministers to reply to questions which he considered to be in order, he would have to devise some suitable form of disciplinary action for cases of refusal. And, if a speaker could force ministers to divulge information, some system would have to be invented for making the speaker or the member who asked the question responsible for the information given. In view of such problems as these, it is no doubt best to leave the ministers themselves responsible for deciding whether or not they will answer members' queries.

In Britain, it has always been understood that a minister might refuse to

[44]Alex. Lewis, *Parliamentary Procedure*, p. 45. The British and Canadian rules may be found in May, *Parliamentary Practice*, p. 351, and Dawson, *Procedure in the Canadian House of Commons*, p. 155.

[45]Chester and Bowring, *Questions in Parliament*, pp. 299–300.

[46]Canada, House of Commons, *Debates*, April 6, 1925, pp. 1916–17. Referred to in Dawson, *Procedure in the Canadian House of Commons*, p. 155.

answer a question only if he can give some good reason – good in the sense that it would be acceptable to the House. In their exhaustive study of questions in parliament, Daniel Chester and Nona Bowring give two main reasons which are considered acceptable: a minister may refuse to answer on the grounds that to give the information sought in the question would be contrary to the public interest, or because it is not his responsibility.[47] If the minister refuses to answer a question and does not give an excuse that the House will accept, or if he renders an answer that the questioner deems unsatisfactory, the constitutional remedy is to put down a motion of censure of the minister. In Ontario, however, until recently such a course of action was not very feasible because all answers were so delayed that members could not know that their questions had been refused replies until after the session was over. In the interval they could not always be certain whether the delay was a result of difficulty encountered in trying to get the answer or was simply due to the decision of the minister not to proceed with the matter. Furthermore, it was not always easy to affix responsibility if an answer was not given because many of the questions were not directed to any particular minister and all answers that were given were tabled by the prime minister, regardless of which department they concerned.

With such a situation prevailing it had become a well-known practice of the Government of Ontario to simply refuse to answer some of the

TABLE 16

WRITTEN QUESTIONS ASKED AND ANSWERED, SELECTED YEARS, 1900–60

Year	Number asked	Number answered	Percentage answered
1900	77	65	84.4
1905	27	27	100.0
1910	16	16	100.0
1915	45	45	100.0
1920	103	103	100.0
1925	118	118	100.0
1930	59	56	94.9
1935	256	241	94.1
1940	65	59	90.8
1945	46	20	43.5
1950	111	102	91.9
1955	64	53	82.8
1960	53	48	90.6

written questions which it did not like. Part of the record for this century is set out in the following Table 16. An average of 83 questions was asked in the years listed in Table 16, but the average number answered was only 76, or 92 per cent. During the 26th Parliament, 1960–63, members asked

[47]Chester and Bowring, *Questions in Parliament*, p. 300.

fewer questions and even a slightly smaller proportion of these were answered.[48] The data for the four sessions are set out in Table 17.

TABLE 17

WRITTEN QUESTIONS ASKED AND ANSWERED IN EACH SESSION OF THE 26TH PARLIAMENT, 1960–63

Session	Number asked	Number answered	Percentage answered
1960	53	48	90.6
1960–61	15	15	100.0
1961–62	17	15	88.2
1962–63	16	13	81.3

Members asked an average of only 25 questions each session and received answers to 90 per cent of those asked. Any reasons that might have been proffered by the Government to excuse this unsatisfactory performance would have had to be remarkable indeed if they were to satisfy any members acquainted with the fact that at Westminster virtually all questions are answered. The old complaint about over-work certainly would not have done. In the United Kingdom, in each of the sessions which roughly correspond to the sessions of the Ontario legislature listed in Table 16, an average of 12,348 questions was asked[49] compared to an average of eighty-three in Ontario. Even the longer session and the larger civil service in the United Kingdom are not enough to account for the ability of the Government of that country to deal with *that* many more questions than seemed possible in Ontario. But, to make the comparison more balanced, the average number of questions asked each day in the two parliaments may be given. In recent years – from 1955 to 1960 – the British ministers have had to answer an average of 105 questions each sitting day,[50] while the Government of Ontario was asked to answer on an average of less than one written question per day during the four sessions of the 26th Parliament.

Enough has been said to substantiate the fact that relatively few questions were put to ministers in Ontario and that even fewer were answered in the sessions prior to 1965. No doubt the latter fact to some extent accounts for the former, since members would be unlikely to ask very

[48]The 1965 session of the legislature saw a revival in the popularity of questions but this was largely due to the efforts of one member, Vernon Singer (Lib. Downsview), who alone asked 91 of the 117 questions put to the Ministry. The Government chose to answer 116 of these.

[49]Calculated from the figures given in Chester and Bowring, *Questions in Parliament*, pp. 87, 88, and 316. These include both starred and unstarred questions.

[50]*Ibid.*, p. 88.

many searching questions when they knew they might be completely ignored by the Government. However, there is another and more important reason why Ontario's MPPs did not bother to ask more questions: even when the Government did answer a question, the answer was usually such a long time in coming that it was of limited value when it did appear. Generally speaking, regardless of his motives for asking the question in the first place, a member wants the information as quickly as possible. Whether he wants it in order that he may enlarge his understanding by it or in the hope that he may use it as ammunition for his attack on the Government, the answer will be of little value if it comes in the dying days of a session.

In the United Kingdom starred questions are answered within two or three days. In 1946 the departments were instructed to answer written questions within seven days, and in 1960 Mr. R. A. Butler, leader of the House, announced that the Government was instructing departments that they should exert every effort to provide answers to unstarred questions within three working days after notice had been given, unless members were kind enough to request the answer on a later date. Where this was impossible the departments were to notify the member as soon as possible.[51] As a result, members generally receive answers to both types of written questions within three days.

In Ontario quite a different situation prevailed, For example, in the 1964 session, which lasted less than four months, it took an average of forty-eight calendar days, or twenty-nine sitting days, for members to get answers to their questions, or, on the average, members had to wait for 40 per cent of the total days of the session before getting answers to their questions. Even this would not be so bad if there were a steady stream of answers once 40 per cent of the session was past, but the trend was to withhold most answers until fairly late in the session. Thus, questions asked early in the session generally took much longer to answer than the average, while those asked in the latter part of the session were answered more quickly. Almost invariably members get most of their questions on the order paper in the first few weeks of the session and then taper off so that few, if any, questions are asked in the last few weeks. The pattern of replies was exactly the opposite before 1965: a very few were answered in the early weeks, more just after the session had reached its mid-point, and the bulk of them in the last few weeks, sometimes on the very day of prorogation. The broad outlines of these two patterns may be seen in Table 18.

[51]British House of Commons, *Debates*, 1959–60, vol. 617 col. 43.

TABLE 18

PERCENTAGE OF WRITTEN QUESTIONS ASKED AND ANSWERED IN EACH THIRD OF EACH
SESSION, 1960–64*

Session	First third		Second third		Last Third		Percentage not answered
	Asked	Answered	Asked	Answered	Asked	Answered	
1960	79.25	1.89	20.75	35.85	—	52.83	9.43
1960–61	53.33	—	20.00	53.33	26.67	46.67	—
1961–62	17.65	—	47.06	—	35.29	88.24	11.76
1962–63	75.00	—	12.50	37.50	12.50	43.75	18.75
1964	83.33	—	16.67	50.00	—	44.44	5.56
AVERAGES	61.71	0.38	23.40	35.34	14.89	55.19	9.10

*The short session in the fall of 1963 is omitted.

Obviously the utility of the parliamentary question as a means of obtaining information is greatly diminished when, as happened in the 1961–62 session, not one answer is given until the session is two-thirds over. In a province, such as Ontario, with a large and competent civil service, there could be no reasons other than those of a political nature for the delays in answering members' questions. The Member who asked more written questions during the 1964 session than anyone else – and who, therefore, probably experienced a greater degree of frustration than any of his colleagues in the House – gave it as his opinion that "the promptness with which questions on the Order Paper are answered seems to depend on two factors: (A) the Minister concerned, (B) whether or not the answer is embarrassing to the government."[52] Perhaps the members' questions would not have received such short shrift if more of them had been directed towards gaining useful information instead of attempting to cause the Government embarrassment. But, on the other hand, members may have become so disheartened by the Government's slowness in replying that they were convinced that questions were useless for any purpose *other than* that of embarrassing the Government. For example, one of the nine members who bothered to ask any written questions during the 1964 session made a practice of not asking questions unless he was already fairly certain as to the answer.[53]

Oral questions before the orders of the day are, of course, answered at the time they are asked, unless the minister should be absent or unable

[52]Kenneth Bryden, in a note in response to the author's questionnaire, May 13, 1965.
[53]From an interview with James Trotter, May 12, 1965.

to gather the information in time because of some difficulty or because he did not receive the notice of the question until it was too late, in which case the answer is usually forthcoming on the following day. The British equivalent of this form of question, the private notice question, is used very sparingly. It is strictly reserved for urgent and important matters and for the leader of the Opposition who does not as a rule use the order paper for his questions. Usually only about forty private notice questions are allowed each year.[54] It would be expected that this type of question would have been much more popular in Ontario before 1965 than it is in Britain because of the unsatisfactory situation of written questions in the province, but such was not the case. In spite of the fact that written questions were usually not answered for weeks, for many years prior to 1960 the Ontario speaker applied to oral questions the same rule of urgency as operates in the United Kingdom. Under this rigidly applied urgency rule, very few questions qualified for the privilege of being asked orally before the orders of the day. Furthermore, those which were accepted for this favoured treatment were subjected to such meticulous editing to ensure that they conformed to the letter of the rules governing questions that they lost much of their value, and particularly any political "punch" that they may have had. As one frustrated member complained to Mr. Speaker: "We have submitted questions before the orders of the day and you have seen fit to edit everything out of them except the simple question. . . ."[55] In more recent years the speaker had allowed most oral questions to be asked and he had not subjected them to the same kind of rigorous editing as heretofore. Perhaps this was because members had given up trying to ask many oral questions and had come to realize that they must abide by the rules when framing those that they did ask. In any case, there was no significant increase in the number of oral questions asked before the orders of the day until the 1966 session, by which time the situation with respect to written questions had also improved.

Robbed of spontaneity by the requirement that notice be given to the speaker, who then informed the minister concerned, and robbed of much political overtone by strict editing, oral questions in Ontario before 1966 provided little excitement. In effect the member read his question and the minister his answer. Only if supplementaries were allowed was the minister left open to attack without all his defences having been previously erected for him by his departmental officials. Thus the question period, which

[54]Chester and Bowring, *Questions in Parliament*, p. 106.
[55]Donald MacDonald, leader of the New Democratic party, *Debates*, December 14, 1961, p. 424.

TABLE 19

NUMBER OF ORAL QUESTIONS BEFORE THE ORDERS OF
THE DAY, 1960–64*

Session	Number of sitting days	Number of questions	Average number per day
1960	50	47	0.94
1960–61	60	57	0.95
1961–62	54	102	1.89
1962–63	67	61	0.91
1964	69	91	1.32

*The short session in the fall of 1963 is omitted.

Jennings called the "cocktails before the oratorial feast" and which has proven to be the most popular aspect of proceedings in the Canadian and British Houses, was practically non-existent in Ontario.

While it is impossible to ascertain exactly how many oral questions were rejected by the speaker, they were probably very few. Thus, Table 19, which shows how many oral questions were actually asked in each of the sessions of the 26th Parliament and in the first full session of the 27th Parliament, is probably also a fairly accurate statement of the number of questions submitted by the members.

During the five sessions covered in Table 19 an average of 1.2 oral questions per day was asked. Even when the time spent on supplementary questions is added, the total length of the question period in Ontario was infinitesimal, amounting to only about four minutes each day in the 1964 session. During the whole session of 1964 approximately four-and-a-half hours were spent on questions before the orders of the day.

What few oral questions were asked were fairly evenly distributed throughout each session, although there was some tendency to ask more questions at the beginning of the session than at the end. It may be that the members' enthusiasm was somewhat dampened by the treatment their first attempts received. The distribution of questions before the orders of the day may be seen in Table 20.

The parliamentary question is another one of those devices available to the legislative branch for exercising some influence over the executive, which is generally used only by members of the Opposition. If members of the Government do ask questions it is often at the instigation of a minister who desires a peg on which to hang a statement. The data for the sessions of 1960 to 1964, set out in Table 21, indicate that the back-benchers of the Progressive Conservative party did not ask any written

TABLE 20

THE DISTRIBUTION OF ORAL QUESTIONS IN THE SESSIONS
OF 1960–64*
(percentages)

Session	First third	Second third	Last third
1960	38.3	25.5	36.2
1960–61	33.3	36.9	29.8
1961–62	52.0	26.4	21.6
1962–63	47.5	23.9	28.6
1964	44.0	26.5	29.5
AVERAGES	43.0	27.8	29.1

*The short session in the fall of 1963 is omitted.

questions in those years, and only in 1964 did they ask any questions before the orders of the day.

The use that each party made of questions in the 1964 session is portrayed graphically in Figure 17. Although the New Democratic party constituted only 7 per cent of the House in that session, its members asked nearly 59 per cent of the questions put to ministers that year. During the five sessions included in Table 21, the Liberals asked an average of 56.5 per cent of the questions each session, the New Democrats asked an average of 42.3 per cent, and the Conservatives, thanks to their unusual contribution in 1964, asked an average of 1.3 per cent of the questions per session.

As expected, the art of asking questions is practised by only a small proportion of the membership of the Ontario House. In the 1964 session only 27 of the 108 members put any questions to the ministers, and that figure includes the 7 Conservatives who normally do not participate in this exercise. Only 9 members attempted to use written questions in that session. Of these, Kenneth Bryden (NDP: Woodbine) asked 6 questions, Donald MacDonald (NDP) asked 3, Reginald Gisborn (NDP), and Robert Nixon (Liberal) asked two each, and the other five each asked one question.

There are some other reasons why members were so loath to ask questions: they expose the Opposition's plan of attack, thus permitting the Government to prepare its defence;[56] they can never lead to a definite debate as they can in the United Kingdom and at Ottawa, where a member who is dissatisfied with the answers he has received may raise the matter

[56]From an interview with Andrew Thompson, then leader of the Ontario Liberal party, May 13, 1965. The fact that certain improvements were made in the Attorney General's Department during the 1965 session soon after Mr. Singer had put down a number of questions on the subject was suggested as a possible illustration of this phenomenon.

TABLE 21

THE NUMBER OF ORAL AND WRITTEN QUESTIONS ASKED BY EACH PARTY IN THE SESSIONS OF 1960–64*

Session	Conservative members			Liberal members			New Democratic members			Total oral and written questions
	Oral	Written	Per cent of total	Oral	Written	Per cent of total	Oral	Written	Per cent of total	
1960	—	—	—	29	31	60	18	22	40	100
1960–61	—	—	—	32	13	62.50	25	2	37.50	72
1961–62	—	—	—	63	10	61.34	39	7	38.66	119
1962–63	—	—	—	38	11	63.64	23	5	36.36	77
1964	7	—	6.42	33	5	34.86	51	13	58.72	109

*Supplementary questions are not included in these figures. The short session in the fall of 1963 is omitted.

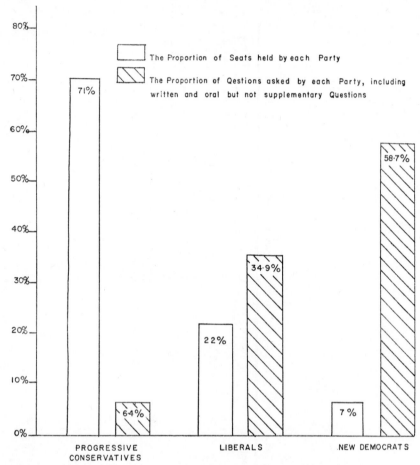

Fɪɢ. 17. Proportion of questions asked by each party in the 1964 session.

"on the adjournment" and have it debated some evening following the regular adjournment hour;[57] they can never come to a vote and, therefore, they can never be used to overthrow a Government.[58]

While it is true that written questions are not always answered promptly in Ontario and sometimes they are not answered at all, this does not mean that the subject matter of the questions cannot be raised on some other occasions. Any of the general debates may provide a member with the opportunity to discuss a question which the Government has failed to

[57]Jennings, *Parliament*, p. 118. The details of the practice in the Canadian House of Commons were provided by Mr. I. Gordon Dubroy, second clerk assistant, in a letter dated July 28, 1965.

[58]Lord Campion and D. W. S. Lidderdale, *European Parliamentary Procedure, A Comparative Handbook* (London: George Allen and Unwin, 1953), p. 33.

answer, but the usual occasion chosen for this purpose is the discussion of the estimates of the department concerned in Committee of Supply. If a member is lucky he may elicit an answer from the minister at that time, and, if he is provocative enough, he may even spark a debate on the subject matter of his question. Two instances of the use of this technique are cited here, partly because they illustrate how forthrightly a member may raise his questions in Committee of Supply, and partly because they reveal how easily and quickly the answers could have been given when they were first put on the order paper. Both questions were raised during the consideration of the estimates of the Department of Labour and both were raised by Kenneth Bryden.

The first instance, in reference to a question submitted on January 24, 1964, occurred when Mr. Bryden spoke on February 14:

Mr. K. Bryden (Woodbine): Mr. Chairman . . . I have a question on the order paper which I think relates to this vote. Unfortunately, one of the practices the new administration has taken over from the old administration, is to fail to answer questions put on the order paper by members until it is too late for the information to be of any use to them.

However, I think the hon. Minister of Labour has had adequate notice of this question since it has been on the order paper almost since the opening of the session. It is question four on page eight, as follows:

1. Has the foundation on automation and employment been established?
2. If so, (a) when was it established? (b) Who is its director or other principal officer? (c) What is its address.

Hon. Mr. Rowntree: At the conclusion of the conference on automation and employment last September, the government declared its intentions. . . . These were to appoint a steering committee. . . . That steering committee . . . has met regularly. . . . It is the intention of the government to move the matter right along.

Mr. Bryden: I assume then that the answer to question one is no, and therefore question two is covered by the first answer.[59]

In this case, the answer which the member had been awaiting for three weeks was a simple "no" and required no research at all by departmental officials. Had Mr. Bryden waited for this answer to be tabled, the occasion for which he required the information – the consideration of vote 1001 of the estimates of the Department of Labour – would have been past. Nevertheless, he was able to get the information he required by this rather unorthodox method.

The second instance of a question being asked during Committee of Supply which merits our special attention occurred on February 18, 1964. The original question had been on the order paper since January 24. The relevant portion of the debates on the day the question was brought up is quoted here.

[59]*Debates*, February 14, 1964, p. 629.

Mr. Bryden: . . . I have a question on the order paper which, like all questions, never seems to be answered. I decided, however, that one can put these questions on the order paper and then, when the estimates come along, the hon. Minister can be considered to have been given due notice. So I am going to refer him to . . . question No. 3, standing in my name. There are five parts to it. To begin with, at any rate I will read only the first part. With regard to section 5 –

Hon. Mr. Rowntree: Well, I can give the hon. member the answer to the whole thing at once. . . . The question on the order paper has to do with section 5 of the Human Rights Code dealing with discrimination between male and female employees. How many complaints have been received? I am instructed that there have been none. . . .

Mr. Bryden: All the rest of the question falls in view of the answer to question 1.[60]

This question, too, could have been answered immediately upon being asked, and it is difficult to imagine any reason why this was not done. However, the fact remains that the Member was able to get a reply to his query when he put it directly to the Minister during the supply proceedings. Perhaps it was the use of this tactic that forced ministers to adopt a more favourable attitude towards members' questions in the 1966 session, but whether this new attitude will become a permanent feature of parliamentary practice in Ontario remains to be seen.

Special Procedures

There are available to private members certain special procedures whereby they may interrupt or delay the normal business of the House. Two of the three are generally considered to be quite useful instruments for checking the executive, and the third is simply a device for interposing delays in the legislative process. The three special procedures considered worthy of some attention here are: motions to adjourn the House to discuss a definite matter of urgent public importance, motions to express lack of confidence in the Government, and dilatory motions.

The revision of the rules in 1939 introduced to Ontario procedure an opportunity which had been available to private MPs in the United Kingdom since 1802 and in Ottawa since 1906: the right to move "the adjournment of the House for the purpose of discussing a definite matter of urgent public importance." A member who desires to move such a motion may do so after routine business has been disposed of and before the orders of the day are read. According to the provisions of rule 38(*a*) previous notice of the matter must have been "submitted to, and approved by the Speaker." In practice this means that a member must give written

[60]*Debates,* February 18, 1964, p. 741.

notice to the speaker before 12 noon on the day he wishes the debate to take place. Unlike the usual procedure in Britain and at Ottawa, the speaker's approval, or more likely his disapproval, is indicated privately to the member concerned before the day's sitting begins, although occasionally the member is permitted to stand and move the motion before it is disallowed by the speaker. Except on those rare occasions when the speaker gives his ruling orally in the House, no record is kept of the attempts on the part of the members to make use of rule 38(a), and it is impossible to examine the specific reasons given for rejecting their motions. As no guidelines are laid down in the rules to assist the speaker in deciding whether or not a particular motion to adjourn the House under this rule is acceptable,[61] it is left to his own discretion to establish criteria for deciding which subjects are definite, urgent, and of sufficient public importance to merit consideration in a special debate. Furthermore, the speaker is given no assistance by the House in this regard.

At Ottawa and Westminster, if the speaker is favourably disposed towards the motion he will ask whether it has the leave of the House, and, if twenty members in the Canadian House or forty members in the British House rise, it is assumed that the motion has the leave of the House. If less than twenty but more than five members of the Canadian House or less than forty but more than ten members of the British House rise, the question whether the member has leave to move adjournment of the House is put forthwith, without debate, and determined, if necessary, by a division.[62] In Ontario, conceivably the speaker could privately reject a motion made under rule 38(a) even though a majority of the House favoured a debate on the subject. On the other hand, there is the remote possibility that a speaker might allow a debate even though fewer than twenty – or even fewer than five – members wanted it. However, in the event that the speaker went to this extreme, the matter would probably be decided by a majority vote of the House on a motion challenging the speaker's ruling.

If a member is able to convince the speaker that his motion to adjourn the House in order to discuss a definite matter of urgent public importance ought to be permitted – and if the speaker's decision is not overruled by the Government's majority – he moves the adjournment and on this motion he may discuss the subject he is interested in for ten minutes. Any other members may then also take part in the debate, with the same time limit

[61]See pp. 141–42.

[62]For descriptions of the Canadian and British practices see Arthur Beauchesne, *Rules and Forms of the House of Commons of Canada* (4th ed.; Toronto: Carswell, 1958), p. 74, and Sir T. Erskine May, *Parliamentary Practice*, pp. 360–9.

applying to each speech. Although no such time limit on speeches is imposed at Ottawa or Westminster, there is a limit on the total length of any debate arising under this head in the British House. There, the debate does not begin until 7 PM and at 10 PM the House reverts to the business that was underway before the debate began. At Ottawa no special time limit is placed on speeches or debates under the provisions of standing order 26 which governs this procedure, but the usual rules governing speeches do apply.

A peculiarity in the Ontario and British procedures governing motions to adjourn the House for the purpose of discussing a definite matter of urgent public importance is that the motions rarely come to any vote. In Ontario the debate ends when the House leader calls for the next order of business. In the United Kingdom the debate usually comes to an end automatically at 10 PM. At Ottawa, however, the debate is usually brought to an end by the member responsible for the motion withdrawing it when everyone who wished to speak has had an opportunity to do so,[63] by the House rising at the end of the day's sitting pursuant to standing order,[64] or, sometimes, by the adoption of a motion that the House now pass to the orders of the day.[65] The use of the latter procedure can give the House the opportunity to divide on the subject that has been discussed.

The importance of rule 38(a) in Ontario is that it provides the private members with one of those rare opportunities to initiate debates on subjects of their own choosing. This makes it the more regrettable that greater use of it is not made. It is true that until recently there had been a steady decline in the number of such motions that were allowed in the British House of Commons: from seventeen between 1920 and 1930, to seven before 1930 and 1940, to four between 1940 and 1950.[66] But even when they were least popular in the United Kingdom – during the war and in the immediate postwar years – they were still more common than in Ontario, and in recent years there has been a renewed interest in their use in Britain. Between 1950 and 1960, for instance, eight urgency motions were allowed in the British House of Commons. In Ontario members have been permitted by the speaker to move the adjournment to discuss an urgent matter on only three or four occasions since the end of the war. The situation with regard to the use of this procedure seems to be quite similar to that existing with regard to questions put by members. Speakers have interpreted the grounds upon which members may move the adjournment

[63]See, for example, Canada, House of Commons, *Debates*, August 10, 1964, p. 6628.

[64]*Ibid.*, March 11, 1964, p. 813.

[65]Arthur Beauchesne, *Rules and Forms of the House of Commons of Canada*, p. 92.

[66]Taylor, *The House of Commons at Work*, p. 65, n. 1.

of the House to discuss an urgent matter in such a narrow fashion and then have applied the rule so strictly that they have all but nullified the original intention of the rule. The rule that was added in 1939 in order to give private members some opportunity to initiate debates on matters which they considered to be of public importance has become little more than another cause of frustration for them. Backbenchers have been so consistently thwarted in their attempts to use rule 38(a) that only the most persistent of them continue to make the effort, and they do so only occasionally. If the members were abusing the privilege and a great deal of the time of the House was being spent in debate on matters of questionable significance to the electorate, the speaker would no doubt be justified in applying the rule in such a rigid fashion. This, however, is manifestly not the case. There can be no doubt that the Government and its nominee, the speaker, would prefer to avoid special debates of this nature – just as it avoids calling private members' business and answering private members' questions – but the *sub rosa* fashion in which special debates are rejected makes such decisions an even greater offence to the House. At least the House and the public are acquainted with the subject matter of members' bills and questions, even if the Government gives them no heed. But only the speaker is acquainted with the subjects members wish debated under rule 38(a) and only he decides whether they shall be extended that privilege.

The second special procedure to be discussed here is the motion of lack of confidence in the Government or the "vote of censure." Even though practically all of the Opposition's words and actions are ultimately aimed at criticizing and, if possible, defeating the Government, under most types of parliamentary government special provisions are made to ensure that from time to time the legislative branch is enabled to pronounce decisively upon either the general policy of the executive branch or upon some particular aspect of that policy. Under the British parliamentary system such opportunities take the form of substantive motions, that is, self-contained proposals submitted for the approval of the House and drafted in such a way as to be capable of expressing a decision of the House.[67] If the Government wants to flaunt its majority or bring about its own defeat and so justify an early election, it may bring in the motion itself, in which case it will be called a "vote of confidence." If the Opposition moves the motion it is known as a "vote of censure." In either case, a defeat of the Government would entail its resignation or the dissolution of Parliament. Instead of initiating a special debate on a substantive motion, Governments will sometimes accomplish essentially the same end without

[67]Lord Campion, *An Introduction to the Procedure of The House of Commons*, pp. 170–1.

any special procedure by simply declaring their intention to consider some ordinary motion to be a vote of confidence. Thus, for example, a Government may say that it is staking its life on a particular bill and that it will consider the ancillary motion for second reading to be a vote of confidence. The defeat of the bill would then become in fact a vote of no confidence in the Government, and the results would be the same as if a special substantive motion had been the occasion for the vote. Actually, it is not common for governments to introduce special votes of confidence but, in Ontario at least, making an ordinary vote a matter of confidence is somewhat more common.

When the Opposition moves a motion of censure, convention demands that the Government immediately allow the motion to be debated unless, of course, the question can be discussed effectively in some other way. On this point, which is rather out of keeping with the usual attitude of the Government towards Opposition tactics, Sir Ivor Jennings has this to say:

The absurdity of a system in which the Government postpones its own business in order to let the Opposition threaten death and damnation is only apparent. The Opposition is not just a nuisance to be tolerated, but a definite and essential part of the Constitution. Once it is accepted that Opposition is not only legitimate but essential to the maintenance of democratic government, the need for arrangements behind the Speaker's Chair follows naturally.[68]

In Ontario special motions of confidence or censure are very rare, and only one, that in 1871, has been of much significance.[69] Following the general election of 1870 the Government found itself in a most unhappy position: it could not command a majority until after a number of by-elections had been held, but the writs for these by-elections could not be issued until the House had met and elected a speaker to issue them. Instead of trying to work out some compromise with the Opposition to ensure that all constituencies would be represented before the beginning of the usual work of the session, Premier Macdonald went ahead as though he did control a majority. The Opposition rose to the challenge, and Edward Blake moved an amendment to the address in reply to the speech from the throne. Although the amendment was altogether out of order – amounting more to a censure of the previous Government than of the existing one – the Government did not recognize this and proceeded to move, through a

[68]Jennings, *Parliament*, p. 158.
[69]The description of the circumstances surrounding the defeat of the Macdonald government in 1871 is taken from Adam Shortt and Arthur G. Doughty, general editors, *Canada and Its Provinces. A History of the Canadian People and their Institutions by One Hundred Associates*, Vol. 17, *The Province of Ontario* (Toronto and Glasgow: Brook, 1914), pp. 120–6, and from Major B. Handley Geary, vc, "Notes on the History of Ontario," an unpublished manuscript.

private member, a resolution calling for the postponement of consideration of the amendment until all constituencies were duly represented. This amendment lost by a vote of 32 to 40, and the Opposition amendment carried, 40 to 33. Technically this could hardly be called a vote of censure on the Government of the day because it dealt only with a measure passed in a previous parliament and Macdonald refused to resign. Blake therefore brought forward another amendment which was a direct motion of no confidence in the Government but which still made reference to the Act passed in the session before the election. Again the Government was defeated, this time by a majority of only one. But, instead of resigning, the Government brought down, in answer to the address, a message from the Lieutenant Governor which explained that the criticism of his advisers was unjustified because they had acted only in accordance with an act passed by the previous House. The proper course of action, according to the Lieutenant Governor, was to repeal or amend the act. No doubt everything the Lieutenant Governor said was true, but it was too late to stem the tide in the House. Blake moved a series of resolutions condemning the ministers for continuing in office against the expressed opinion of the House. Macdonald sought to adjourn the House until January 9, 1872, but the attempt failed, and the motion of censure was carried by a majority of nineteen.

Amendments to the address in reply to the speech from the throne and to the budget motion are usually considered to be so important that they automatically become votes of censure. In view of the shortness of the sessions in the Ontario legislature these two opportunities to move, in effect, no confidence in the Government are perhaps sufficient and account for the fact that specific motions of censure are moved so infrequently. The best illustration of the use of an amendment to the address as a motion of censure occurred in 1945. After about a year and a half in office, the Conservative Premier, George Drew, was convinced that he could win an election and obtain the majority he had failed to secure in the 1943 general election. However, he did not want to accept responsibility for calling another election so soon after the last one. The solution he hit upon was to manœuvre the Liberal party into joining forces with the CCF, thus bringing about the defeat of his Government and hence an election. On March 22 of that year, in the course of the throne debate, Mr. Drew announced "that the Government would regard the amendment proposed to the Motion as a vote of want of confidence and if it carried matters would take their logical course and the people of Ontario would have to decide the issue."[70] By this time the Liberals were in such a position that

[70]*Journals*, 1945, p. 107.

they could not turn back. The main amendment to the motion for an address was carried. The election was called, and Mr. Drew won 66 of the 90 seats in the House.

The dilatory motion is the third type of special procedure which merits some attention. During a debate in the House a member who secures the floor may move "that this House do now adjourn," "that the debate be now adjourned," or, if in Committee, "that the Chairman do report progress and ask to sit again" or "that the Chairman do now leave the chair." As Campion and Lidderdale point out: "The purpose of a dilatory motion is the perfectly legitimate one of persuading the House (or committee) to postpone a decision on the question before it, but such a motion lends itself to obstructive tactics – hence its name."[71] "The previous question" is sometimes given as another type of dilatory motion. This is primarily because in some parliaments, e.g., the British House of Commons, the wording of the question is such that, if it is agreed to, it postpones a decision on the matter being discussed.[72] In Ontario, however, the wording is simply "that this question be now put," and, if this is decided in the affirmative, instead of postponing the matter the debate is immediately closed and the original question is put forthwith without amendment or further debate. In Ottawa, where the House of Commons uses the same wording for the question as in Ontario, if the previous question is *negatived* by the House, the motion under debate is superseded and disappears temporarily from the order paper.[73] In Ontario, apparently, the subject matter of the debate cannot be superseded by either passing or negativing the previous question. If it is passed, the matter is immediately put to the vote; if it is negatived the debate may simply continue.

A motion to adjourn the *House*, if carried in the affirmative, supersedes the main motion; the latter is then dropped from the order paper and cannot be revived during the remainder of the session.[74] The House immediately adjourns until the next regular hour of meeting. If a motion to adjourn the debate is successful the consideration of the main motion is merely postponed until a later date, to be named in the motion or decided by the House before passing to the next order of business.[75] Usually, however, members move such dilatory motions not in the hope that they will

[71]Campion and Lidderdale, *European Parliamentary Procedure*, p. 230.
[72]Lord Campion, *An Introduction to the Procedure of the House of Commons*, p. 175.
[73]Dawson, *Procedure in the Canadian House of Commons*, p. 171.
[74]Alex Lewis, *Parliamentary Procedure in Ontario* (Toronto: King's Printer, 1940), p. 37.
[75]In the British House of Commons, it is impossible to specify a future day in the motion which must be simply that the debate be *now* adjourned. May, *Parliamentary Practice*, p. 404.

pass, but simply to obstruct temporarily the normal proceedings of the House. At Queen's Park and Westminster – but not at Ottawa[76] – these motions are debatable, but the debate must be relevant to the reasons why it is desirable to adjourn the House or the debate.[77] No amendments are allowed and, if a dilatory motion is defeated, it cannot be moved again until some other business intervenes. At Westminster – but not at Queen's Park or Ottawa – the speaker, if he be of the opinion that dilatory motions are an abuse of the rules of the House, is empowered to put forthwith the question thereon from the chair or to decline to propose the question thereon to the House.[78] It was pointed out in the preceding chapter that the committee which studied the rules in 1939 recommended that such powers be given to the Ontario speaker, but their proposal was turned down.[79]

On balance, the members of the Ontario Legislative Assembly are in a better position to use dilatory motions to check the will of the executive branch than the members of either the Canadian or British Houses of Commons. On the one hand, the speaker in Ontario does not have the written authority to refuse these motions as does the speaker in the British House and, on the other hand, Ontario members have an opportunity to debate such motions which is denied Canadian federal MPs. In spite of these advantages, the Ontario members hardly ever use dilatory motions. In fact, as a rule they are used only by the Government to end debates on private members' bills. The most obvious explanation of why Ontario MPPs do not bother to use dilatory motions is that there is very little need to resort to such devices. With no limits on the length of either speeches or debates, the occasion could hardly arise where the Opposition would have anything to gain by moving the adjournment of the House or of the debate on any particular subject. Only if there were the possibility of such a motion succeeding would there be any point in moving it and even they could probably accomplish almost the same end by simply voting against the main motion.

However, the fact that members of the Ontario Assembly have ample time to speak must be seen in the context of the other topics discussed in this chapter. Procedures whereby private members may take the initiative

[76]Dawson, *Procedure in the Canadian House of Commons*, p. 170. However, even the mechanics of dividing the House occupy at least half an hour so that a dilatory motion may accomplish its purpose in the Canadian House of Commons even though it cannot be debated.

[77]Lewis, *Parliamentary Procedure in Ontario*, p. 37, and May, *Parliamentary Practice*, p. 449. In Ontario speeches on all adjournment motions are limited to ten minutes in length.

[78]British House of Commons standing order 28 (1).

[79]See p. 140.

in the House – e.g., by introducing their own legislative proposals, by putting questions to ministers, or by moving the adjournment of the House in order to discuss a definite matter of urgent public importance – were not treated so generously by the Government in the period under study here. Freedom of speech, quantitatively conceived, is not in itself a powerful enough tool to enable the legislative branch to supervise and control the executive. If they are to be effective, members of the legislature must have some opportunity to direct the affairs of the House themselves and to call the Government to account. In this respect there remain two large subjects to be discussed: the opportunities available to the members of the Legislative Assembly to control the powers delegated to the executive branch and to supervise the expenditure of public monies. These topics constitute the subject matter of the next chapter.

7

THE CONTROL
OF DELEGATED
POWERS AND
THE CONTROL
OF FINANCE

THE GROWTH in the size and complexity of government functions in Ontario has made it necessary for the legislative branch to delegate to the executive many of its traditional functions. This development has presented the Legislative Assembly with two of its most perplexing problems: how to direct the use that the executive makes of the powers delegated to it, and, concomitantly, how to control the way in which the executive dispenses the public monies.

The Control of Delegated Powers

No exhaustive analysis of the perplexing subject of delegated powers will be attempted here. Rather, the primary object of this section will be simply to describe the opportunities which members of the Ontario Legislative Assembly have to control the exercise of the powers that have been delegated. We will thus be concerned with the way in which the legislative procedures of the province govern the relationships between the Assembly on the one hand and the cabinet, the civil service, and the semi-independent agencies on the other. Enough has already been said in earlier chapters about the inability of the legislative branch to cope with demands for detailed regulations that the era of the positive state has brought. Here, the need for delegation will be taken for granted, and attention will be directed towards describing the manner in which the Assembly does delegate its traditional powers and the instruments by which it seeks to control the subordinate bodies' use of the powers delegated to them. To begin with, however, something should be said about the factors that have caused much of the inquietude over the delegation of powers to the departments and to extra-departmental agencies.

High on any list of such factors must come the charge that insufficient care is taken in devising the statutes which delegate the powers in the first place.[1] Naturally, it would be difficult to lay down the details of the policy to be followed by any minister exercising delegated powers when new ground is being broken, but sometimes too much freedom is allowed, and there seem to have been too few attempts in Ontario to amend legislation in order to include the details of policy as they evolve. An example of a statute which conferred far greater discretionary powers on a minister than the situation required was an Act to amend the Department of Agriculture Act, passed in the 1964 session. At first reading the Bill provided that "upon the recommendation of the Minister, the Lieutenant Governor in Council may, upon such terms as he deems proper, agree to guarantee and may guarantee the payment of any loan . . . made to such persons and for such purposes as the Lieutenant Governor in Council determines."[2] By this Bill the minister of agriculture was authorized, subject only to the approval of the executive council, to guarantee loans for anyone he chose, up to any amount he desired, and for whatever purpose he liked. Fortunately, the Bill was amended before it received third reading to limit its application to loans made to farmers to pay for purchasing and transporting water to a maximum of $2,500 – which was apparently sufficient to meet the original intention of the Bill.[3]

Similarly, there may be some need to give fairly comprehensive powers to organizations which have responsibility for new fields of jurisdiction,[4] but, in some instances, powers have been conferred which were hardly needed to execute the assigned functions. For example, the Liquor Control Board was given the power to expropriate land. This power was so superfluous that the Board never saw fit to use it. In the 1965 session this power was taken away from the Board.[5]

[1]It is not meant to refer here to the work performed by the legislative counsel's office but to the prior work done by the departmental officials under the direction of the minister.

[2]Ontario, Legislative Assembly, *Bills*, 1964, Bill 9, first reading, s. 1.

[3]*Ibid.*, third reading, s. 1.

[4]It is possible to have too rigorous parliamentary control over subordinate agencies, particularly those carrying out financial enterprises. A study carried out by the Acton Society Trust (*Accountability and Parliament, 1950*) found that in the first experiments in public control in the United Kingdom, in which close parliamentary control was attempted, the method produced "excessive conservatism, caution, avoidance of financial risk, delay in reaching decisions and excessive paperwork." Quoted in Ontario, Committee on the Organization of Government in Ontario, *Report* (Toronto, 1959), (hereinafter cited as the Gordon Committee Report), p. 50.

[5]*Statutes of Ontario SO.*, 1965, c. 58.

The original intention in giving departments and semi-independent agencies the right to make regulations was to enlist their assistance in bringing legislation into operation. Regulations were meant to supplement the substantive provision of statutes by providing for routine matters of administration. However, under the pressures of public demand and bureaucratic suggestion, the tendency now is to draft skeletal legislation and to leave to the executive council or to extradepartmental agencies the task of creating much of the province's substantive law.

Why has the Ontario legislature allowed so large a part of its legislative functions to be delegated to other authorities, and why is not more care taken in the devising of legislation? Several answers to these two questions have already been discussed: the shortness of the sessions, the lack of information on the part of members, and the paucity of funds or services to assist them in getting information, etc. Related reasons are the limited use of committees of the legislature and the inadequacy of the services provided for these committees. But another explanation for the legislature's rather shoddy performance of what has traditionally been conceived of as its central task is the Governments' practice of introducing legislation late in the session.

Before discussing the tendency of Governments to introduce their own legislation – and to call private members' legislation – late in the session, it should be made clear that there is no set length to any session of the Ontario House. Furthermore, prime ministers have in the past intimated that they would be willing to keep the House in session as long as the Opposition wanted. Nevertheless, the history of the Legislative Assembly and the attitudes of the members dictate that the sessions should end fairly early in the spring of each year; hence, psychologically, if not constitutionally, there is a fairly well-established prorogation time. Furthermore, the length of the session is really in the hands of the prime minister, who decides when parliament shall be summoned, when its various items of business will be taken up, and, ultimately through his party majority, when discussion will cease. The average length of the regular sessions of the legislature from 1867 to 1964, omitting the special sessions of five days or less, was 44.3 days, and, although there has been a tendency for sessions to be lengthened in recent years, it is doubtful that they could be made much longer unless fall sessions became the rule.

In fairness to recent administrations it should also be noted that earlier Governments also made it a practice to introduce their legislative proposals quite late in the session. On three occasions in bygone years, such haste was taken in the passage of certain bills that their real import did not dawn upon the Government until after the bills were passed, and the lieutenant governor had to be instructed to withhold his assent to them.

And, in two separate sessions, two bills with the same object were introduced and passed; the lieutenant governor had to veto one of the two on each occasion.[6]

Since the second world war the normal procedure has been to bring very little business before the House in the first month or so and then to introduce more and more bills as the session progresses and the House becomes increasingly involved in Committee of Supply and other activities. The result is that in the last few days of the session members must consider not only the estimates and the new legislation being introduced, but also the bills that went through their first stages earlier in the session. Table 22 sets out some of the relevant data for the sessions from 1960 to 1964. From this it may be seen that in the last three weeks (fifteen sitting days) of each of those five sessions, members had to study an average of 28.6 pieces of new legislation of which they probably had no previous knowledge, and during the same period they were expected to give second reading to an average of 43.8 bills, consider 88 bills in Committee of the Whole House, and give third reading to 88.6 bills. These figures are expressed as percentages in Table 23.

Is it any wonder that little time or forethought is given to the detailed revision of bills in Committee of the Whole House when 60.5 per cent of all bills are taken through that stage in the last fifteen days of the session? And, although Table 23 does express fifteen days as a percentage of each session, it must be borne in mind that fifteen days are still only fifteen days, regardless of what proportion of the session they may constitute. The figure is included in the table simply to demonstrate that a disproportionate amount of the Assembly's legislative output comes in the last three weeks of the session. Of course, if the session were longer, the disproportion would increase. Indeed, this has been the trend: the sessions have grown longer, making fifteen days a smaller proportion of each, and at the same time the amount of legislation taken in the last three weeks of each session has increased. This suggests that perhaps the real problem is the organization of business of the House rather than the relative shortness of the session, and this possibility is given further credence by the fact that, although the 1960 session was the shortest of the five sessions analysed, a smaller proportion of bills was dealt with in the last three weeks of that session than in any other session. Table 24 gives the same information as Table 23 except that it deals only with the last five days of each session. It is a cause of some wonderment that in spite of the activity that is concentrated in the closing days of any session, the Govern-

[6]John T. Saywell, *The Office of Lieutenant-Governor* (Toronto: University of Toronto Press, 1957), p. 222.

TABLE 22

NUMBER OF BILLS DEALT WITH LATE IN EACH SESSION, 1960–64*

Session	Length of session (sitting days)	Total number of bills passed	Number Introduced		Number given second reading		Number considered in committee		Number given third reading	
			in the last 15 sitting days	in the last 5 sitting days	in the last 15 sitting days	in the last 5 sitting days	in the last 15 sitting days	in the last 5 sitting days	in the last 15 sitting days	in the last 5 sitting days
1960	50	132	11	1	23	4	66	11	68	18
1960–61	60	103	16	2	21	4	48	10	51	28
1961–62	54	142	50	6	77	17	127	96	122	94
1962–63	67	145	45	9	53	36	126	94	128	98
1964	69	124	21	1	45	12	73	73	74	74
AVERAGES	60	129	28.6	3.8	43.8	14.6	88	56.8	88.6	62.4

*The short session in the fall of 1963 is omitted.

TABLE 23

THE PROPORTION OF BILLS DEALT WITH IN THE LAST FIFTEEN DAYS OF EACH
SESSION, 1960–64*

Session	15 sitting days expressed as a percentage of the session	Percentage of bills given first reading	Percentage of bills given second reading	Percentage of bills considered in Committee of the Whole House	Percentage of bills given third reading
1960	30.0	7.1	16.0	47.8	59.0
1960–61	25.0	13.1	19.4	46.2	48.1
1961–62	27.8	24.8	41.0	69.4	67.0
1962–63	22.4	27.3	33.8	84.0	85.3
1964	21.7	14.6	33.3	55.3	55.6
AVERAGES	25.4	17.4	28.7	60.5	61.0

*The short session in 1963 is omitted. The number of bills going through each of
the four stages in the last fifteen days of any session is expressed here as a percentage
of the total number of bills that went through each stage during that session. Thus,
for example, in 1964 there were 132 bills considered in Committee of the Whole House,
73, or 55.3 per cent, of which were considered in the last fifteen days. We are not concerned with the fact that only 124 bills were placed on the statute books for that year.

ment nevertheless saw fit to introduce an average of 2.3 per cent of the
year's legislation in the last week of each session. In the 1962–63 session,
which was one of the longest in the province's history, 23.1 per cent of the
bills given second reading were pushed through that stage in the last five
days, and 62.3 per cent of the bills that went to Committee of the Whole
House were dealt with in the same period.

It is, therefore, quite understandable that legislation is not always given
the detailed scrutiny by the House that it requires when so little time is
given over to this function. What would be remarkable would be to find
that this legislation was carefully gone over to ensure that it laid down the
details of policy, defined the limits of any powers which were delegated,
and clearly set out the lines of responsibility.

The constant complaint of the members, however, is not only that an
inordinate amount of work is piled up in the latter part of the session, but
that many of the most far-reaching and controversial pieces of legislation
are introduced then. For example, in the 1964 session, the Bill to create
the new Department of University Affairs was introduced on day 57 of
the 69-day session, was called for second reading only three days before
the end of the session, and was referred to Committee of the Whole House
on the day before prorogation.

The apparent carelessness in formulating those acts of the legislature
that delegate powers has been carried over to the devising of the subordinate legislation necessitated by the delegation of legislative respon-

TABLE 24

THE PROPORTION OF BILLS DEALT WITH IN THE LAST FIVE DAYS OF EACH SESSION, 1960–64*

Session	5 sitting days expressed as a percentage of the session	Percentage of bills given first reading	Percentage of bills given second reading	Percentage of bills considered in Committee of the Whole House	Percentage of bills given third reading
1960	10.0	0.6	2.8	8.0	13.0
1960–61	8.3	1.6	3.7	9.6	26.4
1961–62	9.3	3.0	9.0	52.5	51.6
1962–63	7.5	5.5	23.1	62.3	65.3
1964	7.2	0.6	8.9	55.3	55.6
AVERAGES	8.5	2.3	9.5	37.6	42.4

*The short session in 1963 is omitted. The number of bills going through each of the four stages in the last five days of any session is expressed here as a percentage of the total number of bills that went through each stage during that session.

sibility.[7] The various forms of subordinate legislation – orders in council, regulations, rules, by-laws, or a species known by some other name – have the force of law just as much as the parent statutes by which they are authorized, and equal care should be exercised in their preparation. But, in spite of the far-reaching significance of many items of delegated legislation, there is ample evidence to support the accusation that insufficient thought is given to their conception.[8]

However, a practice which is open to even greater abuse than the shoddy design of specific regulations is that of regulation by reference. The dangers attendant upon such a practice may be clearly demonstrated by one case.[9] At an inquest into the death of a man killed in a major explosion in Ottawa, one of the first matters which required study was the law which

[7]It should be noted again that the carelessness referred to here is not in the actual drafting of bills, orders, etc., but in the initial conception of them and in the instructions that are given to those who do the final drafting. The basic point that is being made is that if all the legislators in the House could spend a sufficient amount of time in the consideration of these pieces of legislation, they could conceivably suggest improvements which had not occurred to the originators of the legislative proposals.

[8]For example, until it was brought to his attention that it was constitutionally impossible, the attempt was made to obtain for the Minister of Agriculture, by means of an order in council, the sweeping powers to guarantee loans that were later outlined in the original Bill 9 of the 1964 session. Had it not been for the insistence of one of the officials of the legislature, the powers that were deemed too great to be conferred upon a minister by statute would have been granted to him by an order in council.

[9]This case was suggested by Mr. E. H. Silk, then assistant deputy attorney general, in a memorandum submitted to the Select Committee on Administrative and Executive Problems of Government on September 19, 1960.

was applicable in the case. It so happened that the procedures to be followed in this instance were set out in a book of rules printed in the United States. The volume, known by a code number, was extremely difficult to obtain, and then it turned out not to be a body of law but merely a compendium of suggestions. Nevertheless, this code book was incorporated by reference into the law of Ontario and remained as such until new regulations were published, over a year after the accident occurred. The obvious difficulties involved in enforcing such adopted provisions suggest that it might have been better to take the time to write adequate regulations in the first place.[10]

It is now well worth asking how items of subordinate legislation, which later prove so contentious, are allowed to pass. First, although it appears that all regulations are in fact reviewed by the legislative counsel and law officers of the crown, this is not mandatory. Secondly, while the large majority of regulations are made or approved by the lieutenant governor in council, there are still many which are approved only by an individual minister, an official of the government, or by a semi-independent agency. This again makes it possible for regulations to come into being without the advantage of prior perusal by that body of men which has final responsibility for governing the province. Thirdly, there is seldom, if ever, any advance knowledge of the contents of regulations given to the public before they are published in the *Ontario Gazette* and by that time the regulations have already come into force, unless they specifically stipulate otherwise. This means that there can be no representations made and no public debate on the merits of the regulations. In the case of bills passed in the legislature, no matter how rushed the Government may be, every legislative proposal is subjected to three readings by the elected representatives of the people; but regulations, which may affect some people far more than the acts which authorize them, may become law without the prior knowledge of more than a handful of people.

To safeguard the public from the misuse of regulations "of a legislative nature," a number of requirements has been written into the Regulations Act. However, the minister who administers the Act may "determine whether a regulation, rule, order or by-law is a regulation within the meaning of this Act and his decision is final."[11] It is impossible to discover how many rules are in force which have not been brought under the require-

[10]The statutory authority for the procedure followed in this case was a subsection of the Energy Act which stipulates that "any regulation may adopt by reference, in whole or in part with such changes as the Lieutenant Governor in Council considers necessary, any code, and may require compliance with any code that is so adopted." *Revised Statutes of Ontario (RSO)*, 1960, c. 122, s. 9 (2).

[11]*RSO*, 1960, c. 349, s. 6 (a).

ments of the Regulations Act but which could conceivably be construed to be "of a legislative nature." For the ordinary citizen, whose usual contacts with government are through the rather remote medium of Her Majesty's Mails, the distinction is not always easy to see. Hence, any departmental regulation or agency rule which frustrates his attempts to find satisfaction might well appear to him to be one more instance of the excessive delegation of legislative power. And he might be right. The problem was aptly summarized by a committee of the Inter-Parliamentary Union:

The delegation by Parliament of its legislative powers to the executive raises one of the most complex and most baffling problems of contemporary constitutional law. Its complexity arises essentially from the difficulty of determining exactly where to draw the line between what is law and what are regulations, the two fields, according to classical theory, being the preserves of Parliament and Government respectively.[12]

When a legislature is too generous in the delegation of its legislative powers and when those exercising delegated powers do not take sufficient care to conform either to the intentions of the assembly that gave them the authority to act or to the public's interpretation of its own well-being, then the whole system of delegated powers is open to abuse.

Another aspect of the system of delegation which has often been condemned is the lack of provision for appeals from quasi-judicial decisions made by those who exercise delegated powers. While this problem of administrative justice is certainly a part of the whole question of the legislature's control of delegated powers, it also is a very large subject in its own right. Only enough will be said here to demonstrate the nature of the problem in Ontario and to indicate how it relates to the larger problem of parliamentary control.

Administrative law recognizes that there are whole areas of social conflict which are too specialized and complex for the ordinary courts to handle effectively, and that a simple and speedy method of handling cases by boards instead of courts eliminates enormous expense and delay and the annoyance of technical court procedure.[13] In many instances, the boards make decisions that are completely beyond the competence of the ordinary courts. For example, when a board decides whether or not to

[12]Inter-Parliamentary Union, *Parliaments: A Comparative Study on the Structure and Functioning of Representative Institutions in Forty-one Countries* (New York and London: Praeger, 1962 [first published in French in 1961]), p. 129.

[13]The contrast between the output of the regular courts and some boards is phenomenal. For example, of the 997 civil cases set down in the 1961 winter and spring assizes for jury trial in York County, only 63 were tried, whereas the Ontario Labour Relations Board disposes of over 2,000 cases each year. See "Justice Delayed and Denied," *Globe and Mail*, August 30, 1962, and the submission of the Ontario Federation of Labour, CLC, to the Gordon Committee, February 16, 1959, p. 17.

grant a franchise to a bus company, it is not so much interpreting a point of law as it is working out its policy towards commercial bus lines. If judicial review of the decision were allowed, the courts would simply be confirming the board's policy or substituting one of their own. The courts would lose their status as unbiased tribunals, and the board would become a redundant institution. Similarly, if appeals to the lieutenant governor in council were allowed, the Government would become directly involved in an infinite variety of administrative details, and the purpose behind the creation of boards would be obviated. On the other side, it must be pointed out that there *is* an aura of aloofness and objectivity surrounding the courts, which is noticeably absent from the boards. Whereas judges are amenable only to the crown in Parliament where there is public debate, there is the strong suspicion that many of the boards are amenable to the cabinet and can be dealt with without any public hearing. And, if the Government openly participated in the board's decision-making, the boards would lose their *raison d'être*. The solution, of course, is to find a *via media* between unchallenged autonomy for the boards on the one hand and the unrestricted right of judicial review by the courts on the other, and to encompass the boards with more comprehensive legislation. The need for more and better legislation is manifest in at least three areas.

First, existing legislation often fails to set forth clearly enough the field of jurisdiction being delegated to the board, the general policy that should guide the board in its actions, and the procedures the board should follow in arriving at its decisions. Too frequently boards with vaguely defined spheres of activity go about working out policies on an *ad hoc* basis as cases arise and, to the dismay of the legal profession, with little regard for such niceties as court rules of evidence or written reasoned decisions.

Secondly, legislation governing the quasi-judicial boards is not consistent or specific enough about the rights of appeal. No system of appeals outside of the courts has been established in Ontario as has been done in Manitoba, Saskatchewan, and British Columbia.[14] In some cases no mention whatsoever is made of appeals. Other statutes contain privative clauses which expressly forbid judicial review of a board's orders.[15] Those who oppose the use of privative clauses see them as a violation of the rule of law but this can hardly be the case because, in spite of the express words

[14]Ontario, Legislative Assembly, Select Committee on Administrative and Executive Problems of Government, *Minutes*, September 20, 1960.

[15]A good example of this type of provision is section 80 of the Labour Relations Act: "No decision order, direction, declaration or ruling of the Board shall be questioned or reviewed in any court, and no order shall be made or process entered, or proceedings taken in any court, whether by way of injunction, declaratory judgment, certiorari, mandamus, prohibition, quo warranto, or otherwise, to question, review, prohibit or restrain the Board of any of its proceedings." *RSO*, 1960, c. 202, s. 80.

of these clauses, the courts in fact *do* review the decisions of the boards, which are supposed to be exempt from such review.[16] If the concept of the rule of law is central to our system of government, the principle of the supremacy of parliament is certainly no less important. When the Ontario Legislative Assembly sees fit to give a board the final jurisdiction over an area of public concern, it does seem curious that the courts should be conceded the right to read these privative clauses out of the statutes. If the problems associated with the delegation of powers are to be solved, legislation must be passed to govern appeal procedures, and that legislation must then be obeyed – even by the courts.

The third area where legislation should be more explicit is in the delineation of responsibility. To whom, to what extent, and by means of what procedures are semi-independent agencies to be kept responsible? The legislation that delegates authority to a board should also specify whether it is to be directly responsible to the legislature or to a minister who would then assume responsibility for the over-all performance of the board.[17] In either case the degree of discretion allowed the agency and the means for maintaining control over it should both be laid out in the statute in as much detail as possible.

So far this section on delegated powers has dealt with three factors which have contributed to the "problem" of delegated powers in Ontario: insufficient care in devising legislation, lack of care in designing and enacting regulations, and failure to make adequate provision for appeals from the decisions of semi-independent agencies. The fourth and last factor to be mentioned is related to the third: the failure to provide for any definite system for legislative review of the regulations passed by those entrusted

[16]Maxwell Bruce, QC, Memorandum to the Select Committee on Administrative and Executive Problems, re: denial of judicial review of administrative action by the "privative clause" device, June 6, 1960. Usually the courts justify their review of boards' decisions by reference to their right to define the bounds of the powers delegated to the boards and their responsibility to ensure that those bounds are respected. In other words, they claim the right of judicial review, i.e., the right to declare board decisions *ultra vires* or "beyond the powers" conferred upon the board by the appropriate act. They also claim the general authority to review administrative procedure to ensure that it is fair and does not violate the canons of "natural justice."

[17]The obscurity of the line of responsibility may be gathered from the statement by a former Deputy Minister of Economics that "even today, there is in fact if not in name, ambiguity as to what Minister the heads of certain boards and commissions should approach to consider policy matters." (G. E. Gathercole, "Outline of a basis for Discussion by the Select Committee on Administrative and Executive Problems," p. 2.) Another indication of this failure to assign responsibility is the practice of the provincial secretary of tabling many of the agency reports as a matter of courtesy instead of these being placed before the House by the ministers of departments with functions related to those of the various agencies. If the ministers tabled the reports they would be expected to assume at least some degree of responsibility for them.

with subordinate rule-making authority. If a semi-independent agency or a departmental body performs a quasi-judicial function, there is usually some semblance of a hearing and even some chance of an appeal from the decision made, but thousands of administrative decisions are made which are never subjected to any public hearing whatsoever. It is felt by many that if the rules and regulations passed by these agencies were subject to regular review by the legislature, many of the abuses which they currently perpetrate would disappear automatically and others could be eliminated eventually. In the meantime, the complete absence of any such formal review procedure must certainly encourage the kinds of excesses which have brought the whole system of delegated powers into disrepute.

Several procedures have been adopted in the United Kingdom and Canada to correct possible abuses and allay fears. In the United Kingdom, Lord Justice Hewart's book, *The New Despotism* (1929), brought the whole problem to the forefront of public attention and resulted in the appointment of the Committee on Ministers' Powers (Donoughmore Committee), which reported in 1932. This Committee was appointed "to consider the powers exercised by or under the direction of (or by persons or bodies appointed specially by) Ministers of the Crown by way of (a) delegated legislation and (b) judicial or quasi-judicial decision, and to report what safeguards are desirable or necessary to secure the constitutional principles of the sovereignty of Parliament and the supremacy of the law."[18] The criticisms and suggestions made in this report and the studies and discussions which followed it, particularly during the second world war, resulted in a number of improvements in the use and control of delegated powers.

Then, in 1955, a second major step was taken with the appointment of the Committee on Administrative Tribunals and Enquiries (Franks Committee). The terms of reference of this Committee corresponded broadly to the second part of the Donoughmore Committee's terms. The 1932 Committee was to look into the question of delegated legislation as well as the question of quasi-judicial decisions, but the Franks Committee, which reported in 1957, was appointed to investigate the latter only. Its terms of reference were "to consider and make recommendations on: (a) The constitution and working of tribunals other than the ordinary courts of law. . . . (b) The working of such administrative procedures as include the holding of an enquiry or hearing by or on behalf of a Minister on an appeal or as the result of objections."[19] Using the criteria of openness,

18United Kingdom, Parliament, Committee on Ministers' Powers *Report* (London: His Majesty's Stationery Office, Cmd. 4060, 1932), p. v.
19United Kingdom, Parliament, Committee on Administrative Tribunals and Enquiries, *Report* (London: Her Majesty's Stationery Office, Cmd. 218, 1957), p. iii.

fairness, and impartiality, the Franks Committee made a number of recommendations, most of which have been implemented, either under the Tribunals and Inquiries Act, 1958, or simply by administrative action.

The provisions governing tribunals and inquiries may be summarized briefly.[20] The Act of 1958 created a new body, called the Council on Tribunals, which keeps the working of over two thousand tribunals and inquiries under constant review. This Council is purely an advisory body with no executive power, but it can publish its views and it does have the blessings of the Government; hence, the tribunals under its supervision are under some pressure to conform to its specifications. The composition of a tribunal has to be related to the kind of work it does and the tendency to appoint chairmen with legal qualifications has been growing.[21] Although no standard code of procedure is laid down for all tribunals, every tribunal must have some carefully formulated rules of procedure, and when new tribunals are set up the Council has to be consulted about the procedural rules which government departments make for them. Appeals are still not always available, but the Franks Committee recommended that, generally speaking, there should be the right of appeal to an appellate tribunal, with a further appeal on a point of law to the courts. And in some cases, an aggrieved citizen may appeal to any of a variety of authorities.

So far as delegated legislation in Britain is concerned, Parliament – which must retain ultimate control – has developed a number of specific procedures for supervising subordinate legislation in addition to the normal opportunities provided in the legislative process.[22] The Statutory Instruments Act, 1946, provided for the numbering, printing, publication, citation, and laying before the House of "statutory instruments," the general term used by the Act to refer to a variety of rules and regulations.[23] About half the British statutory instruments – avowedly those concerned merely with machinery, such as the description of a form – do not have to

[20]Much of the following description is taken from an address to the Administrative Law Section of the American Bar Association on August 29, 1960, by H. W. R. Wade, reader in English law, Cambridge University, England. Professor Wade was one of the original members of the Council on Tribunals.

[21]J. Harvey and L. Bather, *The British Constitution* (London: Macmillan, 1963), pp. 388–9.

[22]The following details have been garnered mainly from Eric Taylor, *The House of Commons at Work* (4th ed.; Middlesex: Penguin, 1961), pp. 187–8 and Harvey and Bather, *The British Constitution*, pp. 378–2.

[23]It is not meant to imply here that there were none of these provisions prior to 1946. For example, instruments of delegated legislation have been systematically published in Britain since 1896. Those interested in the history of the supervision of delegated legislation in the United Kingdom should consult John E. Kersell, *Parliamentary Supervision of Delegated Legislation: the United Kingdom, Australia, New Zealand and Canada* (London: Stevens & Sons, 1960), pp. 6–9, 14–22, 43–67, *passim*.

be laid before Parliament, and those that are tabled are dealt with in one of three ways. Some, approximately 15 per cent, are not subject to any debate whatsoever.[24] In other cases the instrument is "laid" on the table and, unless some member moves a "prayer" to annul it during the period of forty sittings days during which it is vulnerable, it continues in force. This provision covers about 30 per cent of the total number of instruments that are tabled. And, finally, a few very significant statutory instruments require an "affirmative resolution," which means that the order lapses or does not come into effect unless or until the House has passed a resolution to approve it. While this usually takes only a few moments, it may entail a lengthy debate if the order is opposed.[25]

To assist it in considering the statutory instruments that either require its confirmation or are subject to annulment, Parliament appoints in each session a Select Committee on Statutory Instruments, usually referred to as the Scrutiny Committee. It is the responsibility of this Committee to scrutinize the eight hundred or so statutory instruments referred to it to check for such things as the unusual or unexpected use of powers, the need for elucidation, provisions imposing a charge on the public revenues or purporting to have a retrospective effect, etc. The Committee is assisted by speaker's counsel. The terms of reference for the Scrutiny Committee are strictly limited: it cannot comment on departmental policy or on the merits of any particular instrument but can only draw the attention of the House to any orders it thinks merit special consideration. The Committee looks at less than a quarter of the statutory instruments tabled each year, and only about one per cent of these are brought to the attention of the House. Of those which are brought to the attention of the House, only about one in three is debated. Nevertheless, the Committee does have a salutary effect on the departments, and it has also made some useful suggestions concerning the drafting and consolidation of statutory instruments.

24Ibid., p. 159.
25Professor Kersell has estimated that the British House of Commons has devoted 4 per cent of its total sitting hours to the debate of delegated legislation since 1945 (Ibid., p. 160), but this seems rather unlikely. Lord Campion does not even specify this item in his analysis of the parliamentary timetable [Lord Campion, Introduction to the Procedure of the House of Commons (3rd ed.; London: Macmillan, 1958), p. 337], but it is probably included in the category labelled "Incidental Business," which also includes such items as the adjournment of the House under standing order 9, votes of censure and matters of privilege. In the years 1945 to 1954 this whole category only accounted for approximately 8.5 per cent of the time of the House, and the bulk of this was taken up by Government adjournment motions. If only 24 negative resolutions were debated in the House from the time the Scrutiny Committee was set up in 1944 until 1959 (Kersell, Parliamentary Supervision of Delegated Legislation, p. 60), it seems unlikely that the debates on these and affirmative resolutions took up 4 per cent of the time of the House in those fifteen years.

The "problem" of delegated powers is of fairly recent origin in Canada, and provisions for the control of these powers are greatly inferior to those developed in the United Kingdom.[26] A major difference between the systems in these two countries is that, while the Canadian federal government has established a few appeal boards, it does not have anything like the vast network of tribunals that exists in Britain. At the federal level in Canada, as in the provinces, both legislative and judicial powers are often delegated to one and the same agency. This makes matters slightly confusing and makes exact comparisons with the British pattern impossible.[27] Canada has not developed any central administrative machinery such as the British Council on Tribunals to supervise the work of its semi-independent agencies, whether mainly legislative or judicial in nature. Nor, for that matter, has the Canadian government ever sponsored a full-scale investigation of delegated powers along the lines followed by the Donoughmore and Franks committees.

Prior to the second world war there was no systematic requirement for the publication of orders in council or other administrative regulations, though publication of certain designated orders was mandatory. In most cases, the decision as to whether or not certain regulations were to be published rested with the minister of the originating department. However, the enormous increase in the number of rules made by the governor general in council during the war made it imperative that these rules be widely publicized and, by the end of the war, the practice of systematically publishing delegated legislation was thoroughly established.[28] After two years of experience under an order in council which required the publication and tabling of all instruments made under delegated powers, the requirement was given statutory authority in the Regulations Act of 1950.[29]

The passing of the Regulations Act in 1950 was a significant step towards the goal of parliamentary supervision of delegated legislation. The provisions of the Act at least made it possible for Parliament and the public to determine without too much difficulty what the law touching any matter was. However, that is about all that can be said for the system. There are no general provisions for any kind of systematic review of the instruments of delegated legislation once they are laid before Parliament,

[26]J. R. Mallory, "Delegated Legislation in Canada: Recent Changes in Machinery," *Canadian Journal of Economics and Political Science*, vol. XIX (November 1953), p. 462.

[27]This also accounts for the fact that in much of the discussion of the delegation of powers in Ontario and Canada in this chapter, the two types of delegation are treated simultaneously.

[28]Mallory, "Delegated Legislation in Canada," p. 463.

[29]R. M. Dawson, *The Government of Canada* (4th ed., rev. by Norman Ward; Toronto: University of Toronto Press, 1963), p. 293.

although one statute does require affirmation of instruments made under its authority, and two provide for motions to annul.[30] Of course, the Canadian House of Commons, like most legislative bodies, may use the normal opportunities to influence the executive in order to exercise some control over delegated legislation, but such opportunities are not adequate for the task.

Now that the procedures followed at Westminster and Ottawa to control the exercise of delegated powers have been noted it is possible to analyse and evaluate the procedures that have been developed at Queen's Park for this purpose.

While Ontario has had no exhaustive study of this subject, at least two select committees of the House have looked into the question, and the Gordon Committee, which reported in 1959, put much of its emphasis on problems of delegated powers, both legislative and judicial. In 1940 a select committee was appointed to inquire into the administration of justice in the province, and a portion of its report dealt with the subject of the judicial functions exercised by semi-independent agencies of government.[31] Little came of this report, however, and the question of delegated powers was not investigated in any thorough way until the Gordon Committee was set up.[32]

The major impetus for the appointment of the Gordon Committee came from a suggestion made by the then Provincial Auditor, Mr. H. A. Cotnam, in his report for the 1956–57 fiscal year. In this report, Mr. Cotnam pointed out that until 1943 the departments of the Ontario government were largely used as the machinery of government to give effect to tasks imposed by legislation and Government:

The departments were the operative agencies for carrying out the policies and decisions of Government and were each constituted not only to deal with the technical or specialized subject or groups of subjects, but also to provide and administer the actual services and institutions relating to those subjects. The department of health, for example, provided and administered hospitals for the mentally ill; the department of reform institutions provided and adminis-

---

[30]Kersell, *Parliamentary Supervision of Delegated Legislation*, p. 163.

[31]For the report of the Select Committee appointed to inquire into the administration of justice, along with the minutes of its meetings see Ontario, Legislative Assembly, *Journals*, 1941, part II, Appendix 2, and especially pp. 753–4, 1662, 1665, 1731, and 1764. (Hereinafter, the short title, *Journals*, will be used to refer to the *Journals* of the Legislative Assembly of Ontario).

[32]No doubt the problems of delegated powers will also be dealt with by the Royal Commission on Human Rights and Civil Liberties being carried out by Chief Justice J. C. McRuer, and by the Ontario Law Reform Commission, also under the chairmanship of Chief Justice McRuer, but neither of these commissions had reported at time of writing.

tered reform institutions to control the persons committed thereto. Boards and commissions, operating outside of the departments, were relatively few in number and consisted for the most part of The Hydro-Electric Power Commission of Ontario; the Workmen's Compensation Board; the Liquor Control Board of Ontario; The Niagara Parks Commission and the Ontario Northland Transportation Commission. It can, therefore, be said that the general pattern, until near the end of the second world war, was that the actual administration of government business was largely carried out by departments.[33]

The Auditor then listed sixteen boards and commissions that had been added since 1943 and concluded that

In my opinion, a survey to assess the strength and weakness of the present machinery of government is needed. What is envisaged as a result is not a detailed organization chart for recasting the whole organization of government but such a survey would bring thought to bear upon the fundamental problems of government as a whole. Such a survey could be expected to report upon a reallocation of duties between departments themselves and between departments and boards and commissions based on the principle of the nature of the service rendered to the community.[34]

The Standing Committee on Government Commissions considered the Provincial Auditor's report during the 1958 session and suggested that personnel qualified to review the problems of government should be appointed to make a survey for the purpose of inquiring into and reporting upon the relationship of provincial commissions and boards to the Government of Ontario, the Legislative Assembly, and the government departments with a view to: "(a) Preserving governmental responsibility and ensuring effective control by the Legislature over Public Expenditure and decisions; (b) Maintaining high standards of administrative economy and efficiency in all branches of the provincial services."[35]

No more detailed instructions than these were ever laid down for the Gordon Committee. In his letter to the Chairman of the Committee, the Prime Minister said only that "the terms of reference broadly are to examine into the administrative and executive problems of the Government of Ontario in all divisions of the provincial service and to examine into the relationship of Boards and Commissions to the Government and the Legislature,"[36] and referred to the terms of reference of the Haldane Committee on the Machinery of Government, 1918, as a precedent for such broad directives. The order in council appointing the Committee simply

[33]Ontario, Legislative Assembly, *Provincial Auditor's Report, 1956–57* (Toronto: Queen's Printer, 1958), pp. 17–18.

[34]*Ibid.*

[35]*Journals*, 1958, p. 132.

[36]Prime Minister Leslie M. Frost to Mr. Walter Gordon, May 15, 1958, in Gordon Committee *Report*, pp. 87–9.

named its members (Walter L. Gordon, William A. Mackintosh, and Clifford R. Magone, QC) and provided for their payment, giving no further terms of reference than those already quoted from Mr. Frost's letter.[37]

To guide them more directly in their endeavours, the Committee laid down the three goals which they felt administrative or procedural arrangements should achieve in order to "make more explicit the objectives we have had in mind in the course of our work. They are, in effect, our terms of reference."[38] It was the interpretation that the Committee members put upon their terms of reference that made their work so directly relevant to the subject of legislative-executive relations. The Committee felt that to be satisfactory administrative and procedural arrangements for the conduct of government business should:

– contain safeguards against abuses of power and authority. In broad terms this means an insistence upon the accountability of government for all its activities including those conducted by government departments and by separate agencies. It also means there must be adequate protection of the rights of individual citizens.
– provide for adequate supervision and control over all administrative actions performed in the name of government. In both policy and financial spheres, the lines and limits of authority should be clear.
– operate as smoothly, efficiently and economically as possible. This implies, among other things, the avoidance of overlapping and duplication of responsibilities.[39]

The bulk of the Gordon Committee *Report* is taken up with detailed descriptions of the various departments and agencies of government, but some eighty-four pages of commentary include chapters on supervision and control of delegated legislation (which includes a section on delegated judicial functions), departmental organization, and boards and commissions. And, in the introductory statement, stress is laid upon four broad standards that the process of delegation of powers should meet if the objects set out as the Committee's terms of reference are to be met: ministerial responsibility, financial accountability, grouping of related functions, and provision for appeals. Of even greater use to anyone interested in the subject matter of the Committee's deliberations than the *Report* itself are the briefs that were submitted to the Committee by some twenty-three organizations and the various special reports submitted by officials at the Committee's request.[40]

37The order in council was dated June 12, 1958. *Ibid.*, p. 89.
38*Ibid.*, p. 4.
39*Ibid.*, pp. 3–4.
40Unfortunately, these briefs and submissions were not published and are not readily available to the public. However, they were made available to the Select

The Gordon Committee reported on September 25, 1959, and on April 4 of the following year the Select Committee on Administrative and Executive Problems of Government appointed with the same broad terms of reference as had been set out for the Gordon Committee, plus the specific instructions to study the *Report* of that Committee and make recommendations about its implementation.[41] There are a number of indications that the Legislative Assembly took the Select Committee very seriously and that the Committee itself was impressed with its significance. For example, all of the political parties in the House had strong representations on the Committee. Of the eight Progressive Conservatives, three had contested their party's leadership, and three others had served as campaign chairmen for leadership candidates. Another was an able member from the eastern part of the province, and the eighth was a cabinet minister. The CCF was represented by its leader and the Liberals by a former leader and one of the best of their younger members. More than three-quarters of the members of the Committee were lawyers. Reinforcing this legal bias was the Committee Counsel, Maxwell Bruce, QC, and the Secretary of the Committee, Miss C. M. Wysocki, a solicitor in the Attorney General's Department. Virtually all the ministers of Government and senior members of the public service appeared before the Committee, as well as a number of prominent people from outside the service. In response to published invitations, eight briefs were submitted to the Committee, which already had the benefit of the twenty-three briefs submitted to the Gordon Committee. A wealth of special material was also prepared for the Committee by its own Counsel and Secretary as well as by officials in the employ of the Government.

As with the Gordon Committee, the documentation accumulated by the Select Committee on Administrative and Executive Problems is even more useful for the person with a serious interest in the subject than the Committee's reports themselves.[42] The Committee made two reports before it was allowed to lapse. In its first report, tabled in the House on November 7, 1960, the Committee declared its adherence "to the well established principles of responsible government including ministerial and executive responsibility," which it saw as the "key to the whole subject

---

Committee on Administrative and Executive Problems, and the author was granted access to all of the materials collected by that Committee. These documents are sufficiently voluminous to fill at least one large filing cabinet, and it is to be hoped that they will eventually be deposited in a location more accessible to the public.

[41]*Journals*, 1960, pp. 188–9.

[42]The most complete collection of these documents was that of the Hon. A. Kelso Roberts, who was chairman of the Committee.

under consideration."[43] Wherever the Committee found in the governmental structure a tendency to stray from these principles and responsibilities it advocated courses of action suggested in its slogan: "Return to the Legislature." The bulk of the twenty-four-page *Interim Report* dealt with the forty-eight specific recommendations which the Committee had gleaned from the Gordon Committee *Report*, and either approved the implementation of the recommendations, amended them, or rejected them. Seventeen new recommendations were made. The second report of the Committee was not tabled until March 19, 1962.[44] Only seven pages long, it dealt with two matters: the recommendation to set up a statutory public accounts committee, and the proposal to establish a central registry office for filing decisions of administrative tribunals; it recommended the former and opposed the latter.

A few of the detailed recommendations in the Gordon Committee *Report* and in the two reports of the Select Committee on Administrative and Executive Problems of Government have been implemented, but the general suggestions relating to legislative-executive relations had not been given effect at time of writing. Reference has already been made to some of the items included in these three reports and allusions will be made to them later. No detailed discussion of them is warranted here, since they have apparently had only a limited effect on the government of the province. It will be more profitable to turn now to a description of the actual means available to the Legislative Assembly to supervise and control the powers that have been delegated to the various facets of the executive branch of the government in Ontario.

If the Assembly is going to review the use of the legislative powers which it has delegated, two preconditions must be met: the instruments by which those powers are exercised must be published, and they must be laid before the legislature. The first of these prerequisites is provided for in the Regulations Act,[45] which was first enacted in 1944.[46] This Act follows fairly closely the draft legislation adopted by the Conference of Commissioners on Uniformity of Legislation in Canada in 1943.[47] It stipulates that all regulations must be filed with the registrar of regulations and

[43]Ontario, Legislative Assembly, Select Committee on Administrative and Executive Problems of Government, *Interim Report*, p. 4.

[44]Ontario, Legislative Assembly, Select Committee on Administrative and Executive Problems of Government, *Second Interim Report*.

[45]*RSO*, 1960, c. 349.

[46]An Act to provide for the Central Filing and Publication of Regulations. *SO*, 1944, c. 52.

[47]E. H. Silk, assistant deputy attorney general, Memorandum to the Select Committee on Administrative and Executive Problems of Government re: legislation by Incorporation or Reference, September 19, 1960.

published in the *Ontario Gazette* within one month of filing. By section 5 (3) of the Act, a regulation that is not published is not effective against a person who has not had actual notice of it. The Regulations Act also provides for a registrar of regulations and lays down certain terms of reference to guide him in the performance of his duties. The second precondition of the legislative review of regulations is not met by the Regulations Act nor by any other Ontario statute: no general provisions are made for tabling subordinate legislation in the House.

There are a number of other possible aids to legislative review that are absent from the Ontario Act. For example, nothing in the Act requires that regulations should be reviewed by the law officers of the crown or be approved by the lieutenant governor in council, and the terms of reference governing the registrar of regulations are certainly not broad enough to cover such responsibilities. Similarly, the Act does not consider that public discussion might take place before regulations have effect. In fact, regulations normally come into force on the day on which they are filed, which may be a full month before they are even published in the *Gazette*. Although regulations cannot be made effective against an individual until they are published or until the individual has been notified of their existence, they nevertheless come into effect before the public has heard of them. Hence open discussion of the merits of any given regulation is precluded until after the regulation has been promulgated. And, finally, there is nothing in the Act to facilitate any kind of *ex post facto* review of regulations. Such a review could be carried out in a number of ways – by a committee of the legislature, by an officer especially appointed by the House for that purpose, by an outside group, or by a committee of civil servants – but, whatever the body responsible for actually reviewing the regulations, its work would be greatly assisted if the Regulations Act required the registrar of regulations to make an annual report to it, specifying which regulations appeared to require special consideration. Even if no special body were charged with reviewing delegated legislation, informal review would be facilitated if the Act required that more publicity be given to regulations. After all, the *Ontario Gazette* is not a very widely circulated or popular periodical.

One feature of the Regulations Act which bears reiteration is that it does not apply to all subordinate legislation. Section 6(*a*) gives the minister to whom the administration of the Act has been assigned the power to determine whether a regulation, rule, order, or by-law *is* a regulation within the meaning of the Act, and there are no guidelines given to assist him in interpreting what is meant by the phrase, "of a legislative nature." It is not unlikely that different persons would have different opinions about which instruments were "of a legislative nature" and therefore subject to the provisions of the Act. Section 1(d) of the Act specifies certain categories of delegated legislation which are automatically excluded from the jurisdiction of the Act. In general, these exceptions have been made (a) where there is some other machinery to ensure that the regulations are made available to the public, or (b) where the subject matter is not deemed to be of a general public application, or where it is not considered to be primarily of a legislative nature but there is a possible doubt.[48] Exceptions under the first category include: by-laws of municipalities and local boards that require approval; orders of the Ontario Municipal Board and the Ontario Energy Board, other than rules governing their procedure; rules of the Ontario Racing Commission; and the designation of King's Highways. Illustrations of exceptions under category (b) would be: regulations made by the governing bodies of the Broker-Dealers' Association, the Ontario Teachers' Federation, agricultural associations and some regulations made by conservation authorities; by-laws of public hospitals; orders under the Highway Improvement Act designating which roads are to be the responsibilitty of the province or the local municipality; and regulations by the minister of education defining the content of courses and approving text books.

If no regulations are laid before the provincial legislature for specfic approval or debate and if only some regulations are so much as filed and published, what possible means are there available to members to review the use of delegated powers?

The usually suggested channel of review is indirect, through the minister responsible for the agency exercising the delegated power. If the agency concerned is a branch or division of a minister's department, then certainly the constitutional principle of individual ministerial responsibility does afford some opportunity for legislative control over the operations of that agency. But even in this case it is not always easy to give substance to the principle of responsibility: the members must still obtain information about the operations of the agency, and they must have a legitimate opportunity to bring the subject before the House. However, the real difficulty in applying this principle to the problem of controlling delegated powers comes when the agency exercising the power is extradepartmental and possesses a large degree of autonomy. The amount of responsibility that ministers will accept for the activities of semi-independent agencies is of limited usefulness for purposes of legislative review and varies from minister to minister and from agency to agency. It is generally expected

[48]A. N. Stone, assistant registrar of regulations, Memorandum to the Select Committee on Administrative and Executive Problems of Government, September 19, 1960.

that ministers will accept responsibility for the over-all policy followed by an agency, but they are not expected to be responsible for the details of an agency's day-to-day actions.[49] Indeed, the whole purpose in creating such bodies is to take such details out of the Government's hands. However, when seeking to control delegated authority, it is quite often the details about the use of that authority that interest the Legislative Assembly and the public alike. If the need for delegation is accepted at all, then surely the primary problem left is to supervise the detailed use of the power delegated to ensure that it is not abused in individual cases. But ministers will not accept responsibility for the details and are not expected to do so.

If semi-independent agencies are to be controlled by the legislature by means of ministers assuming responsibility for them, then the reports submitted to the House by those agencies become very important – not so much for their specific content, which is seldom of much value, but because they form a tangible link between the MPPs, the ministers, and the agencies. Similarly, if the provincial auditor is given responsibility for auditing their accounts, another tie between the legislature and the agencies is created. And, of course, any information about the province's boards and commissions that the members can obtain will assist them in controlling those agencies. However, if the concept of ministerial responsibility were to operate fully, ministers would have to accept responsibility for, and defend in the House, the reports and accounts of these semi-independent bodies, but this the ministers are unwilling to do since they supposedly have little control over either. The usefulness of the reports submitted by the semi-independent agencies and of the auditor's reports of agency accounts is limited in one other important respect: not all of the agencies make reports, and not all of the accounts are audited by the provincial auditor. The Gordon Committee listed eleven important agencies for which no reports were tabled in the 1958 session.[50] As of July 12, 1960, forty-seven reports are required by statute to be tabled, but in the 1960 session only forty-three of these were in fact tabled. Although not required by statute, eight other reports were filed gratuitously during the same session.[51] The Select Committee on Administrative and Executive Problems listed eleven agencies of the Ontario government

[49]Even when, as often happens, ministers themselves are members of boards and commissions, they generally refuse to accept responsibility for specific actions taken or decisions made by those agencies. The reason for this is apparently that board decisions are group decisions and the minister might be outvoted on specific items of business.

[50]Gordon Committee *Report*, pp. 20–1.

[51]From a letter by R. J. Cudney, deputy provincial secretary, to Miss C. Wysocki, secretary to the Select Committee on Administrative and Executive Problems of Government, July 12, 1960.

that the provincial auditor did not audit.[52] For eight of these, there was express statutory authority to enable the lieutenant governor in council to appoint an auditor or make regulations for auditing. In no case was the appointment of the provincial auditor precluded; an appointment could be made by an order in council in each case. The statutory provisions in the other three cases where the provincial auditor did not carry out the audit did not clearly specify how an auditor was to be appointed, but in no case was there any obvious reason why the provincial auditor should not be given the responsibility.[53] Since 1960 some minor changes have been made, but the general situation is much the same. In his address to the Public Accounts Committee in 1964, the Provincial Auditor listed ten government agencies that were audited by outside firms. His list included one agency that had not been mentioned by the Select Committee in 1960 (Ontario Municipal Retirement Board) and omitted two which had been listed in 1960 (Ontario Water Resources Commission and the Niagara Parks Commission). The semi-independent agencies listed by the Provincial Auditor are given in Appendix D, which also indicates the auditing authority for each.

No special occasion for the review of delegated powers and debate of reports and activities of agencies is available to members, but those agencies included in departmental estimates are reviewed in Committee of Supply. In recent years the Government has also allowed the Committee of Supply to discuss the activities of agencies not dependent on funds voted by the House and therefore not subject to review during supply proceedings: "The practice is to call the agency concerned as if it were the last item of the departmental estimates of the minister through whom it reports."[54] While this unusual procedure is of some value, its effectiveness is limited by the fact that each agency is dealt with as a single item. There is no breakdown of subject matter to focus debate and encourage more detailed analysis. About the only other way for a member to initiate a debate on a particular agency report is to introduce a resolution for the consideration thereof,[55] but such a resolution is not guaranteed any better treatment than is usually afforded private members' resolutions – which

[52]*Interim Report*, p. 13.

[53]Maxwell Bruce, Memorandum to the Select Committee on Administrative and Executive Problems of Government re: Provincial Audits, June 2, 1960.

[54]Kenneth Bryden, "Committees of the Ontario Legislature," an unpublished paper prepared for a graduate seminar in public administration conducted by Professors M. Brownstone and W. Grasham of the Department of Political Science, University of Toronto, April 15, 1965, p. 4.

[55]Ontario Legislative Assembly, Select Committee Appointed April 11th, 1960, to Study and Inquire into Matters Pertaining to the Transaction of Business in the Legislature, *Report*, p. 2. This *Report* was tabled on November 23, 1960, as Sessional Paper 54.

probably accounts for the fact that members rarely attempt to use this device.

Undoubtedly the best opportunity available to members to investigate the use made of delegated powers is in the Standing Committee on Government Commissions.[56] This Committee was first set up in 1951 and meets an average of five times each session. The commissions brought before the Committee are those selected by the members of the Committee, including opposition members, who thus shape the agenda to suit themselves.[57] Usually the chief executive officer of the agency concerned comes before the Committee and makes a prepared statement. As would be expected, such statements are rather grey and present members with as few hooks on which to hang difficult questions as possible. Nevertheless, members do ask questions: members of the opposition parties seek to dig up politically useful material, and members of the Government party try to suggest that their constituencies deserve better treatment. Occasionally the representative of an agency will refuse to answer a question on the grounds that it involves "policy" laid down in the act governing the agency's operation.[58] Some opposition members launch into attacks on the agencies that come before the Committee, and there are usually some members from the Government who content themselves with lauding the efforts of the agency to serve the people of Ontario.

Normally an agency will only appear at one meeting of the Committee lasting about two hours, and the agency's accounts are not laid before the Committee for scrutiny. In short, the Committee never does a very thorough job of investigating the operations of the semi-independent agencies, and it makes virtually no attempt to review either the regulations of a legislative nature originating with the agencies nor the decisions of a judicial nature that the agencies make. Part of the blame for the cursory examinations carried out by the Standing Committee on Government Commissions must rest with the MPPs who simply do not prepare themselves for the job they are to perform, but they are also hindered by the fact that so little information is provided for them and no assistance is given them by anyone qualified for the task.

In the 1960 session, following the recommendation of the Gordon Committee,[59] a series of motions proposed by Premier Frost referred

[56]Some useful opportunities to fulfill this purpose have also been made available in the Energy, Health and Legal Bills committees which sometimes investigate the operations of the Hydro-Electric Power Commission, the Ontario Hospital Services Commission, and the Securities Commission, respectively.

[57]From an interview with John H. White, PC: London South, May 25, 1965.

[58]From an interview with James Trotter, Lib. Parkdale, May 12, 1965.

[59]Gordon Committee *Report*, p. 21.

eighty-five agencies to thirteen standing committees.[60] The motions were identical and the first of the series is quoted here to demonstrate the purposes the Prime Minister had in mind when he brought them before the House.

That in order to promote economy, efficiency and improved service in the operation of Crown Agencies it is deemed advisable to invite the observations of the Committee on *Agriculture* on the present organization and methods of procedure of the undernoted Crown Agencies with a view to determining whether the procedures, methods and organization generally are well adapted for the most economical operation as is possible consistent with the efficient and comprehensive conduct of the affairs of the respective Crown Agencies. [There follows a list of eighteen Agencies.] Further, That there be referred to the said Committee on Agriculture the most current annual reports and their accompanying audited statements of the Crown Agencies mentioned in this resolution.

While this innovation was not a sufficient solution to the problem of how to control the semi-independent agencies, it was certainly a large step in the right direction. If nothing else, it was an encouraging sign of awareness and concern on the part of the Government. Nevertheless, the whole grand design fell through. None of the standing committees departed to any significant extent from the routine it had followed in previous years, and no committee reported on the agencies that had been referred to it.[61] No similar attempt to distribute the agencies among the committees has been made since.

Although the question of judicial review of decisions made by subordinate agencies is not obviously germane to a study of legislative-executive relations, to the degree that the legislature defines the nature and extent of this review it is definitely relevant. Even if the Legislative Assembly created for itself every possible technique for reviewing delegated powers, it would still be hampered in this task by the fact that it only sits for three or four months of the year. Realizing this, it is quite conceivable that the legislative branch of government would transfer some of its responsibility for review to the courts. Thus, judicial review might in some cases serve as an alternative to legislative review.

Despite the privative clauses that remain in some statutes,[62] all statutory tribunals existing in Ontario are subject to judicial review by means of one or more of certiorari, mandamus, prohibition, and injunction or declaration, depending on whether the agency is judicial, quasi-judicial,

---

[60]*Journals*, 1960, pp. 56–63.

[61]Bryden, "Committees of the Ontario Legislature," p. 10.

[62]The Gordon Committee *Report* (p. 23), listed six statutes that included privative clauses.

or administrative in nature.[63] However, the procedural maze that confronts a person who seeks judicial review by such means is enough to dissuade most persons from ever making the attempt. The Ontario section of the Canadian Bar Association has for a number of years been concerned with the difficulties confronting those who wish the courts to review board decisions and it has made a number of proposals,[64] but thus far no action has been taken. The privative clauses remain and no significant steps have been taken to make available appeals to the courts, the lieutenant governor in council, a responsible minister, or to appeal boards within the administrative system itself. It should also be added that no formal steps have been taken to establish standard procedural safeguards within the judicial and quasi-judicial agencies themselves. The Gordon Committee rejected the suggestion that a minimum code of procedure should be imposed upon all government agencies, but it did recommend that the individual agencies should draft their own codes and that these should then be subject to review by the law officers of the crown and to approval by the lieutenant governor in council.[65] Little has been done to implement this proposal. The Select Committee on Administrative and Executive Problems also considered a proposal to establish a central registry office for filing decisions of administrative tribunals, but it rejected the suggestion on the ground that interested parties could apply for decisions directly to the appropriate agencies.[66]

Thus, while the Legislative Assembly of Ontario has been only slightly less prone to delegate legislative and judicial powers to semi-independent agencies than either the British or Canadian parliaments, it has been slow to adopt methods for controlling the powers so delegated. Ill-defined powers are delegated to semi-independent agencies, and few rules of procedure are laid down for them to follow in the execution of their responsibilities. The lines of responsibility are blurred, and the principle of ministerial responsibility is more observed in the breach than in the practice thereof. Few channels of appeal have been developed within the administrative structure, and the right of appeal from a government board to the regular courts is so circumscribed with procedural difficulties as to be close to non-existent. The Government's effort to bring the various semi-independent agencies under the scrutiny of the House was rendered

[63]M. A. R. Laird, then senior solicitor, Department of Attorney General, in a memorandum to the Hon. A. Kelso Roberts, QC, then attorney general, February 5, 1959.

[64]See the brief to the Gordon Committee filed by the Ontario section of the Canadian Bar Association, January 6, 1959, esp. p. 28 and Appendix A.

[65]Gordon Committee *Report*, p. 28.

[66]*Second Interim Report*, p. 5.

ineffectual by the members who refused to rise to the opportunity. The instruments of delegated legislation are not tabled in the House and are not subjected to any kind of formal review. In short, the Legislative Assembly has only provided itself with three specific tools by which to supervise the exercise of delegated powers: it has required that all regulations of a legislative nature must be published so that members of the legislature and other citizens of the province may know that laws have been enacted by the agencies; it has created a Standing Committee on Government Commissions to keep a watchful eye on the over-all operations of the agencies; and it has perverted the purpose of Committee of Supply to allow some debate there on the general questions arising from a delegation of powers. Obviously, a number of other techniques of control must be devised if the executive branch is to be held clearly responsible to the legislature.

The Control of Finance

In this study of legislative-executive relations, as in most similar studies, the subject of parliamentary control over matters of public finance is treated as merely one aspect of the larger topic. However, it is well to remember that in the history of British constitutional development the first type of power achieved by parliament was over public finance. It was around this right to exercise control over the collection and the expenditure of public revenue that the key instiutions of modern parliamentary government took shape. Even the right to legislate is derived from parliament's control of the public purse, combined with the ancient right of petition: by forcing the crown to assent to its wishes before it would grant supply, parliament established its right first to suggest and then to impose legislation. Today, however, the situation is nearly the opposite: with the advent of political, and, more latterly, a degree of social, democracy, parliaments have become less concerned with keeping executives from spending public funds and more concerned with forcing their respective executives to expend ever greater amounts. Hence, the legislators' original function of keeping public expenditures within reasonable bounds has been taken over by members of the executive who are primarily responsible for governing and who are therefore expected to produce sound budgets.

Nevertheless, the legislative branch still has some functions to perform in the field of public finance. It is called upon to authorize the collection of revenue and to approve the ways in which the executive proposes to spend the money thus collected. But, perhaps most important if responsible government is to be maintained, it must oversee the actual expenditure of public funds to ensure that the executive uses the money only for the purposes approved and only in the amounts authorized. It is impossible under our system of government to completely separate executive and legislative responsibilities in the field of public finance but, in general, it may be said that the executive branch has primary responsibility for preparing the budget and the legislative branch has the final responsibility for seeing that the terms of the budget are obeyed. The roles played by both branches of government must be considered here. Since the subject is large and the general features of financial procedure well known, the discussion here will be limited almost entirely to the situation existing in Ontario; reference will be made to other jurisdictions only where the Ontario practice is unique or where it is thought that Ontario could profit from experience elsewhere.[67]

Probably the most logical place to begin a discussion of financial procedures is with the estimates, which are compiled as follows.[68] Usually in June of each year, the provincial treasurer writes to his colleagues in the executive council requesting each of them to have the estimates for his department for the following year prepared and submitted to the Treasury Board in the early autumn. The estimates submitted by each department were traditionally divided into amounts needed for salaries, maintenance, etc. However, this did not reveal the various programmes or projects that a department intended to carry out and thus made proper analysis and evaluation difficult. To make the estimates more meaningful, the Treasury Board requested that the departments begin including programme descriptions and costs in their 1963–64 submissions. Furthermore, the departments were asked to list their proposed new programmes in the descending order of their importance. When the departmental estimates of revenues and expenditures are received, they are compiled into a consolidated statement indicating the approximate financial position

[67]Those interested in making more detailed comparisons with the financial procedures developed at Ottawa and Westminster are directed to the following sources: Basil Chubb, *Control of Public Expenditure, Financial Committees of the House of Commons* (Oxford: Clarendon Press, 1952); W. F. Dawson, *Procedure in the Canadian House of Commons*; Saskatchewan, Legislative Assembly, Special Committee on Public Accounts Procedures, *Report*, February, 1964, tabled in the House on February 13, 1964, as Sessional Paper 41; Eric Taylor, *The House of Commons at Work*; Norman Ward, *The Public Purse: A Study in Canadian Democracy* (Toronto: University of Toronto Press, 1962).

[68]Many of the details about how the estimates are compiled are taken from an address given by C. E. Brannan, secretary of the Treasury Board, to the Ontario Public Accounts Committee, February 28, 1964.

of the province and giving a broad picture of the financial demands and resources available for the coming year. When this statement is ready the Treasury Board[69] reviews it, considering along with it a paper on the economic situation and outlook, a statement of projected revenue, and a statement of the impact on the public debt of the projected revenue and expenditure programme. Out of this review, over-all decisions are made about the general financial framework for the ensuing fiscal year.

To assist the Treasury Board with its decision-making function, an analyst from the permanent staff studies the various programmes in each department's estimates, to find out, for example, what levels of attainment have been achieved in these programmes in the past, how estimated staff requirements for the coming year compare with the requirements in past years, what the fundamental purpose of the programme is, and how it is organized. The Treasury Board analyst also makes certain that existing programmes are separated from proposed expansions and suggested new programmes. The latter are considered policy matters and are supposed to be approved by the Treasury Board and the executive council.

When the reports of the analysts are in and the Treasury Board has laid down the general guidelines for the ensuing fiscal year, the Board reviews with each minister the estimates for his department with a view to adjusting the estimates to conform to the over-all policy of the Government and to anticipated income. If reductions are necessary, an attempt is made to secure these by curtailing lower priority programmes and by practising administrative economies. This done, the estimates are printed and recommended to the Legislative Assembly by the lieutenant governor. The Legislative Assembly then reviews the estimates in a Committee of the Whole House known as the Committee of Supply.

Proceedings in Committee of Supply take up the bulk of the sitting time and embrace nearly every topic that ever comes before the Ontario House. In the 1964 session, 53.6 per cent of the time of the House was spent in this Committee. In the United Kingdom the business of supply is now allotted only twenty-six days and, from the 1945–46 session to the 1954–55 session, an average of only 17 per cent of the time of the House was used for this purpose.[70] Most of the time used by the Committee of Supply at Queen's Park is spent on the general debates that take place when each department's estimates are first introduced. The normal practice now is for each minister to introduce his estimates with a general

[69]For a description of the Treasury Board and its functions see chap. 3, pp. 55–61.

[70]Calculated from the information provided in Lord Campion, *An Introduction to the Procedure of the House of Commons*, p. 337. It must be remembered that the British House of Commons has an Estimates Committee which does much of the detailed work left to the Committee of Supply in Ontario.

statement of the department's recent activities and future plans. Naturally, the opposition critics of that department desire to respond so that usually a least two more general speeches follow. Quite often these speeches in Committee of Supply reiterate the points made in similar speeches during the throne and budget debates. In fact, in the opinion of the clerk of the House, the debates that initiate the review of each department's estimates amount to a "whole series of Throne and Budget Debates, and to excessive duplication and repetition."[71] When the general debate on a particular department is over the Committee of Supply begins the work for which it is primarily intended, namely, the detailed consideration of the proposed expenditures of the Government. Although proceedings at this point are focussed to a certain extent by the specific "votes" set forth for each department,[72] discussions are still quite wide ranging and cover anything from individual problems affecting particular constituencies to broad implications of Government policy. As has already been noted, opportunity is taken during supply proceedings to ask questions which the Government has been slow to answer[73] and to discuss the activities of semi-independent agencies, even though some of them are not dependent on funds voted by the legislature and therefore should not come before the Committee of Supply.[74] In short, Committee of Supply has become an undefined and poorly disciplined "catch-all."

Because the scope of the subject matter dealt with in Committee of Supply is broad and because its proceedings are rather informal does not necessarily hamper its over-all effectiveness as a tool for controlling the executive. However, the Committee of Supply does have certain defects which limit its usefulness. In the first place, the practice of rotating the chairmanship of the Committee of the Whole each year, giving the responsibility to backbenchers with few apparent qualifications for the job, has often left the Committee with completely inadequate supervision from the chair. Speaking from ample experience, one member has complained that if an opposition member touches a sensitive spot in the Government's defences "he will often have to cope with more than a reasonable amount of heckling and obstruction" and "sometimes proceedings in Committee of Supply degenerate into pure shouting matches."[75]

[71]Roderick Lewis, clerk of the Legislative Assembly, Memorandum to the Select Committee on Administrative and Executive Problems of Government, p. 19.

[72]The Estimates for the fiscal year that ended on March 31, 1965, totalled approximately $1,243 million and were divided into 185 separate votes, an average of $6,716,756 per vote.

[73]See chap. 6, pp. 202–4.

[74]See chap. 7, pp. 236–37.

[75]Bryden, "Committees of the Ontario Legislature," pp. 4–5. As anyone who has visited the Ontario legislature knows, not infrequently the shouting matches are initiated by the Member for Woodbine, Mr. Kenneth Bryden.

A second feature of supply procedure in Ontario which limits its effectiveness is the nature of the estimates themselves. The estimates tabled in the House do not contain all the information submitted to the Treasury Board by the departments and made available to the Treasury Board analysts who first study them. In fact, the Committee of Supply is labouring under even greater disadvantages than those experienced by the staff of the Treasury Board before the changes introduced in the 1963–64 estimates. The estimates give no description or explanation of programmes and no figures for previous years. No indication is given as to whether a proposed expenditure is for a new project or for a programme that is already in existence. Table 25 sets out the first vote in the estimates of the Treasury Department for the 1964–65 fiscal year and shows exactly what information the members are given. The notation "S" in the second column indicates that the item is "statutory": the minister's salary, etc., is provided for by legislation and does not have to be voted annually.

In its 1964 report, the Public Accounts Committee recommended that in order to provide the basis for a better appraisal of the estimates by the Legislative Assembly, they should include the following: (a) the approved estimate for the last completed fiscal year, (b) the actual expenditure for the last completed fiscal year, (c) the approved estimate for the current fiscal year, and (d) the interim forecast for the current fiscal year, in addition to the proposed expenditure for the forthcoming fiscal year which is normally given.[76] The Public Accounts Committee also recommended that the estimates and the accounts of the province should show a more detailed classification of the items included under the heading "maintenance," so that the cost of office equipment, supplies, and other categories of expenditure would be more immediately apparent and, likewise, that all grants under the heading "miscellaneous" should be designated by name and amount so that no grant would be made without the prior approval of either the legislature or the Treasury Board.[77]

Another shortcoming of the estimates is that they do not show the financial requirements of certain advisory committees – sometimes included in lists of semi-independent agencies – as separate entities. The estimated expenditures of these "departmental agencies," to use the term suggested by the Gordon Committee,[78] are presently included, but they

[76]Ontario, Legislative Assembly, Standing Committee on Public Accounts, *Report*, 2nd Session of the 27th Legislature May 7, 1964 (Sessional Paper 71), p. 2.

[77]For example, in the Estimates of the Department of Education for the 1964–65 fiscal year, miscellaneous grants, "to be paid as may be directed by the Minister," totalled $125,400. Legislative Assembly, *Estimates of Ordinary Expenditure and Capital Disbursements for the Fiscal Year Ending March 31st, 1965*, p. 45.

[78]Gordon Committee *Report*, p. 53.

TABLE 25

TREASURY DEPARTMENT ESTIMATES, 1964–65*

No. of Vote	No. of Item	Service	Amount
		ORDINARY EXPENDITURE	
2301		General Administration	
	1	Salaries	$ 427,000
	2	Travelling expenses	14,000
	3	Maintenance	34,000
	4	Premium on Fidelity Bonds	31,000
	5	Dominion–Provincial Conferences	10,000
	6	Expenses for special studies, etc.	300,000
		Grants:	
	7	Canadian Standard Bred Horse Society (in amounts as may be authorized by the Treasurer)	60,000
	8	Canadian Thoroughbred Horse Society (in amounts as may be authorized by the Treasurer)	70,000
	9	The Ontario Society for the Prevention of Cruelty to Animals	20,000
	10	St. John Ambulance Association	25,000
			991,000
	S	Minister—R.S.O. 1970, Chap. 127, Sec. 3	12,000
		Total for General Administration	$ 1,003,000
		Public Debt	
	S	Public Debt:	
		Interest, etc.	94,696,000
		Provision for Sinking Fund	40,000,000
		Total for Public Debt	$134,696,000
		Total for General Administration and Public Debt	$135,699,000

SOURCE: Ontario, Legislative Assembly, *Estimates of Ordinary Expenditure and Capital Disbursements for the Fiscal Year Ending March 31st, 1965* (Toronto: Queen's Printer, 1963–64) (Sessional Paper No. 2, 1964); p. 124.

are not always identified as such. Of course, the agencies that are completely divorced from the departments and which have sources of funds independent of the supply granted yearly by the legislature are not included in the estimates considered in Committee of Supply, and no statements of their financial positions are tabled in the House unless they appear in their annual reports or in the auditor's report.

The third reason why the Committee of Supply has been unable to function as a check on the executive as well as might otherwise be expected is perhaps more basic than any of the other reasons suggested here and probably was in the minds of the members of the Public Accounts Committee when they recommended that the estimates for each year should include the estimates for the preceding year *and* a statement of actual expenditure for that year. The problem is that for a number of years government departments have consistently asked for more money than they have spent. Although the supply voted must still be spent only for the purposes specified in the estimates, the individual votes are broad enough and the surplus amounts large enough to leave the Government a good deal of leeway as to how it will dispense the public monies. Only a detailed comparison of approved estimates and actual expenditures for past years would reveal to what extent the executive has used the opportunities that such a situation presents in order to spend public revenue on certain programmes without the prior knowledge or approval of the legislature. The over-all discrepancies between estimated and actual expenditures for the years 1955 to 1964 are set out in Table 26.

It is important to notice that Treasury Board orders are included in the expenditure figures in Table 26. These orders account for a very significant proportion of total disbursements, but they are in excess of the amounts voted for the purposes to which they are applied. This means that the discrepancies between the estimated and actual expenditures on certain other votes is even greater than the average percentage given for each year. Of course, all these discrepancies may be simply the results of poor forecasting on the part of the departments and the Treasury Board, but the consistency of the pattern would seem to suggest some other explanation. If it is not a desire to have extra funds to dispose of without too close supervision, it may be a liking for the appearance of thrift – that comes when not all funds voted are spent – that moves the Government to request larger amounts of revenue than it ever uses. In any case it makes the task of the Committee of Supply that much more difficult, particularly when the figures needed to thoroughly investigate the matter are not set out in the estimates themselves. However, it appears that the introduction of programme descriptions in the original departmental estimates is resulting in a reduction of the discrepancies between estimated and actual expenditures.

A fourth factor that impedes the Committee of Supply in its task of checking the executive in financial matters is the tendency to allow the estimates to pile up towards the end of the session. This situation is much the same as that existing with public bills. In the 1964 session, four votes were passed in the first third of the session, ninety-five votes in the second third, and eighty-six in the last third of the session. In the last fifteen days of the session, 35.7 per cent of the votes were passed, and 13.5 per cent

TABLE 26

ESTIMATED NET ORDINARY AND CAPITAL VOTED EXPENDITURE COMPARED
WITH ACTUAL NET ORDINARY AND CAPITAL VOTED EXPENDITURE FOR THE
TEN YEARS ENDED MARCH 31, 1964

Year	Estimated net ordinary and capital expenditure	Actual net ordinary and capital expenditure[a]	Excess of estimated over actual expenditure[b]
			(percentages)
1955	$ 400,486,100	$ 383,079,270	4.5
1956	465,260,000	419,861,646	10.8
1957	532,380,000	497,112,230	7.0
1958	643,152,500	590,726,897	8.8
1959	762,486,500	690,732,865	10.3
1960	819,923,000	750,973,597	9.1
1961	863,803,400	796,645,161	8.4
1962	985,039,500	888,554,884	10.8
1963	1,077,527,000	1,005,380,515	7.1
1964	1,107,831,000	1,063,629,308	4.1
AVERAGES	$ 765,788,900	$ 708,669,637	8.1

SOURCE: Ontario, Legislative Assembly, *Provincial Auditor's Report, 1963–64*, pp. 42–43.
[a]Including Treasury Board orders.
[b]The excess of estimated net ordinary and capital expenditure over actual net ordinary and capital expenditure is expressed as a percentage of the latter.

were passed in the last week of the session. Fourteen votes, totalling $33,846,000 were passed on the sixty-seventh day of the session, just two days before prorogation. The Government must bear some responsibility in this situation because the Prime Minister controls the business of the House, but there is nothing to force members to rush the estimates through if they want to spend more time with them. Only the natural urge to have done with it and the subtle pressures put upon them by the "Hallelujah Chorus"[79] to give up, compel the members of the opposition parties to allow the estimates through the Committee of Supply without all the attention they merit. The shortness of the session and the tendency for the members' workload to increase as the session progresses would not be such great handicaps if the Ontario legislature had a Standing Committee on Estimates such as the British House of Commons has had for over thirty years and the Canadian House since 1958. Then, the Committee of Supply could deal with general policy and administration, as it tends to do now anyway, and the Standing Committee could do the

[79]This is one of the more euphemistic terms applied to the "overflow" of Progressive Conservative members who are forced to sit to the left of the speaker, next to the members of the Opposition. The name derives from the alleged fact that the utterances from that section of the House are limited to interjections praising the Government.

detailed investigation that is presently being neglected. And, if such a committee were provided with qualified staff in much the same way as the Treasury Board is today, a major step towards truly responsible government would be taken.

Finally, a further reason for the ineffectiveness of the Committee of Supply is the division in the opposition. If there were only one party in opposition, or if the two parties in that position now would co-ordinate their efforts, the analysis of the estimates could be better organized. As it is, a member often finds that he has no sooner breached a subject than he loses the floor to another member who has an altogether unrelated point he wants raised or complaint he wants aired. A united opposition would permit members to pursue each item to some sort of conclusion.

In spite of these defects in Committee of Supply proceedings, the Committee still affords the opposition its best opportunity to criticize and, through that criticism, to control the executive. The informality of the Committee, coupled with the firm direction given to the debate by the estimates, makes it the best forum for the confrontation of opposing views that the rules of procedure ever present. "The opportunity to pursue Ministers with questions, to comment on their answers and to suggest new approaches makes for much more pointed interchanges than is possible in the formal, rambling debates on the Speech from the Throne and the Budget."[80] Probably the debates that take place in Committee of Supply, particularly those that follow the more formal speeches made at the introduction of the estimates for each department, are the closest the Ontario Legislative Assembly ever comes to the popular image of parliament as a place where men of differing views and opinions face each other in animated and largely extemporaneous exchange.

If the estimates are meant to explain how the Government expects to spend the public funds placed at its disposal in the ensuing fiscal year, the purpose of the budget is to describe how those funds are to be raised and what effect the whole operation will have on the economy. Until it is delivered in the House by the provincial treasurer, the budget is the best-guarded secret in the province, and the exact procedures followed in its preparation are still cloaked in some mystery. The chief responsibility for its contents rests with the provincial treasurer, and the detailed drafting is done by the Research and Statistics Branch of his Department.[81]

[80]Bryden, "Committees of the Ontario Legislature," p. 5.

[81]Until 1961, the budget was the concern of the Department of Economics and Federal-Provincial Relations, which was under the provincial treasurer, but in the autumn of that year the Department was merged with the Department of Commerce and Development to form the Department of Economics and Development under a separate minister. The jurisdiction over the budget was then transferred to the

Proposed important changes in the tax structure are brought before the Treasury Board for approval, and general policy considerations are almost certainly discussed in the cabinet, but the details of the budget statement are seldom known to the ministers until the moment of its presentation in the House on the motion that the speaker leave the chair and that the House resolve itself into Committee of Ways and Means. The formal procedures governing the budget debate and the Committee of Ways and Means have already been described, as has the nature of the budget debate itself.[82]

This is one of the major debates of the session and, although it centres around the fiscal policy of the Government, it is usually so general in scope that it hardly deserves special mention under this section dealing with financial control. The proceedings in the Committee of Ways and Means do not warrant any further consideration here either because they are purely formal. Debate rarely, if ever, takes place at this stage, because there has already been the widest possible discussion of the estimates on which the resolution referred to the Committee of Ways and Means is based. The resolution appropriating the total amount of the estimates approved by the Committee of Supply is referred to the Committee of Ways and Means and is immediately reported back to the House. Thereupon, the provincial treasurer introduces the annual supply bill which is given three successive readings immediately. Once this stage of financial procedure is over, the only role that the legislature has to play is *ex post facto*, ensuring that the executive has spent the money it has been voted for the purposes stated and in the amounts specified by the House.

To enable it to perform this function, the legislature must first be given an account of how the Government has in fact spent the money it has been given. This information is provided in the Public Accounts and in the auditor's report, both of which are prepared by the provincial auditor as directed by the terms of the Audit Act.[83] However, it must be born in mind that both the Public Accounts and the auditor's report for any fiscal year only become available to the legislature after a considerable lapse of time. They are usually completed some time in November for the fiscal year that ended on March 31 of that year, but they are not tabled in the House until the beginning of the first session in the following calendar year. For example, the auditor's report for the fiscal year 1962–63 was

---

Department of Provincial Treasurer. From an interview with Mr. Donald Stevenson, then director of the Economics Branch of the Department of Economics and Development, July 26, 1965.

[82]See chap. 5, 158–61.

[83]*RSO*, 1960, c. 27, s. 16 and 20.

presented to the lieutenant governor on November 29, 1963, and was tabled in the House on January 20, 1964. Thus, expenditures made in April 1962 were not officially brought to the attention of the House until nearly two years had elapsed. However, even when the necessary information is finally laid before it, the legislature as a whole is unable to investigate the record; it therefore delegates that responsibility to its Standing Committee on Public Accounts, which, in turn, is assisted by the provincial auditor.

Although the Ontario Legislative Assembly has had a Public Accounts Committee since 1869, only since 1960 has it begun to function in anything like the manner of its British equivalent. Until that time, the opposition and the Government tended to look upon this Committee as an organized witch hunt; hence it was ignored unless specific charges or allegations were brought up and referred to the Committee. Meetings of the Committee were held in only half a dozen sessions from 1934 to 1960, and the only occasion on which the Committee functioned in anything like the manner of its counterpart in the United Kingdom was in 1949, when Mr. John G. Brown, Liberal member for Waterloo North and a chartered accountant by profession, made a number of suggestions about the manner in which the Public Accounts were kept. The Public Accounts Committee was called to consider these suggestions, and several amiable meetings were held in which Mr. Brown and the provincial auditor discussed the technicalities of keeping the province's accounts. Eventually a report was brought in, termed the "Brown Report" by Mr. Frost, and some minor changes were made in the province's accounting procedures.[84]

However, between that session and the session of 1960, the Public Accounts Committee did not so much as meet, and members lost all interest in it. An indication of the lack of enthusiasm for the Committee was given in 1956. In that year, the whips asked members what committees they wished to serve on and then assigned them only to those committees for which they had expressed a preference. The result was that only fourteen members indicated a desire to serve on the Public Accounts Committee, only one more than the number wanting to be on the Committee on Legal Bills, the smallest committee in the House.[85] When the size of the Committee came to light, the Leader of the Opposition protested and urged that its membership be increased. On the next sitting day thirty-five names were added to the Committee,[86] but this made

[84]From an interview with Mr. Roderick Lewis, August 19, 1964.
[85]Journals, 1956, pp. 19–20.
[86]Ibid., p. 24.

little difference because the Committee did not meet during that session anyway.

In 1960 a renewed interest was taken in the Committee, and it did in fact meet a few times during the course of the session, mainly to investigate charges of inefficiency and conflict of interest of certain members of the Niagara Parks Commission. During the remaining sessions of the 26th Parliament, the Opposition continued to press for a more constructive attitude towards the Public Accounts Committee, but the Government was slow to act for fear that the Committee would be used by the Opposition as a kind of political factory for the manufacture of ammunition for forthcoming election campaigns. However, even some members of the Conservative party were convinced that there was much to gain by putting the Public Accounts Committee on a proper footing and referring the Public Accounts to it. Mr. Irwin Haskett, Conservative member for Ottawa South who later became a member of the executive council, said in May 1961 that the Government need have little fear of an efficient Public Accounts Committee because it would not investigate the Government or members of the cabinet but only how the civil servants spent the money voted to their departments by the legislature. There would be scant opportunity for the Public Accounts Committee to challenge the Government, claimed Mr. Haskett, because it would deal with procedure rather than policy.[87] The Committee met a few times each year from 1960 to 1963, but it never was given the opportunity to do any serious work. In 1963 an important step was taken when the membership of the Committee was reduced from fifty to nine, but nothing more was done in that session and the Committee did not meet until so near the end of the session that it could not even undertake a perfunctory review of the Public Accounts.

During the 1964 session the Public Accounts Committee of Ontario performed its proper function for the first time in the history of the province. The Committee met sixteen times under the chairmanship of Mr. Allan F. Lawrence, the Conservative member for St. George, who had already demonstrated an independence of mind such as is not often found in the members of the majority party in the Ontario House.[88] Four meetings were taken up with appearances before the Committee of the Provincial Auditor, the Deputy Provincial Treasurer, and the Secretary of the Treasury Board, and seven meetings were devoted to a review of

[87]Irwin Haskett, Memorandum to the Select Committee on Administrative and Executive Problems of Government, May 16, 1961.

[88]Much of the description of the work of the Public Accounts Committee in 1964 is taken from the report of the Committee itself. Sessional Paper 71.

the entire 1962–63 expenditure of the Department of Education. A total of twenty-three Government officials appeared before the Committee, and seventeen sets of documents were presented to it. The general purpose of the Committee's programme was, first, to acquaint its members with the framework of financial control, and, second, to review certain expenditures made in the fiscal year 1962–63.

As a result of its deliberations, the Public Accounts Committee in its report made fifteen specific recommendations under three headings: the auditing of the accounts of the province, the estimates, and future Public Accounts Committees. These recommendations touched on such matters as the desirability of giving the provincial auditor jurisdiction over the accounts of all government agencies, the need for more information in the estimates, the possible economies that would result from more bulk buying, the false economy of inadequate salary schedules in at least one department, the extensive and expensive use of firms supplying temporary office help, and the benefits of constituting a Public Accounts Committee in each session in the same manner and with the same terms of reference as their own Committee. The Committee also made two written recommendations to the Minister of Education in the belief that, while they might result in economies, they really had to do more with Government policy than with the Public Accounts.

The Provincial Auditor, Mr. George H. Spence, FCA, was present at all the meetings of the Public Accounts Committee in 1964 except during the drafting of its report. The position of this official is somewhat different than that of his opposite numbers at Ottawa or Westminster and merits some description here. The appointment of an auditor was first provided for in 1886 by section 2 of the original Audit Act.[89] Since that time detailed changes have been made in the Act, probably the most significant being those made in 1947. In that year a subsection was added to the Act stating that "the salary of the Auditor shall not be reduced except on address of the Assembly." The purpose of this addition was to assure the auditor's independence from the executive.[90] Section 2 of the Act was also meant to secure the independence of the auditor from executive interference by providing that he shall hold office during good behaviour, but shall be removable for cause by the lieutenant governor on address of the Assembly. To ensure that he has the power to obtain all of the answers

[89]SO, 1886, c. 4.

[90]SO, 1947, c. 5. At the same time the provision for a set salary was replaced with a stipulated minimum salary to obviate the necessity of an amendment to the Act whenever an upward revision of the auditor's salary was deemed advisable. A cynic, upon reading this Act, could be forgiven if he saw the first change as an attempt to make it impossible for the executive to *threaten* the auditor and the second change as attempt to make it possible for the executive to *entice* him.

and explanations he may require, section 7 of the Audit Act stated that every department of the public service shall furnish him with whatever information or material he needs, and section 22 empowered him to examine any person under oath on any matter pertinent to any account submitted to him for examination.

The distinctive feature of the duties of the provincial auditor in Ontario is that he not only carries out the conventional post-audit function normally expected of a Government auditor but also is responsible for pre-auditing the provincial accounts. In fact, he relies mainly on the work done at the pre-audit stage of his work. By the terms of the Act he is to "satisfy himself that every account requisitioned for payment is in accordance with the terms and conditions of the grant to which the account relates." The Act also provides that, with a few exceptions, "no cheque for the payment of public money shall issue without the certificate of the auditor that there is legislative authority for the payment."[91] At Ottawa and Westminster the pre-audit function has long since been taken out of the hands of the auditor general, or the comptroller and auditor general as he is known in Britain. In those jurisdictions the auditor is purely a servant of Parliament with no responsibility whatsoever for controlling the disbursement of funds.[92]

The argument in favour of limiting the auditor to post-audit functions is obvious: when performing a pre-audit he is in fact performing a service for the executive, although the Act specifies that this is done on behalf of the Assembly; when he turns to serve the House by means of a post-audit, it is highly unlikely that he will uncover any errors or indiscretions that may have escaped his notice during the pre-audit stage of his work. Hence, the legislature is left without the benefit of an independent *ex post facto* investigation of the manner in which the Government has disposed of the public monies. The weakness of such a system is partly corrected by the separation of the provincial auditor's office into two divisions, one of which is responsible for the pre-audit and the other for the post-audit. However, these divisions can never be as strict as is depicted in a formal organization chart. If they were, there would be even fewer arguments in favour of leaving the two functions under the jurisdiction of one official.

No doubt it is partly because of the dual nature of the provincial auditor's functions that his reports contain so few remarks that are of any assistance to the Public Accounts Committee. In Britain and at the federal

[91]*RSO*, 1960, c. 27, s. 9(2) and 11(1).

[92]The "running audit" carried out by the British comptroller and auditor general ought not to be confused with the "pre-audit" in Ontario. The running audit is mainly a device for keeping abreast of accounting developments, and only occasionally is it used to correct errors before they have been made. The pre-audit in Ontario is to ensure that no expenditures are made that ought not to be.

level in Canada, the auditor's reports draw attention to expenditures that seem to be contrary to the express wishes of Parliament, situations where the financial administrative rules of government have been broken or need correcting, clear cases of waste or inefficient use of funds, new developments that involve considerable expenditure but have not been debated at length in Parliament, and any other developments in the field of public expenditure which are likely to be of interest to Parliament. In Ontario it is only very rarely that the auditor mentions any such items, and members of the Public Accounts Committee – or members of the legislature at large if the Public Accounts Committee does not meet – are left to search out such matters for themselves. Of course it could be that provincial auditors have been so tough-minded and thorough in carrying out pre-audit functions that no such problems exist in Ontario, but the possibility of this being the case seems rather remote.

Before ending this section on the Public Accounts Committee, a few of the details about its operations must be set out. In the United Kingdom, and in Ottawa since 1958, the chairman of the Public Accounts Committee has been chosen from the ranks of the Opposition. At Westminster the person selected by the Committee for this position has usually been a member of the Committee for a number of years and has often had ministerial experience. In Ontario, since the reactivation of the Committee in 1964, the chairman is informally chosen by the Government and then formally "elected" by the Government's majority in the Committee. Nevertheless, the two chairmen who have presided over the revived Committee have shown themselves to be independent and capable. As long as the Government sees fit to choose men of this calibre there should be no problem but, of course, having a member of the Opposition as chairman would be a better guarantee that the Committee's investigations would be vigorously directed without fear or favour.

One practice that the Ontario Public Accounts Committee has copied from the United Kingdom is that of calling as its witnesses the officials of departments rather than the political heads of departments. When the Committee acted only as special inquiry committee it was customary for ministers to go before the Committee to defend themselves against political attack, and civil servants were naturally very reluctant to be drawn into such conflicts. The same was true in the Canadian Public Accounts Committee until 1958. Calling officials instead of politicians before the Committee has a number of salutary effects: their presence tends to preclude policy debates; their guidance is based on a more intimate knowledge of the facts; their testimony is less likely to be subjected to political screening; and the fact that they are investigated directly, without their ministers to act as buffers, impresses them with the importance of their own duties and with the supremacy of parliament. In connection with this last point, it is important to remember that in many cases it is the permanent officials of the departments who conduct the financial business of the department.[93] In Britain the practice is to designate the administrative head of a department as the "accounting officer," thus placing definite responsibility on him for the financial transactions of his department and requiring him to appear before the Public Accounts Committee. While the responsibility of officials is not always so clearly stated in Ontario, selecting them for appearance before the Committee is certainly sound administration.

So far as reports and publicity are concerned, the Ontario Public Accounts Committee has not adopted the procedures followed by either the Canadian or British Committees. At Ottawa and Westminster verbatim records of Committee proceedings are kept and published with the committees' reports, but at Queen's Park no verbatim record is kept, and not even the report of the Public Accounts Committee is published for general distribution. At one time it was quite common for the Ontario Committee's report to be read in the House, and sometimes it was even debated. The report thus appeared in the *Journals* and in Hansard in those years in which the debates have been recorded. Such publicity was necessary in order to clear the air following an inquiry by the Committee. Now that the nature of the Committee's work has been changed, it is no longer so important to debate its reports. In fact, to subject its reports to political debate would jeopardize the whole basis upon which the reconstituted Public Accounts Committee operates. But, on the other hand, one of the strengths of the Public Accounts Committee is its opportunity to publicize its findings and recommendations, and it is doubtful that sufficient steps have been taken in this regard in Ontario.

The reports for 1964 and 1965 were very short and included no minutes of meetings. They were tabled late in each session and were made sessional papers, but they were not printed. This meant that the only copies available to the general public were those single copies on file in the office of the Clerk of the Legislative Assembly. The reports were not debated and they could hardly even have been studied by members, because they were tabled so late in each session. In Ontario, as at Ottawa, the meetings of the Public Accounts Committee are public so that there is the possibility of publicity while their investigations are underway. However, these meetings are not well attended by the press or the public, and, if they were, it might do the Committee more harm good because any reports that issued

[93]See, for example, *RSO*, 1960, c. 27, s. 8.

at that stage of the Committee's proceedings could not benefit from all the evidence gathered by the Committee and might, therefore, be misleading. In the United Kingdom the Public Accounts Committee meets *in camera* and is thus freed from the dangers of premature publicity. Publishing a verbatim record of proceedings ensures that the public gets the whole story at one time, beside serving as proof that the Committee has proceeded in a fair manner, that the Government has not prevented thorough investigation, and that the Opposition chairman has not misused his powers. A complete report of this nature also makes it possible for administrators and researchers to assess the validity of the Committee's recommendations in the light of the evidence it received.

If the Government responds to the Public Accounts Committee report in a positive fashion, the need for publicity is to a large extent obviated. While experience with a properly constituted Public Accounts Committee is still too limited in Ontario to make any generalizations, judging by the attitude taken by the Government to the 1964 Public Accounts Committee report, publicity may not be very necessary. The over-all purpose of a Public Accounts Committee is, after all, quite similar to that of the Treasury Board and it might be reasonably expected that the Committee's reports would be well received by the Provincial Treasurer's Department. This was evidently the case as far as the 1964 report was concerned and, at the first meeting of the Public Accounts Committee in the 1965 session, the Provincial Treasurer indicated to the Committee which of its recommendations the Government had accepted and why it had not seen fit to accept certain others. If such a relationship between the Committee and the Government becomes formalized and differences of opinion are intelligently pursued and discussed, the Committee may find it quite unnecessary to enlist the aid of public opinion to ensure that its recommendations receive due attention from the Government.

The Select Committee on Administrative and Executive Problems of Government recommended that the Assembly set up a statutory Public Accounts Committee which would continue for the life of a whole legislature and sit between sessions, but nothing has been done to implement this far-reaching proposal.[94] Nevertheless, since its reconstitution in 1964 the Public Accounts Committee of the Ontario Legislative Assembly has served an extremely useful purpose: it has given a few members of the House a real opportunity to become familiar with the details of some of the operations of government; it has strengthened the legislature's control over public expenditures; it has probably had a positive effect on the civil servants who have encountered it; and it has already had an influence on

[94]*Second Interim Report.*

the administration of the province's public affairs. In short, the changes made in the Public Accounts Committee in 1964 probably constituted the greatest advance made by the legislature since the second world war in its perennial struggle to control the executive.

Despite the tendency to over-estimate expenditures, occasions still arise when appropriations for particular projects prove inadequate or when projects must be started, although no provision was made for them in the estimates. At Ottawa and Westminster, the usual method of providing for such situations is to go back to Parliament and ask it to approve "supplementary estimates" or "excess votes," but at Queen's Park the session is so short that such devices are seldom used and flexibility in financial administration is provided for by the use of special warrants, Treasury Board orders, and commitments.

Special warrants are used to create new appropriations to cover unforeseen expenditures, Treasury Board orders increase inadequate appropriations by specified amounts, and commitments are, in a sense, delayed Treasury Board orders that are used when the amount of over-expenditure is not certain.[95] Within the executive branch, a number of checks on the issuance of both special warrants and Treasury Board orders have been established.[96] Steps have also been taken to acquaint the legislature with appropriations made by the use of these instruments through publication in both the Public Accounts and the annual auditor's reports, although, as has already been pointed out, these reports are only made available some time after the end of the fiscal year to which they relate is over.

The important point to notice here is that, in spite of the fact that these instruments of the executive actually create appropriations which have never been approved by the Assembly, they are not subject to any kind of formal review by the legislature as a whole. Thus the executive has usurped a part of what has historically been considered the key power of the legislative branch of government – and the legislature has not been left with even the opportunity to review the executive's use of this power. Furthermore, the executive has not been very hesitant to resort to the use of these instruments, as is amply demonstrated by the figures included in Table 27.

In spite of the fact that the estimates have exceeded actual expenditures by an average of 8.1 per cent each year for the past five years,[97] the Government has found it necessary to create and spend new appropriations to

[95]For descriptions of these three instruments and of the procedures by which they are passed, see chap. 3, p. 57.

[96]See, for example, the description of these checks in the Gordon Committee Report, p. 31.

[97]See Table 4.

TABLE 27

TREASURY BOARD ORDERS AND SPECIAL WARRANTS ISSUED FOR THE FISCAL YEARS,
1959–60 TO 1963–64

	Treasury Board orders*		Special Warrants	
Year	Authorized	Expended	Authorized	Expended
1959–60	$ 9,535,300	$ 8,022,734	$1,665,363	$1,410,187
1960–61	15,492,476	12,723,064	1,356,072	1,272,455
1961–62	12,841,313	11,092,812	1,432,734	1,411,125
1962–63	12,439,177	10,696,505	588,717	519,903
1963–64	37,119,351	25,661,364	1,216,573	1,157,441
AVERAGES	$17,485,524	$13,639,296	$1,251,892	$1,154,223

SOURCE: Ontario provincial auditor's reports for the years concerned.
*Both ordinary and capital Treasury Board orders are included

an average amount of $14,793,519 in those same years. Although this sum accounts for only 1.5 per cent of the average total expenditures for those years, in absolute terms it is much larger than entire Ontario budgets were before the first world war and is still a very considerable sum by today's standards.

At Ottawa, the equivalent of Ontario's special warrant and Treasury Board order is known as the governor general's warrant. Until 1958, amounts appropriated by means of this instrument were not only published in the *Canada Gazette* within thirty days of their issuance and reported to Parliament early in each session, but were also covered by supplementary estimates for the various relevant projects. However, in 1958 the new Government did not see fit to bother the House with estimates for the money that had already been appropriated and spent under warrants. As a result of the protests that ensued over this violation of parliamentary custom, the Minister of Finance introduced a short bill to amend the Financial Administration Act, the most important provision of which was the stipulation that "the amounts appropriated by a special warrant shall be deemed to be included in, and not to be in addition to, the amounts provided by the next appropriation act enacted by parliament."[98] Thus all appropriations made under governor general's warrants must now be subsequently approved by Parliament.

In conclusion it may be said that, although the Ontario Legislative Assembly is beginning to develop a useful tool for the *ex post facto* review of the Public Accounts through its efforts to revive the standing committee charged with that responsibility, it has so far failed to adopt many of the most basic procedures that some other parliaments have

[98]Quoted in Norman Ward, *The Public Purse*, p. 254.

developed to assist them in controlling public expenditures. The Committee of Supply is used for such a multitude of purposes that it neglects its primary function of investigating the estimates. The estimates themselves do not include enough information to make intelligent assessment possible, and invariably they call for larger amounts than are actually required. No estimates committee has been established to assist the House with its review of the Government's proposed expenditures. The Public Accounts Committee still labours under a number of handicaps that have been removed elsewhere: the provincial auditor, who is supposed to serve as its key source of information, also serves the executive, and the Committee's reports are not distributed much beyond the clerk's vault. Finally, the executive itself appropriates large sums of money without reference to the legislature, and these appropriations are never even reviewed by the House. Plainly, then, much remains to be done if the legislative branch of government in Ontario is going to exercise its proper degree of control over public expenditure.

CONCLUSION

8

PERHAPS, in the years before the democratic ideal began to push the government along that collectivist road which leads eventually to some kind of welfare state, the liberal democratic institutions which had previously been devised in Britain did serve their intended purpose in Ontario. In those early days of limited government, when expenditures were small and virtually all Government programmes were administered by a small bureaucracy operating through the regular departments of government, private members did play an active and positive part in the legislative process. Parliament was supreme, and the principles of collective and individual ministerial responsibility did correspond to the realities of the system.

Today, the forms and formulae of liberal democracy remain, but they have been made to serve ends so different from those they were originally designed to serve that their essential natures have been transformed in the process. In fact, it may well be that the principles of parliamentary government which liberalism produced exist now only as myths. Although these myths have concrete roots in constitutional history, they no longer reflect the real power relations in modern society, and they do not adequately describe the legislative process as it operates in Ontario. Instead of members being elected to parliament for the purpose of making laws, checking expenditures, and curbing the propensity of the executive to arrogate power unto itself, members now go to parliament to watch laws being made and to urge the Government on to ever greater responsibilities. The result has been not only a phenomenal growth in government functions at the provincial level but, concomitantly, a continual shift of power and responsibility away from the legislative branch to the executive.

The size of the executive branch of government has grown in proportion to the increase in government functions, and its machinery has constantly been adapted to meet the new demands placed upon it. The legislative branch, on the other hand, has remained relatively static. The tendency has been to pour the new wine into the new skins fashioned for the executive branch rather than to jeopardize the very existence of the traditional apparatus of the legislative branch. Thus, the much-cherished institutions of parliament remain intact, and even a parliament on the scale allowed at the provincial level in Canada manages to retain many of the formal trappings of an irrelevant past – the mace, the throne, royal assent, etc. But instead of being an effective partner in the process of government, the legislative branch has become "an ineffective appendage employed to make noises of approval or discontent."[1] Members of the Legislative Assembly of the Province of Ontario meet during three or four of the slack winter months and use the Government's legislative programme as an occasion to wax loquacious according to their respective versions of received truth. But the actual effect that private members have on legislative output is extremely limited, and the control they exercise over the executive is virtually nil. There is no doubt that it is the Government that governs; the question is whether the legislature is able to control or, more specifically, whether the Opposition is able to oppose executive power effectively.

Several factors that would help to explain the fact of cabinet domination in Ontario could be listed, but most of these are related to two features which characterize the provincial legislature as contrasted with the parliaments at Ottawa and Westminster: the short session, and the tendency towards one-party dominance. It is not suggested here that other parliaments are not dominated by their respective executives, for this is patently the case. Nor is it suggested that Parliament at Ottawa, for instance, is not dominated by one party for extended periods of time or that it does have long enough sessions. What is contended here is simply that the Ontario Legislative Assembly is certainly dominated by the Government, and that the continuance of short sessions and the tendency towards one-party dominance are more pronounced in this province than at either Ottawa or Westminster.

Excluding the special short sessions, the Ontario legislature sat for only 44.3 days in each year from 1867 to 1964. It is indicative of the static nature of the legislative branch and also of the declining importance of that branch in relation to the executive that the sessions of the legislature

[1]Brian Chapman, "Wanted: A Whitehall Revolution," *Sunday Times Weekly Review*, September 1, 1963.

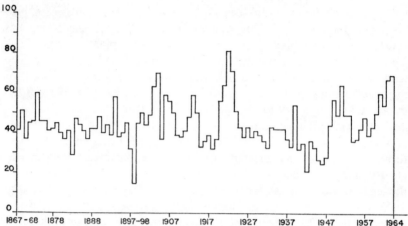

FIG. 18. Length of regular sessions of the Legislative Assembly of Ontario, 1867/68–1964, in sitting days.

have not lengthened appreciably over the years. Figure 18 demonstrates that while there have been fluctuations in the lengths of sessions there has been no consistent tendency for them to become longer. During the depression and the second world war there was an understandable shortening of the legislature's sessions, but in the decade following the war, when government activity was expanding apace, the sessions averaged only 45.5 days, one day less than the average length of the sessions in the first ten years of the province.

The shortness of the session has a number of consequences. Most obviously, it means that all the business of governing the province that is of concern to the Assembly (and what is not?) must be crowded into a very short space of time. The simple fact that the legislature "gets through" most of the business brought before it each year is not to be taken as evidence that the sessions are long enough. Any member could easily list dozens of additional aspects of government concern which could be profitably considered by the House if it had time and opportunity to do so: the reports of the numerous semi-independent agencies could be discussed; committees could be set up to review the work of these bodies and report to the House; committees could also be established to survey the mass of delegated legislation and report to the House any instruments they considered worthy of its attention; the estimates could be submitted to committees for more detailed attention than the Committee of Supply is able to give them; and many other equally important activities could be engaged in if the legislature only had time. Of course, more than time is needed if such tasks are to be performed: there must also be a desire on the part of the members and the Government to see them done or else the extra time will be wasted in much the same way as many hours are presently wasted. Secondly, the short session does not allow the legislature enough time to perform adequately many of the tasks it has already assumed. For instance, the specialized committees of the House do not have the time to do the long-range work necessary to make them effective legislative bodies. Items of legislation submitted to them must be dealt with seriatim, instead of as parts of an over-all design. It is doubtful whether the legislators sitting on the committees have adequate time to study the implications of the bills referred to them and still meet all of the other commitments that are pressed upon them during the session. Furthermore, it should be remembered that only about half of the public bills passed in each session ever go to the standing committees. Thirdly, members who live outside the provincial capital are not encouraged to do research – and may even be prevented from doing research – by the short session. Certainly they cannot be expected to do much serious research during the session, when it is crammed full of regular sittings, committee meetings, caucus meetings, and other activities associated with the session. If a member is unable to remain in Toronto between sessions, he can do very little research indeed. In connection with this, the short session probably confirms the belief that being a member of the provincial legislature is a part-time job and thus gives them an excuse to neglect their parliamentary responsibilities for the rest of the year. Finally, if questions put to ministers are to be considered a form of research, it should be pointed out that the short session prevents them from being fully utilized. Questions still take so long to be answered that the session is often nearly over before the information is provided.

However, the most fundamental consequence of the short session is that it leaves the executive in unchallenged control of the province's affairs for long periods of time. Although the Legislative Assembly may not be very effective in controlling the executive, at least during the session it is able to keep the Government under constant supervision, and it is always ready to focus the spotlight of public attention on any indiscretion it may discover. But during the bulk of the year the Government governs as it sees fit, and members who wish to oversee its work must do so without any assistance. Should they discover an abuse of the trust placed in the Government, they are left to their own devices to find remedies. No forum exists for them to air their complaints until the next session begins, and by then it may be too late to do anything about it.

The second distinctive feature of the Ontario Assembly that helps to explain cabinet domination in the province is the tendency for one party to dominate the House completely for long periods of time. Not counting the first four years, when the Government was supported by a loose coalition, Ontario has gone through four periods of one-party dominance. From 1871 to 1905 the Liberal party was in charge of the affairs of the province and for nearly twenty-five of these thirty-four years the party was led by Sir Oliver Mowat. During that whole period there was never a time when the Liberals were dependent on the support of any minority group, and on the average they held 57.2 per cent of the seats in the House.[2] For the next fourteen years the House was completely dominated by the Conservative party which never held less than 70 per cent of the seats and held an average of 76.2 per cent of the seats during the whole period. After a four-year interval, when the United Farmers formed the Government, the Conservatives returned to power for another eleven years, again with substantial majorities. From 1934 to 1943 the Liberals held office with majorities averaging 71.7 per cent and since then the Conservatives have been in power with an average majority of 70.1 per cent. In essence this means that, following the breakdown of the original coalition, the Liberals dominated the nineteenth century and the Conservatives have thus far ruled the twentieth. Since 1905 there have only been thirteen years of Government by parties other than the Conservatives, four of which were taken up by the minority United Farmers' government. In the ninety-four years since the dissolution of the original Government of the province, there have been only five changes of Government, and even when the four-year United Farmers' government is taken into the calculations, each party has ruled the province for an average of fifteen-and-a-half years at a time. If the peculiar phenomenon of 1919 to 1923 is omitted, the average length of one-party dominance is eighteen years.

The situation has been quite different at the federal level in Canada and in the United Kingdom. Taking essentially the same time period, i.e., counting from the federal election of 1872, there have been nine changes of Government at Ottawa in the last ninety-three years, almost twice as many as in Ontario. The average length of one-party dominance has been just over nine years, about half the average length of the periods of one-party dominance in Ontario. Furthermore, the size of the Government majorities in Ottawa has consistently been smaller than in Ontario, averaging 59.6 per cent of the seats, compared to 67.2 per cent at Queen's Park.

The contrast between the situation in Ontario and the United Kingdom

[2]Following the election of 1894 the Liberal party alone held only 47.9 per cent of the seats of the House, but when the Patron Liberals were included with them they accounted for 60.6 per cent of the total.

is even greater. In this century alone there have been twice as many changes of Government in Britain as there have been in the whole history of Ontario since 1871, and the proportion of seats held by the winning party has been considerably smaller in the United Kingdom than in Ontario. In fact, in only four elections did the winning party in Britain gain as high a proportion of the seats of the House as the successful parties' *average* in Ontario. Thus, the phenomenon of one-party dominance is far more pronounced at Queen's Park than at either Ottawa or Westminster, and this situation is aggravated by the fact that Government majorities are so large.

This means that in Ontario, for periods averaging more than a decade and a half, the direction of Government action in response to public issues is discussed and decided within the confines of one political party. Parliament – which a century ago was seen as the agora of society where issues were debated and consensuses achieved – has in Ontario been left with the unsatisfying function of debating questions only after they have already been decided and placed before it in the form of Government proposals. Since party discipline is no less evident in Ontario than in Canadian federal politics or in Britain, the Government may be confident of the solid backing of its backbenchers once a measure is introduced in the legisalture. It is immaterial whether the members of the House who are of different political persuasions agree with or disapprove of a proposal, for, barring unforeseen complications, the measure will be passed. In a situation such as this debates take on that hollow sound of fury which signifies nothing, and the life of the private member of a minority party becomes little more than a series of frustrations.

Furthermore, with one party so completely dominating the whole legislative process, it is inevitable that after twenty-two years, or thirty-four years, the distinctions between executive and party or between legislature and administration tend to break down. Members of the civil service are found equating the Government with the majority party and seeing themselves as servants of the party instead of as servants of the administration. Publications concerned with various aspects of Ontario government seem as a matter of course to become vehicles for expounding the virtues of the Government of the day. In a thousand little ways it becomes evident that civil servants see their prime loyalty to be to a particular party instead of to the general public they are meant to serve. This is not the result of any insidious design – in fact, in recent years in Ontario the Government has made a conscious effort to counter such tendencies through the improvement and extension of the operations of the Civil Service Commission – but is primarily a natural outgrowth of the long association of one party with the administration of the province. Having the same people doing ordinary work in departments, clerking committees of the legislature, and preparing materials for election campaign speeches all at the same time apparently becomes acceptable practice when one party has dominated the Government, the legislature, and the political life of the province for a generation or more.

While the practice of government in the province becomes ever more remote from the classical principles of parliamentary government, the slogans which have expressed those principles continue to be repeated. "Separation of powers," "parliamentary sovereignty," "ministerial responsibility," and other clichés come readily to the lips of both those who are critical and those who laud the existing frame of things, even though these high-sounding phrases have ceased to bear much relation to the realities of the governmental process in Ontario. In the circumstances the possibility of the executive acting beyond its rightful powers and contrary to the best interests of the people is substantially enhanced. Usually, when the dangers attendant upon such a situation are considered, defenders of the status quo fall back on the principle of ministerial responsibility as the primary safeguard against executive abuse.

The phrase "ministerial responsibility" has many nuances of meaning.[3] It may mean simply that ministers are responsible to parliament for their individual acts or it may imply that they are the people who are accountable to parliament for the acts of others and who must therefore bear the constitutional consequences for those deeds as well as their own. Historically this was a legal responsibility enforced by the instrument of impeachment of ministers at the instance of the Commons, but impeachment is now unnecessary, having been replaced by the newer conventions of cabinet government.

Today, ministerial responsibility means essentially two things. First, it means that all members of a Government are expected publicly to support its actions and policies or, if they are not prepared to do so, to resign their offices: all ministers must accept responsibility for all of the activities carried out in the name of the Government. If parliament should refuse to support the Government's policy, then the whole Government must resign or submit itself to a general election. And, if at any election the people refuse to give the Government the requisite support to keep it in power, it must resign. Secondly, ministerial responsibility means that each individual minister is accountable for his own decisions and for all the

[3]For an extended discussion of the meaning of the phrase see Geoffrey Marshall and Graeme C. Moodie, *Some Problems of the Constitution* (2nd ed.; London: Hutchinson, 1961), pp. 67–84.

actions of the government department under his control. He must present his department's programmes to the House, defend its policies, and answer questions concerning it. If he commits a personal indiscretion or blunder he is, according to theory, expected to resign.

If this is what ministerial responsibility means in theory, how does the principle work out in practice in a province where one-party dominance is the rule and where large disciplined majorities ensure that the Government's will becomes law? How useful is it as a tool for controlling the executive? In short, does Ontario enjoy "responsible government"?

In a sense, one-half of the concept is negatived by the other half: individual responsibility is cancelled out by collective responsibility. Under a disciplined party system, so long as a minister has the confidence of his leader and his colleagues in the party his position is secure. The Government then merely accepts responsibility for the performance of the minister, either explicitly or tacitly, and he immediately falls under the protective cloak of collective responsibility. Whether his performance meets with the approval or disapproval of other members of the House is inconsequential. As long as he remains in the good graces of the premier, the legislative branch has no more control over his tenure of office than the United States Congress has over the tenure in office of a member of the American cabinet. If a minister in the Ontario cabinet is let go, it is because the premier no longer desires his services and not just because the Government refuses to accept responsibility for his blunders. In fact, in one of the most dramatic cases in recent years, the Premier explicitly assumed responsibility for the act in question and still accepted the resignation of the minister who had introduced the act.[4]

The principle of collective responsibility has no more utility than the concept of individual responsibility. It is no great concession for a Government to accept responsibility for its deeds of omission and commission, because neither the legislature nor the general public has the wherewithal to call it to account. During the relatively brief period the House is sitting, members who are not of the majority party have some opportunity to criticize the Government, but with their meagre resources they have slight effect when they come up against a Government which commands the services of thousands of civil servants. And even during the session, the

[4]"I would say at the outset, Mr. Speaker, that as leader of the government I accept full and complete responsibility for this bill and for its introduction into this Legislature." Premier Robarts, speaking on his motion that the order of the day for second reading of Bill 99, the Police Act, be discharged and the Bill be referred forthwith to the Standing Committee on Labour, Legal, and Municipal Bills. The resignation of the Minister who introduced the bill was accepted on the same day. *Debates*, March 23, 1964, pp. 1862 and 1916.

cabinet, through its control of the majority and of the speaker, is able to direct virtually every facet of the legislature's activities. Without the assistance, or at least the consent of the Government, it is impossible for the Opposition to get the information and carry out the investigations that are necessary if it is to understand the operations of the government and check the powers of the executive. And, even if the Government does assist Opposition members and they do find evidence of the abuse of executive powers, what can they do about it? Unless there is a breakdown in party solidarity, the only recourse open to them is to raise as great a commotion as possible and hope that the electorate will remember the incident when the next election finally comes. There is virtually nothing they can do to remedy the situation.

If this is the plight of the legislature, what can be said about the electorate? Every four years or so it is asked to pass judgment on the Government, but it must do so on the basis of its own observations, assisted only by the members of the opposition parties and a few others who, because of their positions, have been able to uncover certain facts about the administration of the affairs of the province. If the members of the legislature find it difficult to get the facts about those matters for which the Government has assumed responsibility, it is virtually impossible for the ordinary citizen. He is therefore left to judge the Government's stewardship without the benefit of an objective account. Indeed, when the Government assumes responsibility for its activities without allowing full and impartial investigations of those activities it is really ensuring that it will never in fact be held responsible for them. Thus, in the given situation, the principle of ministerial responsibility has little usefulness as a tool for checking the powers of the executive.

"In the Liberal language," says Professor A. H. Birch, "Parliament is a corporate entity wielding power. It possesses sovereignty, it holds ministers to account, it controls the executive."[5] But the liberal view of the legislative branch no longer conforms to the realities of the governmental process in Ontario, and to continue to use the language of liberalism with reference to the existing situation serves only to perpetuate and heighten misconceptions. Giving lip service to such myths as "ministerial responsibility" may have some salutary psychological effect on the ministers and civil servants who are charged with a degree of discretionary authority, just as carrying on the business of government in the name of the crown may instill in some individuals a sense of awe and a predisposition to service. But for serious commentators on the Ontario scene to use such

[5]A. H. Birch, *Representative and Responsible Government: An Essay on the British Constitution* (London: George Allen and Unwin, 1964), p. 166.

terms with the intent of describing actualities is at best anachronistic and at worst entirely misleading.

For those who are interested in the reform of the parliamentary institutions of Ontario there appear to be but two alternatives: they can either reject the liberal institutions of government and the terminology associated therewith and seek to build new forms of government which will reflect the real (as opposed to the formal) decision-making process in the province, or they can retain the old forms and attempt to give them the capability of performing their intended purposes. Insofar as any new model of government did take into account the actual power relationships in the provincial society, it would enable the governed to concentrate their attention on the real locus of power instead of dissipating their energies in useless efforts to mold public policy by means of a powerless legislature. Conceivably such a new set of institutions would have places for those organized groups that presently operate outside of the regular institutions of government and would provide some opportunities for them to put forward their respective interests and some machinery to assist them at arriving at a consensus. The legislature would perhaps remain as it is today: a forum for contending parties to exchange their contradictory conceptions of the proper direction for Government activity.

However, the seeds cast by would-be reformers are more likely to find root if they land squarely within the existing institutions of government. In this case, the over-all aim would be to provide specific means for the legislative branch (in effect the Opposition) to exercise continuing supervision over the operations of the executive branch. More particularly, reforms of existing institutions would need to furnish members with opportunities to acquire all the information they required and occasions for them to publicize their findings. Both aspects of their work should be completely removed from the control of the premier. The ultimate objective of reforms in these matters would be to ensure that the executive was made continuously accountable for its acts, regardless of how long any political party remained in power and no matter how large its majorities were. And, without attempting to set out a list of specific reforms that might be made, the general areas most in need of reform can be isolated.

If members are to get the information necessary for intelligent evaluation of the performance of the executive, they must have access to the resources of the civil service as well as research assistants under their own jurisdiction. It may be that ministers must continue to act as the channel of communication between members and public servants, but they should not use this privilege as a means of interposing delays. Members must be left with the right to decide what questions they would like answered; the civil servants should provide the information desired as quickly as possible. Oral questions should be encouraged as they were in the 1966 session, and the British procedures governing starred questions should be reintroduced into the Ontario legislature. The question period should then be used both for eliciting information and for keeping ministers on their toes. But parliamentary questions are not enough, and members should either have access to the services of a trained staff of researchers or else be provided with funds to hire their own assistants. Office space and secretarial services should be adequate so that no member's efficiency is hindered by a lack of such facilities. The committees of the legislature should also have whatever resources they require to do as thoroughly as possible the tasks referred to them.

The sources of information which are under the control of the executive branch should be improved. For example, the estimates tabled in the House should contain the kind of information that is included in the estimates presented to the Treasury Board. The reports of the departments and the semi-independent agencies should give balanced pictures of their operations and include the types of information requested by the members of the House. The provincial auditor should be relieved of his pre-audit functions so that he could provide members with a completely independent analysis of the Public Accounts. Besides getting information of a factual nature for specific purposes it is of the utmost importance that members have the opportunity to carry out extensive investigations of certain aspects of government operations. Again, such investigations should be removed from the control of the Government. The terms of reference of the committees should be broad enough to allow them to initiate discussions or inquiries within their areas of concern without waiting for references sponsored by the Government. Full powers to send for persons, papers, and things and the right to examine under oath, should also be granted them. In some cases the members of the House may want outside experts to make investigations on their behalf, and this type of inquiry should be allowed. But, whether the investigatory body be made up of members of the legislature or of experts selected by the legislature, or both, it should be provided with staff and facilities adequate for its purpose – and this decision should also rest with the legislative branch and not with the Government. If members themselves wish to carry out long-range enquiries or studies, then either the session should be lengthened to allow time for such work or else they should be permitted to carry on this type of activity between sessions, regardless of whether the body involved is a select or a standing committee.

Having armed themselves with the facts, members must be given the opportunity to use them. There is at present ample opportunity for members to speak, but what is required are specific and frequent occasions for them to take the initiative in debate. Whether they wish to bring to light certain shortcomings on the part of the Government or to put forward their own ideas about what legislation should be passed, they should be able to do so without the prior permission of the prime minister. The elected representatives of the people should be trusted not to abuse the opportunities provided for them in the written rules. If an MPP feels that a certain subject warrants a motion to adjourn the House for discussion of the matter and a quorum of the House supports him, debate should be allowed. His own party caucus and his constituents will soon dissuade him from abusing such privileges. The 1966 experiment with regular private members' hours should become a part of the formal rules of procedure. The stipulation that half these periods be reserved for members of the majority party should be removed, and private members' bills and resolutions should be allowed to come to a vote. If members desire to debate the reports of the semi-independent agencies, review certain instruments of delegated legislation, analyse the use of Treasury Board orders and special warrants, or do anything else they feel is important, opportunity should be provided for them to do so.

Time for such activities could easily be provided by extending the length of the session and by reorganizing the business of the House. Much more efficient use could be made of the time available, particularly towards the beginning of each session, and now that members are receiving a reasonable indemnity there is no reason why the House could not sit for a few more months in the year if necessary. If insufficient time ever did become a factor, it would be up to the House to decide whether it should use the time available for debating Government legislation or whether it would rather pass Government legislation quickly and proceed with other interests. The Government's legislative programme could always be passed by the Government majority, either with or without debate. But one important principle needs to be given effect: the subjects of debate and the types of activities carried out by the House ought not to rest solely in the hands of the premier.

Naturally, such innovations would completely change the style of government that currently holds sway in Ontario. No longer could the Government "accept responsibility" for refusing to debate certain matters, for not allowing certain investigations, or for failing to answer certain questions put to ministers. Instead, the Government would in fact be made responsible for its actions, not necessarily to the legislature – which still would not have the means of over-throwing a cabinet or dismissing a minister – but to the people, who would at least be given some basis for assessing the performance of the Government before casting their votes.

It is also true that no Government whose highest purpose was the extension of its period of dominance would ever admit such changes to be made in the structure of government. No Government is perfect, and the revelation of this truth in its naked detail would soon have its expected result. On the other hand, most Governments include men who are dedicated to ideals which are higher than the advancement of party advantage, and piecemeal reform is better than no improvement at all. Although responsible government may be an elusive ideal, it is well worth striving after, and immediate benefit will be derived from the pursuit itself.

APPENDICES, INDEX

OATHS SWORN BY MEMBERS OF THE EXECUTIVE COUNCIL OF ONTARIO

Oath of Allegiance

You ———— do sincerely promise and swear that you will be faithful and bear true allegiance to Her Majesty, Queen Elizabeth the Second.

So Help You God.

Oath of Office

I, ————, do solemnly and sincerely promise and swear that I will duly and faithfully and to the best of my skill and knowledge execute the powers and trusts reposed in me as ———— of the Province of Ontario.

So Help Me God.

Oath of Member of the Council

You, ———— do sincerely promise and swear that you will serve Her Majesty truly and faithfully, in the place of Her Council in this Her Majesty's Province of Ontario. You will keep close and secret all such matters as shall be treated, debated and resolved in the Executive Council without publishing or disclosing the same or any part thereof by word, writing or any otherwise, to any person out of the same Council, and yet if any matter so performed, treated and debated in any such Executive Council shall touch any particular person sworn of the same Council upon any such matter as shall in any wise concern his loyalty and fidelity to the Queen's Majesty you will in no wise open the same but keep it secret as you would from any person, until the Queen's Majesty's pleasure be known in that behalf.

You will in all things to be moved, treated and debated in any such Executive Council faithfully, honestly and truly declare your mind and opinion to the honour and benefit of the Queen's Majesty and the good of her subjects without partiality or affection of persons in no wise forbearing so to do from any manner of respect, favour, love, need, displeasure or dread of any person or persons whatsoever.

In general you will be vigilant, diligent and circumspect in all your doings touching the Queen's Majesty's affairs.

All which matters and things you will faithfully keep and observe as a good Councillor ought to do to the utmost of your power, will and discretion.

So Help You God.

STANDING COMMITTEES OF THE ONTARIO LEGISLATURE, 1900–60

(Decennial years only)

Committee	Membership	Quorum
1900		
Standing Orders	39	7
Private Bills	68	9
Railways	66	9
Municipal Law	72	7
Legal Bills	17	5
Printing	14	5
Public Accounts	30	7
Privileges and Elections	40	9
1910		
Privileges and Elections	36	9
Railways	67	9
Private Bills	61	9
Standing Orders	46	7
Public Accounts	39	7
Municipal Law	71	9
Printing	17	5
Legal Bills	19	5
Agriculture and Colonization	48	9
Fish and Game	25	7
1920		
Privileges and Elections	41	9
Railways	71	9
Private Bills	72	9
Standing Orders	49	7
Public Accounts	48	7
Municipal Law	72	9
Agriculture and Colonization	52	9
Printing	14	5
Legal Bills	19	5
Fish and Game	32	7

Committee	Membership	Quorum
1930		
Standing Orders	37	7
Private Bills	75	9
Railways	54	9
Municipal Law	73	9
Agriculture and Colonization	63	9
Public Accounts	67	7
Privileges and Elections	38	9
Legal Bills	24	5
Labour	25	7
Printing	20	5
Game and Fish	66	7
1939–40		
Standing Orders	41	7
Privileges and Elections	45	9
Railways	54	9
Private Bills	71	9
Public Accounts	69	9
Printing	28	5
Municipal Law	60	9
Legal Bills	29	5
Agriculture	54	9
Fish and Game	61	9
Labour	36	7
1950		
Privileges and Elections	17	7
Education	33	9
Private Bills	51	9
Standing Orders	31	7
Public Accounts	55	9
Printing	23	7
Municipal Law	47	7

Legal Bills	21	7		Health	50	7
Agriculture and				Highway Safety	50	7
Colonization	47	9		Labour	35	5
Fish and Game	51	9		Lands and Forests	50	7
Labour	30	9		Legal Bills	25	5
Mining	30	9		Mining	35	5
				Municipal Law	50	7
1960				Printing	25	5
Agriculture	50	7		Private Bills	60	7
Conservation	35	5		Privileges and		
Education	50	7		Elections	15	5
Energy	25	5		Public Accounts	50	7
Game and Fish	50	7		Standing Orders	25	5
Government				Travel and		
Commissions	35	5		Publicity	50	7

APPENDIX C

WRITTEN QUESTIONS IN THE 1964 SESSION*

I. Questions asked for which answers were tabled

1. **Mr. K. Bryden** (Woodbine): Inquiry of the Ministry: (1) Has the Hydro-Electric Power Commission of Ontario acquired title to the lands described as "the remaining lands" in the agreement between Dimensional Investments Limited and the commission dated March 11, 1959? (2) If so, (*a*) what amount or amounts were paid for the said lands; (*b*) when; and (*c*) to whom? (3) If not, what steps are being or have been taken to acquire title to these lands?

6. **Mr. R. F. Nixon** (Brant): Inquiry of the Ministry: (*a*) On what date did the regulation requiring principals of schools with over 300 pupils to have university degrees come into force? (*b*) How many schools in this category have principals without such degrees at the present time? (*c*) On what basis does the department award letters of permission under these circumstances?

7. **Mr. R. Gisborn** (Wentworth East): Inquiry of the Ministry: (1) Have lands been acquired for the development of the Queen Elizabeth Highway to a limited access road from Hamilton to the Lincoln county line? (2) (*a*) If so, what lands have been acquired? (*b*) From whom were they purchased? (*c*) And at what cost? (3) (*a*) Is any land being expropriated for this purpose at the present time? (*b*) If so, who is the owner of the land presently being expropriated?

9. **Mr. F. Young** (Yorkview): Inquiry of the Ministry: (1) Has the farm machinery board, recommended by the Ontario farm machinery investigating committee, been set up? (2) If it has, would the hon. Minister inform the House (*a*) of the names of its members; (*b*) its terms of reference? (3) If the committee has not yet been set up, can the hon. Minister state when it will be?

12. **Mr. J. B. Trotter** (Parkdale): Inquiry of the Ministry: (1) How much money did the Department of Lands and Forests lose as a result of the introduction of the three-day non-resident fishing license in 1963? (2) (*a*) How much money was collected for the said license in 1963? (*b*) How much did the collection costs of the licenses increase?

*Ontario, Legislative Assembly, *Debates*, March 3, 1964, pp. 1165–66; March 9, 1964, pp. 1384–85; April 29, 1964, pp. 2576–77.

2. **Mr. K. Bryden** (Woodbine): Inquiry of the Ministry: (1) How many loans have been guaranteed under The Economic Development Loans Guarantee Act, 1962–1963? (2) What was the total amount of these loans? (3) What was the amount of (*a*) the largest; (*b*) the smallest loan guaranteed under the Act?

8. **Mr. D. A. Paterson** (Essex South): Inquiry of the Ministry: Does the Liquor Control Board of Ontario intend to allow any new wine manufacturing licenses as a result of the increased importation and consumption of wines in Ontario?

10. **Mr. M. L. Belanger** (Windsor-Sandwich): Inquiry of the Ministry: (1) What school boards in Ontario have adult day classes where elementary subjects are taught? (2) Are all school board meetings public meetings, or are there provisions in The Schools Administration Act to hold meetings in camera?

11. **Mr. D. C. MacDonald** (York South): Inquiry of the Ministry: (1) What were the total sales of spirits by the LCBO in the last fiscal year for which figures are available? (2) (*a*) Which companies whose products are retailed by LCBO had sales of more than two per cent of the total; (*b*) what was the amount of sales for each company?

13. **Mr. K. Bryden** (Woodbine): Inquiry of the Ministry:
   (1) Does the Canadian Thoroughbred Horse Society give the Provincial Treasurer an accounting of its distribution of the annual grant made to it?

   (2) If not, on what basis is the amount of the grant arrived at?

   (3) If so, how many breeders received grants in (*a*) the fiscal year ended March 31, 1963; and (*b*) the current fiscal year to date?

   (4) In each of the said periods, what breeders received individual grants in excess of $1,000, and how much did each of them receive?

14. **Mr. R. Gisborn** (Wentworth East): Inquiry of the Ministry:
   (1) On what date did the OPP occupy their present station on Bronte Street in Milton?

   (2) Is there a lease, and, if so, what period does it cover?

   (3) How much rent does the OPP pay for the premises?

16. **Mr. E. G. Freeman** (Fort William): Inquiry of the Ministry:
   (1) How many trees were raised in government nurseries and planted on Crown lands for the last year for which figures are available?

   (2) For the same year, how many trees were raised by all private corporations and planted on their licensed limits?

(3) Specifically, how many trees were raised in their own nurseries and planted on their own limits by: (a) Spruce Falls Pulp and Paper; (b) Great Lakes Paper; (c) Marathon; (d) Ontario and Minnesota; (e) Abitibi; (f) Kimberly-Clark?

15. **Mr. D. C. MacDonald** (York South): Inquiry of the Ministry:
(1) Did any Minister of the Crown during the months of August and September 1963, appear in person and turn over, either to representatives of municipal bodies or to executives of private voluntary organizations in the communities of Terrace Bay, Gull Bay, Geraldton, Macdiarmid, Nakina, Longlac, Manitouwadge or Beardmore, in the riding of Port Arthur, any cheques or letters confirming payments from the provincial Treasury?

(2) If so, (a) who was the Minister; (b) what were the organizations; and (c) what was the authorization for such practice either in statute or regulation, or in any constitutional reference confirming the practice?

17. **Mr. D. C. MacDonald** (York South): Inquiry of the Ministry:
(1) What hotels, inns, taverns, restaurants or public houses in the Municipality of Metropolitan Toronto were granted licences by the Ontario Liquor Licensing Board during the years 1960, 1961, 1962, and 1963?

(2) Who was the lawyer, or legal firm, representing the successful applicants in each case before the Ontario Liquor Licensing Board?

18. **Mr. K. Bryden** (Woodbine): Inquiry of the Ministry:
(1) Will the cost of the dinner and dance, scheduled for Thursday, March 19, 1964, to which the Prime Minister and Members of the Government have invited the Press Gallery of Ontario and other Press, Radio and Television guests, be defrayed out of public funds?

(2) If so, (a) what is the estimated cost; and (b) out of what appropriation will it be paid?

II. Questions for which no answers were tabled†

3. **Mr. Bryden:** Inquiry of the Ministry: With regard to section 5 of The Ontario Human Rights Code, 1961–62, dealing with discrimination between male and female employees:

(1) How many complaints have been received by the Ontario Human Rights Commission of discrimination contrary to this section from the coming into force of the Act to date.

†In fact two of these questions [(3) and (4)] were answered orally during proceedings in Committee of Supply.

(2) In how many cases was the Commission able to effect a settlement of the complaints without a board of inquiry being appointed.

(3) In how many cases was a board of inquiry appointed, and in how many of these cases did a board find a complaint to be supported by the evidence.

(4) In how many cases did the Commission recommend that the Minister issue an order, and in how many of theses cases did the Minister in fact issue an order.

(5) In how many cases did the Minister consent to prosecution.

4. **Mr. Bryden:** Inquiry of the Ministry: (1) Has the Foundation on Automation and Employment been established. (2) If so, (*a*) when was it established; (*b*) who is its director or other principal officer (*c*) what is its address.

5. **Mr. Nixon:** Inquiry of the Ministry: (1) How much tobacco was removed from the market during the 1962–63 sales season as "no sale" tobacco. (2) To what extent is the Government of Ontario financially involved in this stored tobacco. (3) (*a*) How much of this tobacco has already been sold; (*b*) to whom and at what prices.

SEMI-INDEPENDENT GOVERNMENT AGENCIES IN ONTARIO AS OF SEPTEMBER 30, 1963, SHOWING THE AUDITING AUTHORITY FOR EACH AGENCY*

I. Agencies audited by the provincial auditor as parts of departments of government

ADVISORY BODIES

Department of Agriculture

Advanced Registry Board for Beef Cattle
Artificial Insemination Board
Milk Industry Advisory Committee of Ontario
Milk Producers Co-ordinating Board
Ontario Fertilizer Board
Stallion Enrolment Board

Department of the Attorney-General

Committee on Obscene Literature
Committee on the Process of Arbitration

Department of Education

Advisory Committee on University Affairs

Department of Health

Cemeteries Advisory Board
Commission for the Investigation of Cancer Remedies
Council of Nursing
Air Pollution Advisory Committee

Department of Labour

Committee for the Designated Building Trades
Committee for the Designated Trade of Barber
Committee for the Designated Trade of Hairdresser
Committee for the Designated Trade of Motor Vehicle Repairs
Committee for the Designated Trade of Worker in Servicing and Installing
    Air-Conditioning and Refrigerating Equipment
Labour Safety Council of Ontario

Department of Mines

Sulphur Dioxide Committee

*Compiled from the information submitted to the Public Accounts Committee of the Ontario legislature in 1964 by Mr. G. H. Spence, provincial auditor, and the Gordon Committee *Report*, pp. 465–67.

Department of Municipal Affairs

Municipal Advisory Committee

Department of Public Welfare

Board of Review
Medical Advisory Board
Committee on Child Welfare
Committee on Indian Welfare Services
Advisory Council for Public Welfare Training
Advisory Committee with respect to development and provision of rehabilitation services

Department of Reform Institutions

Training Schools Advisory Board

Department of Transport

Research Advisory Committee

Department of Travel and Publicity

Ontario Archaeological and Historic Sites Advisory Board

DEPARTMENTAL AGENCIES

Department of Agriculture

Co-operative Loans Board of Ontario
Agricultural Research Institute of Ontario
Ontario Producers, Processors, Distributors and Consumers Food Council
Ontario Food Council

Department of the Attorney-General

Ontario Provincial Police
Ontario Police Commission
Emergency Measures Organization of Ontario

Department of Civil Service

Civil Service Commission
Public Service Grievance Board
Classification Rating Committee
Joint Council

Department of Economics and Development

Ontario Economic Council
Ontario Development Agency
Ontario House

Department of Education

Defence Training Board

Department of Labour

Industry and Labour Board
Ontario Human Rights Commission
Jurisdictional Disputes Commission

Department of Lands and Forests
Lake of the Woods Control Board

Department of Municipal Affairs
Royal Commission of Metropolitan Toronto

Department of Prime Minister
Ontario Committee on Taxation

Department of Transport
Committee on overall transportation policy for Metropolitan Toronto and surrounding municipalities
Motor Vehicle Accident Claims Fund Advisory Committee

MINISTERIAL AGENCIES

Minister of Agriculture
Milk Industry Board of Ontario
Farm Products Marketing Board and local marketing boards
Agricultural Rehabilitation and Development Directorate of Ontario

Minister of Labour
Board of Examiners of Operating Engineers

Minister of Reform Institutions
Board of Parole

Minister of Travel and Publicity
Ontario-St. Lawrence Development Commission

Treasurer of Ontario
Public Service Superannuation Board
Ontario Parks Integration Board
Pension Commission of Ontario

QUASI-JUDICIAL AGENCIES

Minister of Municipal Affairs
Ontario Municipal Board

Minister of Transport
Ontario Highway Transport Board

Attorney General
Ontario Securities Commission

Minister of Energy Resources
Ontario Energy Board

Minister of Mines
Mining Commissioner
Sulphur Fumes Arbitrator

Minister of Labour
Ontario Labour Relations Board

II. Agencies audited by the provincial auditor as separate entities

DEPARTMENTAL AGENCIES

Department of Agriculture

Ontario Telephone Service Commission
Ontario Telephone Development Corporation
Ontario Junior Farmer Establishment Loan Corporation
Board of Regents of the Federated Colleges of the Department of
    Agriculture

Department of the Attorney General

Office of the Fire Marshal

Treasury Department

Ontario Municipal Improvement Corporation
Province of Ontario Savings Office
Housing Corporation Limited
Commissioner of Agricultural Loans

MINISTERIAL AGENCIES

Minister of Agriculture

Ontario Food Terminal Board
Ontario Stock Yards Board

Minister of Economics and Development

Ontario Northland Transportation Commission
Star Transfer Limited

Minister of Education

Province of Ontario Council for the Arts

Minister of Health

Ontario Hospital Services Commission
Ontario Mental Health Foundation
Alcoholism and Drug Addiction Research Foundation

Minister of Municipal Affairs

Ontario Water Resources Commission

Minister of Travel and Publicity

Board of Censors

Treasurer of Ontario

Ontario Racing Commission
Liquor Control Board of Ontario

Other

Niagara Parks Commission

QUASI-JUDICIAL AGENCIES

Provincial Secretary
Liquor License Board

OTHER AGENCIES

Treasurer of Ontario
International Transit Company, Limited

III. Agencies audited by someone other than the provincial auditor

DEPARTMENTAL AGENCIES

Department of the Attorney-General
Accountant of the Supreme Court of Ontario
Official Guardian
Public Trustee

MINISTERIAL AGENCIES

Minister of Economics and Development
Ontario Research Foundation

Minister of Education
Teachers' Superannuation Commission

Minister of Health
Ontario Cancer Institute (Princess Margaret Hospital)

Minister of Municipal Affairs
Ontario Municipal Employees Retirement Board

Minister of Public Welfare
Soldiers' Aid Commission

QUASI-JUDICIAL AGENCIES

Minister of Labour
Workmen's Compensation Board

OTHER AGENCIES

Minister of Energy Resources
Hydro-Electric Power Commission of Ontario

PREMIERS OF ONTARIO

	Party	Term of Office
*Hon. John Sandfield Macdonald†	Liberal	1867–1871
*Hon. E. Blake	Liberal	1871–1872
*Hon. Sir Oliver Mowat	Liberal	1872–1896
*Hon. A. S. Hardy	Liberal	1896–1899
*Hon. G. W. Ross	Liberal	1899–1905
*Hon. Sir J. P. Whitney	Conservative	1905–1914
*Hon. Sir Wm. Howard Hearst	Conservative	1914–1919
*Hon. Ernest Charles Drury	United Farmers	1919–1923
*Hon. G. H. Ferguson	Conservative	1923–1930
*Hon. G. S. Henry	Conservative	1930–1934
*Hon. M. F. Hepburn	Liberal	1934–1942
*Hon. G. D. Conant	Liberal	1942–1943
*Hon. H. C. Nixon	Liberal	May 1943–Aug. 1943
Hon. George A. Drew	Progressive Conservative	1943–1948
*Hon. T. L. Kennedy	Progressive Conservative	1948–1949
Hon. Leslie M. Frost	Progressive Conservative	1949–1961
Hon. John P. Robarts	Progressive Conservative	1961–

*Deceased.
†Unionist Government.

LIEUTENANT-GOVERNORS OF ONTARIO

1867   Henry William Stisted
1868   William Pearce Howland
1873   John Willoughby Crawford
1875   Donald Alexander Macdonald
1880   John Beverley Robinson
1887   Alexander Campbell
1892   George Airey Kirkpatrick
1897   Oliver Mowat
1903   William Mortimer Clark
1908   John Morison Gibson
1914   John Strathearn Hendrie
1919   Lionel Herbert Clarke
1921   Henry Cockshutt
1926   William Donald Ross
1932   Herbert Alexander Bruce
1937   Albert Matthews
1946   Ray Lawson
1952   Louis Orville Breithaupt
1957   John Keiller Mackay
1963   William Earl Rowe
1968   W. Ross Macdonald

APPENDIX G

SPEAKERS OF THE ONTARIO LEGISLATURE

Speaker	Constituency	Party affiliation	Date of election	Parliament
John Stevenson	Lennox	Conservative	December 27, 1867	1st
R. W. Scott	Ottawa	Liberal	December 7, 1871	2nd
J. G. Currie	Welland	Liberal	December 21, 1871	2nd
R. M. Wells	Bruce South	Liberal	November 24, 1875	3rd
C. Clarke	Wellington Centre	Liberal	January 7, 1880	4th
C. Clarke	Wellington Centre	Liberal	January 25, 1884	5th
J. Baxter	Haldimand	Liberal	February 10, 1887	6th
T. B. Ballantyne	Perth South	Liberal	February 11, 1891	7th
W. D. Balfour	Essex South	Liberal	February 21, 1895	8th
F. E. A. Evanturel	Prescott	Liberal	August 3, 1898	9th
W. A. Charlton	Norfolk South	Liberal	March 10, 1903	10th
J. W. St. John	York West	Conservative	March 22, 1905	11th
T. Crawford	Toronto West	Conservative	April 8, 1907	11th
T. Crawford	Toronto West "A"	Conservative	April 16, 1909	12th
W. H. Hoyle	Ontario North	Conservative	February 7, 1912	13th
D. Jamieson	Grey South	Conservative	February 16, 1915	14th

Name	Riding	Party	Date	Parliament
Nelson Parliament	Prince Edward	Liberal	March 9, 1920	15th
Joseph E. Thompson	Toronto Northeast "B"	Conservative	February 6, 1924	16th
William D. Black	Addington	Conservative	February 2, 1927	17th
Thomas A. Kidd	Kingston	Conservative	February 5, 1930	18th
Norman O. Hipel	Waterloo South	Liberal	February 20, 1935	19th
Norman O. Hipel	Waterloo South	Liberal	December 1, 1937	20th
James H. Clark	Windsor-Sandwich	Liberal	March 8, 1939	20th
Wm. J. Stewart	Parkdale	Conservative	February 22, 1944	21st
Wm. J. Stewart	Parkdale	Conservative	July 16, 1945	22nd
James de C. Hepburn	Prince Edward-Lennox	Conservative	March 24, 1947	22nd
M. Cooke Davies	Windsor-Walkerville	Conservative	February 10, 1949	23rd
M. Cooke Davies	Windsor-Walkerville	Conservative	February 21, 1952	24th
A. W. Downer	Dufferin-Simcoe	Conservative	September 8, 1955	25th
Wm. Murdoch	Essex South	Conservative	January 26, 1960	26th
Donald Hugo Morrow	Ottawa West	Conservative	October 29, 1963	27th
Fred M. Cass	Grenville-Dundas	Conservative	February 14, 1968	28th